Qualitative Inquiry and Human Rights

We need to assert our allegiance to the human race.

Howard Zinn

Qualitative Inquiry and Human Rights

Norman K. Denzin
Michael D. Giardina

Editors

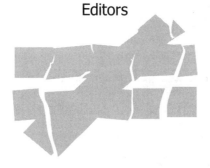

Left Coast
Press Inc.

Walnut Creek, California

Left Coast Press Inc.

LEFT COAST PRESS, INC.
1630 North Main Street, #400
Walnut Creek, CA 94596
http://www.LCoastPress.com

ISBN 978-1-59874-537-5 hardcover
ISBN 978-1-59874-538-2 paperback

Library of Congress Cataloging-in-Publication Data

Qualitative inquiry and human rights / Norman K. Denzin, Michael D. Giardina, editors.
    p. cm.
  Includes bibliographical references and index.
  ISBN 978-1-59874-537-5 (hardcover : alk. paper)—ISBN 978-1-59874-538-2 (pbk. : alk. paper)
1. Mass media—Technological innovations. 2. Mass media—Moral and ethical aspects. 3. Mass media—Social aspects. I. Denzin, Norman K. II. Giardina, Michael   1976-

  P96.T42Q36 2010
  370.7'2--dc22

                              2010010037

Printed in the United States of America

 ∞™ The paper used in this publication meets the minimum requirements of American National Standard for Information Sciences—Permanence of Paper for Printed Library Materials, ANSI/NISO Z39.48–1992.

10 11 12 13   5 4 3 2 1

Table of Contents

Introduction   13

Norman K. Denzin and Michael D. Giardina
University of Illinois, Urbana-Champaign

Section 1: Theory   43

1. *Theories for a Global Ethics*   45

   Clifford G. Christians
   University of Illinois, Urbana-Champaign

2. *Human Rights Theory: Criteria, Boundaries,*   66
   and Complexities

   A. Belden Fields
   University of Illinois, Urbana-Champaign

3. *Human Vulnerabilities: Toward a Theory of Rights for*   82
   Qualitative Researchers

   Svend Brinkmann
   Aalborg University, Denmark

4. *Human Rights, Social Justice, and Qualitative Research:*   100
   Questions and Hesitations about What We Say about
   What We Do

   Julianne Cheek
   Atlantis Medical College, Norway

5. *Affirming Human Dignity in Qualitative Inquiry:*   112
   Walking the Walk

   Frederick Erickson
   University of California, Los Angeles

Section 2: Method 123

6. *In the Name of Human Rights: I Say (How) You (Should) Speak (Before I Listen)* 125

   Antjie Krog
   University of the Western Cape, South Africa

7. *Autoethnography and Queer Theory: Making Possibilities* 136

   Stacy Holman Jones
   University of South Florida

   Tony E. Adams
   Northeastern Illinois University

8. *Some Ethical Considerations in Preparing Students for Performative Autoethnography* 158

   Tami L. Spry
   St. Cloud State University

Section 3: Politics 171

9. *This Is Our Moment (So) Yes We Can: Shifting Margins, Centers, and Politics of Difference in the Time of President Barack Obama* 173

   Cynthia B. Dillard
   The Ohio State University

10. *Triangulation of Micro-Perspectives on Juvenile Homelessness, Health, and Human Rights* 186

    Uwe Flick
    Alice Salomon University of Applied Sciences, Germany

11. *Poverty and Social Exclusion: The Everyday Life of the Poor as the Research Field of a Critical Ethnography* 205

    Elisabeth Niederer
    Carinthian Network Against Poverty and Social Discrimination

    Rainer Winter
    University of Klagenfurt, Austria

12. *Human Rights and Qualitative Health Inquiry:*   218
   On Biofacism and the Importance of Parrhesia

   Geneviève Rail
   Concordia University, Canada

   Stuart J. Murray
   Ryerson University, Canada

   Dave Holmes
   University of Ottawa, Canada

Coda: Meaningful Research, Aging, and   243
Positive Transformation

   Carolyn Ellis
   University of South Florida

   Laurel Richardson
   The Ohio State University

   Mary Gergen
   Pennsylvania State University, Brandywine

   Kenneth Gergen
   Swarthmore College

   Norman K. Denzin
   University of Illinois, Urbana-Champaign

   Arthur P. Bochner
   University of South Florida

Index   275

About the Authors   281

International Congress Of Qualitative Inquiry

The International Congress of Qualitative Inquiry has been hosted each May since 2005 by the International Center for Qualitative Inquiry at the University of Illinois, Urbana-Champaign. This volume, as well as four proceeding ones, are products of plenary sessions from these international congresses. All of these volumes are available from Left Coast Press, Inc.

Qualitative Inquiry and Human Rights
Edited by Norman K. Denzin and Michael D. Giardina 2010, based on the 2009 Congress ISBN 978-1-59874-537-5 hardcover, 978-1-59874-538-2 paperback

Qualitative Inquiry and Social Justice
Edited by Norman K. Denzin and Michael D. Giardina 2009, based on the 2008 Congress ISBN 978-1-59874-422-4 hardcover, 978-1-59874-423-1 paperback

Qualitative Inquiry and the Politics of Evidence
Edited by Norman K. Denzin and Michael D. Giardina 2008, based on the 2007 Congress ISBN 978-1-59874-321-0 hardcover, 978-1-59874-322-7 paperback

Ethical Futures in Qualitative Research
Edited by Norman K. Denzin and Michael D. Giardina 2007, based on the 2006 Congress ISBN 978-1-59874-140-7 hardcover, 978-1-59874-141-4 paperback

Qualitative Inquiry and the Conservative Challenge
Edited by Norman K. Denzin and Michael D. Giardina 2006, based on the 2005 Congress ISBN 978-1-59874-045-5 hardcover, 978-1-59874-046-2 paperback

Another product of the congress is the quarterly refereed journal of the institute. *International Review of Qualitative Research* is a peer-reviewed journal that encourages the use of critical, experimental, and traditional forms of qualitative inquiry in the interests of social justice. We seek works that are both academically sound and partisan, works that offer knowledge-based radical critiques of social settings and institutions while promoting human dignity, human rights, and just societies around the globe. Submissions to the journal are judged by the effective use of critical qualitative research methodologies and practices for understanding and advocacy in policy arenas as well as clarity of writing and willingness to experiment with new and traditional forms of presentation. Linked to the annual Congress for Qualitative Inquiry, much of the journal's content will be drawn from presentations and themes developed from these international meetings. The journal is published by Left Coast Press, Inc.

International Review of Qualitative Research
Editor: Norman K. Denzin
Quarterly in May, August, November, February ISSN
1940-8447

For more information on these publications, or to order, go to
www.LCoastPress.com

Acknowledgments

We thank Mitch Allen at Left Coast Press for his continued enthusiastic support of our endeavors. He is the editor of all editors. We also thank Carole Bernard for her editorial expertise and patience with us throughout the production process and Hannah Jennings for the production design of the volume.

Many of the chapters contained in this book were presented as plenary or keynote addresses at the Fifth International Congress of Qualitative Inquiry, held at the University of Illinois, Urbana-Champaign, in May 2009. We thank the Institute of Communications Research, the College of Media, and the International Institute for Qualitative Inquiry for continued support of the congress, as well as those campus units that contributed time, funds, and/or volunteers to the effort.

The congress, and by extension this book, would not have materialized without the tireless efforts of Dong Hong, Christina Ceisel, David Haskell, Melba Vélez, Koeli Goel, Li Xiong, Yiye Liu, Robin Price, and James Salvo (the glue who continues to hold the whole thing together). For information on future congresses, please visit http://www.icqi.org.

Norman K. Denzin
Michael D. Giardina

Champaign, Illinois
December 2009

Introduction[1]

Norman K. Denzin and Michael D. Giardina

University of Illinois

*The social sciences ... should be used to improve quality of life
... for the oppressed, marginalized, stigmatized and ignored
... and to bring about healing, reconciliation and restoration
between the researcher and the researched.*

— John H. Stanfield, 2006, p. 725

*Each time a man stands up for an ideal, or acts to improve
the lot of others, or strikes out against injustice, he sends
forth a tiny ripple of hope, and crossing each other from a
million different centers of energy and daring, those ripples
build a current which can sweep down the mightiest walls of
oppression and resistance.*

— Robert F. Kennedy,
Cape Town, South Africa, June 6, 1966

Proem

Poverty. Oppression. Homelessness. Discrimination. Persecution. Pain and suffering. War. Hallmarks of everyday life in even the most "civilized" of our societies today.

Thus, for all of the talk of human rights—the basic rights and freedoms to which all persons are entitled (e.g., those expressed in the 1948 United Nations' "Universal Declaration of Human Rights," such as all human beings are born free and equal in dignity and rights, no one shall be subjected to torture, all persons are equal before the law, everyone has the right to freedom of

13

movement, and so forth)—reality often conflicts with the ideal).[2] Look at a slice of life from our own shameful history in the United States in the last century alone: the subhuman working conditions and blatant exploitation of wage labor (such as the kind immortalized in Upton Sinclair's *The Jungle* [1906]); the "Ludlow Massacre" of 1914, in which the National Guard was called in to suppress striking union workers and resulted in sixty-six deaths; the internment of some 110,000 Japanese Americans on the West Coast during WWII; the atomic bombs dropped on Hiroshima and Nagasaki, which killed an estimated 200,000 civilians; the tragic legacy of Vietnam; the savage brutality of racism on display during the Civil Rights era; the invasion and occupation of Iraq; the list could go on and on.

And, if we want to be more specific with regard to the historical present, we can also add such recent large-scale events and their after-effects as worldwide financial sector meltdowns, rapidly rising rates of unemployment, ever-receding civil liberties,[3] the creation of legal justifications for torture,[4] the political suppression of the vote, most noticeably in Iran, and the subsequent violent crackdown on peaceful protesters, and the horrific impact of natural disasters on historically impoverished and federally neglected cities (e.g., New Orleans), or on countries (e.g., Haiti, Sri Lanka) lacking sufficient infrastructure through years of prolonged neglect from the international community. And behind each of these examples we see human beings suffering through it all, or trying to resist in the face of such suffering.

Yet to students of history, none of the above injustices should come as anything short of business as usual, whether among developed capitalist societies or in Third World countries.

In the midst of such an assault on human rights, it is becoming ever clearer that we must be honest about the role of qualitative research and researchers in such a context: It is not *just* about "method" or "technique." Rather, *qualitative research is about making the world visible in ways that implement the goals of social justice and radical, progressive democracy.* To such an end, this volume represents our ongoing conversation (see Denzin & Giardina, 2006a, 2006b, 2007, 2008, 2009) about qualitative inquiry as it relates to ethics, evidence, social justice, human rights, and the global community. The global interpretive community seeks forms of qualitative inquiry that make a difference in everyday lives by promoting human dignity and social justice. Critical performance pedagogy, spectacle pedagogy, critical minstrelsy theory, and ethno- and performance drama, for example, advance this agenda by exposing and critiquing the pedagogies of terror and discrimination that operate in daily life (Garoian & Gaudelius, 2008, p. 126; Kaufman, 2001; Madison, 2005; Madison & Hamera, 2006, pp. xx–xxi; Smith, 2004). The current historical moment requires morally informed disciplines and interventions that will help people recover meaning in the shadows of a post-9/11 world, in a world after George Bush—a world entering the possibility of transformational change inaugurated by President Obama. There is a deep desire to transcend and overcome the psychological despair fostered by wars, economic disaster, and divisive sexual and cultural politics. As global citizens, we lived through 8 long years of cynicism, fraud, and deceit. *Enough!*

Taking Stock of Qualitative Inquiry in an Age of Uncertainty

What is the role of critical qualitative research in a historical present when the need for social justice has never been greater? This is a historical present that cries out for emancipatory visions, for visions that inspire transformative inquiries, and for inquiries that can provide the moral authority to move people to struggle and resist oppression. The pursuit of social justice within a transformative paradigm challenges prevailing forms of inequality, poverty, human oppression, and injustice. This paradigm is firmly rooted in a human rights agenda. It requires an ethical framework that is rights- and social justice-based. It requires an awareness of "the need to redress inequalities by giving precedence ... to the voices of the least advantaged groups in society" (Mertens, Holmes, & Harris, 2009, p. 89). It encourages the use of qualitative research for social justice purposes, including making such research accessible for public education, social policy making, and community transformation.

This is a vision that is open to myriad ways of doing progressive, activist-based work: social workers handling individual clients compassionately; graduate students serving as language translators for non-English-speaking migrant workers and their children; health researchers collaborating with communities to improve health care delivery systems; qualitative researchers engaging their students in public interest visions of society; indigenous scholars being trained to work for their own communities using their own values; teachers fostering the ethical practices of qualitative research through publications, presentations, and teaching in both traditional classroom and professional development settings, both nationally and internationally (Bloom, 2009, p. 253).

The social justice community is huge, consisting of multiple disciplines, professions, religions, scholarly societies, individual researchers using multiple methodologies, a thousand different paths to the same ends. The International Congress of Qualitative Inquiry (ICQI) is part of the global social justice movement. Over the past decade, the international community of qualitative research scholars has come together to debate and resist these pressures, namely at the ICQI and in the pages of its affiliated journals. The ICQI was born out of a desire to demonstrate the promise of qualitative inquiry for social justice and human rights in an age of global uncertainty. At the inaugural ICQI in 2005, delegates from more than forty nations were committed to an ethically responsible form of qualitative inquiry, a form that would listen to the voices of the oppressed, bear witness to the power structures that control people's lives, offer resistance narratives, and imagine utopian alternatives (Keifer-Boyd, 2009, p. 2). This would be critical inquiry that operated at all levels, from the local, to the global. *It would embrace an activist agenda.* The theme of the first congress, "Qualitative Inquiry in a Time of Global Uncertainty,"[5] anticipated this desire and commitment.[6]

Critical qualitative inquiry scholars are united in the commitment to expose and critique the forms of inequality and discrimination that operate in daily life (Garoian & Gaudelius, 2008).[7] Together, they seek morally informed disciplines and interventions that will help people transcend and overcome the psychological despair fostered by wars, economic disaster, and divisive sexual and cultural politics. As global citizens, we are no longer called to just *interpret* the world, which was the mandate of traditional qualitative inquiry. Today, we are called to *change* the world and to do it in ways that resist injustice while celebrating freedom and full, inclusive, participatory democracy. *Such is the mandate of this volume.*

This challenge mobilizes members of the interpretive community in two ways. It offers an answer to those who express doubt and reservations about qualitative research, people who say "It's only a qualitative study!" The answer is this is NOT JUST A QUALITATIVE STUDY. This is ethically responsible activist research. The avowed social justice commitment focuses inquiry on research that makes a difference in the lives of socially oppressed persons.

As Thomas Schwandt (2006) has noted:

The 2005 ICQI issued what amounted to a call to arms to the international community of interpretive scholars ... the Second Congress continued the call to arms by exploring experiences with institutional review boards; investigating the over-reliance of audit cultures on evidence-based models of inquiry; promoting ways of decolonizing traditional methodologies and examining how ... participatory forms of critical inquiry can advance the goals of social justice. (p. 808)

These invitations open up spaces for dialog and careful examination of criticisms that have been made of qualitative inquiry. These discourses will always be about the local, about human justice in lives lived under neoliberalism. The focus will be on human beings as universal singulars, individuals and groups universalizing in their singularity the transformative life experiences in their historical moment. The desire is to create an ethically responsible agenda that would have goals of the sort enumerated by Leslie Bloom and Patricia Sawin (2009) in their article "Ethical Responsibilities in Feminist Research: Challenging Ourselves to Do Activist Research with Women in Poverty":

(1) It places the voices of the oppressed at the center of inquiry;

(2) It uses inquiry to reveal sites for change and activism;

(3) It uses inquiry and activism to help people;

(4) It affects social policy by getting critiques heard and acted on by policy makers;

(5) It affects changes in the inquirer's life, thereby serving as a model of change for others. (pp. 338, 340–342, 344)

These are moral criteria that celebrate resistance, experimentation, and empowerment. They honor sound partisan work that offers knowledge-based critiques of social settings, and institutions. And they promote human dignity, human rights, and just societies around the globe.

Justice Now: A Play in One Act[8]

"Justice Now," a short one-act play, pushes back against those discourses that would marginalize an ethically responsible social justice agenda for qualitative inquiry. The play imagines a space that celebrates utopian commitments to human rights, peace, and the sacred (see Diversi & Moreira, 2009). This space is required if the promises of an international coalition of critical inquiry are to be realized. The play unfolds in five scenes: Taking Control; The Many Ghosts of Paulo Freire; Justice and Democracy; Justice and Healing; and Hope and Transformations.

Characters: Speaker One, Speaker Two

Staging Notes: Performers are seated around a seminar table on the third floor of Gregory Hall, a four-story, 125-year-old brick classroom on the campus of the University of Illinois. There are twenty-five chairs along the walls and around a 40-foot long wooden table. Two large nature paintings on loan from the Art Department hang on the north and east walls of the room. There is a pull-down screen at the south end of the room for projecting video. Overhead lights are dimmed. Sun streams in through the two north windows. It is 1:00 pm. The time is the present. The text of the play is handed from speaker to speaker. The first speaker reads the text for Speaker One, the second speaker reads for Speaker Two, and so forth, to the end.

Scene One: Taking Control

Speaker One:

Fred Erickson says we have to take control of our own destiny. If we don't become proactive, standards, criteria and guidelines for good and bad work, fundable and not fundable scholarship will be imposed on us by others.

Speaker Two:

Our work fosters social justice. It directly addresses the needs of the oppressed. It offers performance vehicles for illuminating and representing the voices of the oppressed.

Speaker One:

International organizations like ICQI seem evenmore necessary. They reinforce efforts to help people say what they have to say and to make it politically audible. They encourage us to redouble efforts to understand and make sense of what is going on in this world, to expand and promote qualitative inquiry, its quality, ethics, and its commitment to social justice. These organizations ensure that new qualitative inquiry researchers are trained and supported all around the world. They provide communication mechanisms and communities of meaning where scholars can share experience, and receive political support.

Speaker Two:

In this way, working through networks of shared meaning, and with collaborating sites located around the world, critical inquiry becomes a vehicle for advancing human rights.

Speaker One:

Members of the social justice alliance reject the argument that they are introducing extra-scientific considerations into the research equation! They believe it is impossible to keep politics out of science.

Speaker Two:

We endorse a wide-gauged interpretive project, one that is critical, rigorous, open-ended—one that is dialogical. We seek to find common ground between critical theoretical positions, one which critiques colonial, postcolonial and geopolitical social economies, one which advances indigenous methodologies, one which "re-enchants" social inquiry with its sacred and spiritual commitments to social life, one which honors native lifeways, one which wrests social science away from a dominant and domineering Western model of use and commodification (Lincoln & Denzin, 2008, p. 563).

Speaker One:

Under the heading of activism, we believe there must be an inevitable political character to our work. We believe that our work should be directed to bringing about social change of the sort that challenges the conditions that surround homophobia, patriarchy, sexism, and racism.

Speaker Two:

I became a qualitative social scientist so I could make the world a better place to live in. You cannot separate science from politics. We are developing alliances across the human and health disciplines, from sociology to education, from social work to nursing, from public health to community psychology, from anthropology to business, from communications to political science. In each of these fields there is an emphasis on interpretive methodologies that engender social change. This is what we mean by an ethically responsible social science agenda.

Speaker One:

This means we build a firm firewall protecting us from those who say we are being too political, not scientific enough.

Scene Two: The Many Ghosts of Paulo Freire[9]

Speaker One:

The ghosts of Paulo Freire are everywhere. This play is written in and through his language, his words, his dreams: resisting oppression, critical pedagogy, praxis, freedom, hope, love, decolonizing knowledge, justice, ethics.

Speaker Two:

Paulo taught us that critical pedagogy takes many different forms: indigenous, queer, critical race, critical social disability, red, black, endarkened, performance, postcolonial, feminist, stand-point, transnational, non-Western, Asian, African.

Speaker One:

It's all tangled up in theory, in decolonizing performances, in indigenous pedagogies and methodologies, resistance narratives, in clashes between regimes of power, truth and justice. Everything is always, already performative. Each of these pedagogies exists on the public performance stage—moving from decolonizing discourses, toward decolonizing praxis, toward dreams of freedom, and liberation towards spaces where we each become experts in our own struggles to be free (Diversi & Moreira, 2009, p. 28, paraphrase).

Speaker Two:

A commitment to Freire's critical pedagogy means the conversation criss-crosses discursive communities, it moves across humanity. It confronts layers and levels of oppression. It addresses forms of violence and social injustice that come from the intersections of race, class, gender, religion, and sexual orientation. It confronts the experiences of misery, violence, poverty, hatred, and self-loathing.

Speaker One:

What does it mean to embrace indigenous pedagogies and methodologies, indigenous poetics?

Speaker Two:

We use our bodies and our identities, our colonized experiences to theorize these poetics, pedagogies and methodologies. Like Gloria Anzaldua, we invent our own roots, our own histories, we theorize and live in the spaces between cultures, races, ethnicities, identities, oppressions and liberations (Diversi & Moreira, 2009, p. 23).

Speaker One:

We need to work through an indigenous politics of critical inquiry. We are in the second Decade of Critical Indigenous Inquiry. In this decade there will be a thorough-going transition from discourses about and on method, to discourses centering on power, ethics and social justice. This discourse will bring new meanings to these terms. It will also involve a rethinking of terms like social justice, democracy, science and education.

Speaker Two:

We want a set of proactive understandings that give indigenous persons increased self-determination and autonomy in their own lives. Individuals should be free to determine their own goals and make sense of their world in terms of culturally meaningful terms. This call for autonomy is not a call for separatism, but rather is an invitation for a dialog between indigenous and non-indigenous persons. It asks that work done with indigenous persons be initiated by them, benefit them, represent them without prejudice, be legitimated in terms of their key values, and be done by researchers who are accountable for the consequences of their work.

Speaker One:

This translates into a culturally responsive social justice pedagogy. This pedagogy extends from schools into family, community, into culture and language.

Speaker Two:

This may involve collaborative storytelling, the co-construction of counter-narratives, and the creation of classrooms as discursive, sacred spaces where Maori values were experienced. Out of these practices emerge students who were able to exercise self-determination in their own education, students able to achieve their own sense of cultural autonomy and healthy well-being (Bishop, 2005).

Speaker One:

Culturally responsive pedagogy moves in several directions at the same time. The classroom obviously becomes one site for social justice work; clearly there are other sites for social justice activism.

Speaker Two:

I use social justice theater and Augusto Boal's Theatre of the Oppressed to help my students think about the connection between Paulo Freire, critical pedagogy and critical consciousness (Yellow Bird, 2005, p. 13; also quoted in Diversi & Moreira, 2009, p. 7).

Scene Three: Justice and Democracy

Speaker One:

Let's consider democracy and indigenous models of governance. Indigenous models of democracy involve inclusion and the free and full participation of all members of a society in civic discourse. The architects of American democracy subverted this full-inclusion model when they wrote the U.S. constitution. They denied citizenship rights to Native Americans, African Americans, and women.

Speaker Two:

There is a need to return full sovereignty to all Native Americans. Their indigenous models of democracy should be allowed to flourish under full federal financial sponsorship. In a truly legitimate democratic society, the discussion of democracy and education would be irrelevant because everyone would be free to participate and express themselves regarding the welfare of the community. Sadly, this has not been the case for Native Americans in the United States (Begaye, 2008, p. 465).

Speaker One:

Can colonizer-oppressor and colonized-oppressed ever speak to one another? Who speaks for whom here? Can there be a collaboration between oppressed and oppressor?

Speaker Two:

It is never straightforward. There is an inevitable tangle of passion, ignorance, ambivalence, desire and power which shapes the colonizer-colonized collaborating relationship. For example, the hyphen that connects Maori and non-Maori defines a colonial relationship. Each term forces the other into being. The hyphen can never be erased. There may be, however, an impulse for indigenous (and non-indigenous) persons to write from both sides of the hyphen—the outsider-within (Jones & Jenkins, 2008).

Speaker One:

Isn't this an impossibility?

Speaker Two:

Collaborative social justice inquiry can be guided by a set of ethical principles that include respect, care, equity, empathy, a commitment to fairness and a commitment to honoring indigenous culture and its histories.

Speaker One:

Colonizer-colonized collaboration can become a site of learning from difference rather than learning about the Other. Such a commitment respects and upholds difference. Remember, the Other is fundamentally unknowable, visible only in their cultural performances.

Speaker Two:

We are all exposed in these uneasy social justice spaces where we come in contact with the poverty, pain, illness and sadness in the lives of suffering people. We do not know how to write about it (Martinez-Salgado, 2009, p. 309).

Speaker One:

Indigenous people must have control over their own knowledge. They must have mechanisms that protect them when research is being done on, among, or with them. How can you create ethical mandates and ethical behavior in a knowledge system contaminated by colonials and racism?

Speaker Two:

Indigenous persons should be the guardians and interpreters of their culture. They have the right and obligation to exercise control to protect what is theirs. All research should be approached as a negotiated partnership, and all participants should be treated as equals.

Speaker One:

Research ceases to be research within an ethical social justice perspective. It becomes, instead, a transformative practice, a form of social justice theater where utopian models of empowerment are explored.

Speaker Two:

> This involves a huge struggle, a commitment to principles before personalities, a nonjudgmental commitment to respect, kindness, caring and love for the other, an honoring of personal experience, a belief in practical wisdom, the desire to heal and end pain.

Scene Four: Justice and Healing

Speaker One:

> It is possible to extend the social justice model to include justice as healing. This means getting outside the colonizer's legal cage where "might makes right." It means embedding justice within a moral community. Legal positivism, a cousin of epistemological positivism, oppresses indigenous persons. It has caused great harm and destruction in Native communities by undermining indigenous concepts of community and natural law (McCaslin and Breton, 2008).

Speaker Two:

> We advocate a restorative view of justice based on indigenous ways of healing, not scapegoating and punishing offenders. Restorative justice represents a paradigm shift, violations to persons and their properties are regarded as violations of relationship and only secondarily of the law. Punishment of offenders is not practiced. We do healing circles (McCaslin and Breton, 2008).

Speaker One:

> The key features include speaking the truth, healing, respect of the other person, an honoring of their voice, the prevention of future harm. Restorative justice can be achieved through various practices, including mediation, sentencing circles, healing circles, and community conferencing. Restorative justice is like a spiritual process. It celebrates balance, harmony, making persons whole again. It honors the intrinsic worth and good of each person.

Speaker Two:

> Exactly. It is dialogic. Healing is not about fixing persons, or getting even. It is about transforming relationships, about being good relatives and good neighbors. Healing is spiritual, involving

sincere and genuine efforts by all those involved to practice values such as fairness, honesty, compassion, harmony, inclusiveness, trust, humility, openness, and most importantly, respect.

Speaker One:

Healing, in combination with restorative justice, works to restore dignity. It refuses to engage in negative labeling, including applying harmful labels to disempowered youth. This is the core challenge; that is, to confront the colonizing cage that traps both indigenous and non-indigenous people in genocide, fraud, theft, institutional racism and abuse.

Speaker Two:

Yes! But restorative justice should not become yet another tool of colonizing institutions. The goal is to remove the cage altogether, and to rebuild our long house, hogans, iglus, pueblos, wikiups, earth lodges, wigwams, plank houses, grass houses, or chickees.

Speaker One:

Justice as healing has some similarities with the South African Truth and Reconciliation Commission. In those commission hearings there was an attempt to hear the voices of the persons who suffered under Apartheid.

Speaker Two:

Exactly. Here is an example. Mrs. Konile is a native South African whose son was killed by military security forces. Mrs. Konile testified before the Truth and Reconciliation Commission (TRC). Her narrative included a dream episode and an incident with a goat. Mrs. Konile testified in her mother tongue. Difficulties arose when it was translated and an official transcript was produced. Her testimony seemed ill-fitting, strange, incoherent. The court was inclined to disregard her testimony. The TRC laughed at her. They said she was crazy (Krog, Mpolweni-Zantsi, Ratele, 2008, pp. 531–532).

Speaker One:

A deeper interpretation suggested that her narrative was coherentand that she was resisting other frameworks that were imposed on her. Her dream with the goat connects her to her culture, to her ancestral worlds, far from the world where her son was killed in the struggle to liberate his and her country (Krog, Mpolweni-Zantsi, Ratele, 2008, pp. 531–532, 542).

Speaker Two:

The case of Mrs. Konile is instructive. She is trapped. She occupies multiple spaces within the discourses of the TRC and yet they would not hear her. Mrs. Konile uses her agency—her narrated dream—to resist racial and political oppression. Her courtroom story reinforces the need for a critical pedagogy framed around the tenets of restorative justice, justice as healing. It took special listeners to hear her story!

Speaker One:

This is how ethically responsible inquiry should work. Krog, Mpolweni-Zantsi, and Ratele located the court, the hearings and the transcriptions as sites of intervention. They challenged the ways in which the court was treating TRC testimony. They initiated change for social justice purposes. They used their story as a model of change for others.

Scene Five: Hope and Transformations

Speaker One:

We need a politics of hope. We are the children of Paulo Freire. We believe hope is an ontological need.

Speaker Two:

Write what you believe should be written. Dare to take chances (Yvonna Lincoln).

Speaker One:

We want to write in an in-between space. We are in a transitional moment with new decolonizing narratives. Resistance stories written over, around and behind the hyphen, hopeful, utopian narratives, narratives that dare to dream, stories that imagine pedagogies of freedom. Narratives that create new spaces of resistance—classrooms, courtrooms, nursing homes, hospitals, bus stations, street corners, faculty meetings, the hallways of the academy, sporting fields, cyberspace, treatment centers, journals, conferences, churches, books, new battlegrounds (Diversi and Moreira, 2009, pp. 208–209).

Speaker Two:

Hope, faith and hard work will transform the world. This is a hope grounded in the belief that the demand for basic human rights, and the demand for social justice will prevail. But it requires a fight, and an investment of great emotion and passion.

Speaker One:

Remember: A pedagogy of hope enacts a politics of resistance and imagines a utopian future. Hope makes radical cultural critique and racial social change possible.

Speaker Two:

Paulo Freire (1999 [1992]) tells this story about himself:

> Listen. From the ages of twenty-two to twenty-nine I would be overcome by a sense of despair, sadness, even depression. It would hit me suddenly and often last for days (p. 27). I stepped back from my depression and made it an object of investigation. I observed that it happened more often in the rainy season. ... It was connected to rain and mud, the green of the cane brakes and the dark sky. ... In seeking for the deepest "why" of my pain, I was educating and inventing the concrete hope which one day would deliver me from my depression. (pp. 29–31)

Speaker One:

The story continues:

> I needed to discover that lace in my past which brought all of these terms—rain, mud, green—together. And so, one rainy afternoon... under a leaden sky. ... I paid a visit to Morro de Saude, where I had lived as a child. I stopped in front of the house where my father died in the late afternoon of October 21, 1934. ... I saw ... the lawn ... the mango trees, their green founds. I saw my feet ... my muddy feet going up the hill. ... I had before, as on a canvas, my father dying, my mother in stupefaction, my family lost in sorrow. ... That rainy afternoon, with the sky dark as lead over the bright green land ... I discovered the fabric of my depression. I became conscious ... of the deeper core. ...

I unveiled ... its "why.".... Since then, never again has the relationship between rain, green and mud ... sparked in me the depression that had affected me for years. (Freire 1999 [1992], pp. 30–31)

Speaker Two:

So he found the why. He went back home, to the scene of his father's death, his family in pain and suffering, the place where rain, mud, and the color green came together.

Speaker One:

Freire continues:

I had to move forward. I had to act. ... I threw myself into my work. I worked to transform the concrete conditions that were producing the oppression. So hope moves in two directions at the same time. It liberated me and lead me to become hopeful about how I could help others overcome pedagogies of oppression. The hope of remaking the world is basic to the struggle. (Freire 1999 [1992], pp. 30–31)

Speaker Two:

Let's summarize. Hope alone will not produce change. First there must be pain, and despair. Persons must make pain the object of conscious reflection, the desire to resist, to change. This desire must be wedded to a conscious struggle to change the conditions that create the pain in the first place (Freire 1999 [1992], pp. 30–31). Hope makes change possible. You can call this Paulo's pedagogy of hope.

Speaker One:

Let's come full circle. Back to the beginning. A social justice agenda for qualitative inquiry is based on a politics of hope. Scholars who follow this fork in the road experience transformations in their own lives. These transformations lead them to embrace pedagogies of hope.

The Chapters

With the above in mind, *Qualitative Inquiry and Human Rights* actively inserts itself into the unfolding landscape of human rights and social justice in the post-Bush era. To this end, the volume is loosely organized around three sections: (1) Theory; (2) Method; and (3) Politics.

To begin Section 1, Clifford G. Christians ("Theories for a Global Ethics") discusses the urgent need for a global media ethics that matches the international impact and reach of modern media formations, especially as oriented around social justice and human rights. Christians begins by reviewing various scientific theories of communication ethics (e.g., ethical formalism) as well as alternative, anti-Enlightenment models of ethics (including those of Benhabib, Hamelink, Nussbaum, and Wiredu). He then proposes a three-dimensional theory for global media ethics—one composed of presuppositions, principles, and precepts—and which is opposed explicitly to single-strand Enlightenment universals.

In Chapter Two ("Human Rights Theory: Criteria, Boundaries, and Complexities"), A. Belden Fields explores the possibilities of grounding human rights theoretically. To that end, he (1) examines arguments that such an attempt is futile because the concept itself is flawed; (2) considers arguments that the concept is a valid one and only becomes flawed when it is overextended in scope; and (3) presents his own "holistic" argument that some of the arguments for constraining the scope do not hold up under deeper scrutiny.

Svend Brinkmann follows in Chapter Three ("Human Vulnerabilities: Toward a Theory of Rights for Qualitative Researchers"), which takes up the question of whether or not the advancement of human rights is a legitimate goal for qualitative research practices. In so doing, Brinkmann critically addresses those who question such a goal because of a sense of researcher neutrality, as well as those who reject the goal outright because of beliefs that rights-talk is too firmly tied to neoliberal individualism.

In Chapter Four ("Human Rights, Social Justice and Qualitative Research: Questions and Hesitations about What We Say about What We Do"), Julianne Cheek raises a series of questions and hesitations concerning the researcher's location to questions and practices of social justice and human rights in the production and consumption of our research endeavors. To wit, she turns her gaze on the research process itself, conceived of as a series of social practices that are shaped by, and in turn shape, understandings of social justice and human rights. In particular,

Cheek wants us to consider or think through our location to our research, how we (and our generally privileged positions as researchers) inform the dynamics of a given study, and how our position may be implicated in our findings.

The section closes with Frederick Erickson's chapter ("Affirming Human Dignity in Qualitative Inquiry: Walking the Walk"), which examines the conduct of qualitative inquiry itself as it relates to various methodological concerns. Critically discussing "plain old ethnography," "critical ethnography," "auto-ethnography," "participatory action research," and "performance ethnography," Erickson argues for the need to practice humility and self-critical awareness in the ways in which we go about our inquiry and report what we have learned. In so doing, he calls for more reflexive and self-critical qualitative inquiry than naively realist ethnography was able to achieve, while at the same time acknowledging that "it is not easy to do good, even when that is what we want to do."

Section 2 opens with Antjie Krog's chapter ("In the Name of Human Rights"), which draws from her work on the South African Truth and Reconciliation Commission (TRC) and focuses on the rights of two groups: (1) those living in margin-alized areas but who produce virtually on a daily basis intricate knowledge systems of survival, and (2) scholars coming from those marginalized places, but who can only enter the world of acknowledged knowledge in languages not their own and within discourses based on foreign and estrange-ing structures. More specifically, Krog shows us the backstage process of her collab-orative work with one particular individual who testified before the TRC (Mrs. Konile), addressing in the process questions of "academic authority" and voice, of whose voice carries authority to speak, of the limitations of "disciplines" and "theory." She con-cludes by imploring us to find ways in which "the marginalized can enter our discourses on their own genres and their own terms so that we can learn to hear them."

The next two chapters both take up different perspectives on autoethnography with respect to a human rights agenda. In Chapter Seven ("Autoethnography and Queer Theory: Making Possibilities"), Stacy Holman Jones and Tony E. Adams offer a co-constructed narrative that illustrates "what can happen when a method and a theoretical perspective are put into conversation" toward the aims of honoring the sanctity of life and human dignity. Drawing from Della Pollock's work on the "performative I," their chapter begins with a kind of relational inventory, exploring what joins and holds apart autoethnography and queer theory and asking why these practices and politics are good for each other. They then offer deeply personal and moving narrative examples to demonstrate this collision in action.

In Chapter Eight ("Some Ethical Considerations in Preparing Students for Performative Autoethnography"), Tami L. Spry reminds us that we must be cognizant of the human rights of students in the pedagogical performance process, arguing that "it is an ethical imperative of their human rights for students to be provided the theoretical and methodological foundation in the study of performance when we ask them to engage the vulnerable, transformational, and dangerous terrain of critical autoethnographic performance." To illustrate this ethical imperative of aesthetical epistemology, she shares with us several student autoethnographic performances (a critical reflection on rape, an autoethnography of "driving while black," and critical work on the gay body in a Catholic church), which are at once moving and empowering.

Section 3 moves the discussion into four specific case studies conducted on such divergent—yet nevertheless interconnected—topics of poverty, homelessness, health care, and racial politics. Cynthia Dillard's chapter ("This Is Our Moment (So) Yes We Can: Shifting Margins, Centers, and Politics of Difference in the Time of President Barack Obama") opens the section. Utilizing the election of Obama as the backdrop upon which to reveal the fundamental shifts and disruptions of individual and collective interactions across differences, Dillard leads us on an exploration of endarkended feminist perspectives related to both "margin" and "center." At its core, she speaks about a kind of "new collective consciousness," which are represented by four lessons gleaned from the Obama campaign—that of "new connections, "a new set of recognitions," "a new site of accountability," and the sense of a "new source of power."

In Chapter Ten ("Triangulation of Micro-Perspectives on Juvenile Homelessness, Health, and Human Rights"), Uwe Flick explores the issue of juvenile homelessness and its links to health issues. To that end, he offers insight on a recent qualitative project—driven largely by triangulation—that looks into risks of becoming homeless, the living conditions of being homeless and its implications for health, the specific contextual phenomenon of homeless youth, and the systemic barriers homeless youth face in terms of acquiring health care and services. The words and experiences of his research participants are especially revealing of the predicament faced by homeless youth.

Elisabeth Niederer and Rainer Winter follow with Chapter Eleven ("Poverty and Social Exclusion: The Everyday Life of the Poor as the Research Field of a Critical Ethnography"), which is an exploratory study on poverty and social exclusion in a wealthy country (Austria). Focusing on single parents, welfare recipients, immigrants, retirees, and the unemployed, the authors endeavor to reveal the everyday cultures of poverty their research participants negotiate and experience. Here the voices and experiences of their participants, many of whom are speaking of their particular predicaments for the first time, illustrate the social injustices and inequalities they face on a regular basis. Yet Niederer and Winter's project is not solely to *hear* the voices of the poor, but to enable their participants to join the social, cultural, and political dialog and to participate with equal rights in society.

And in Chapter Twelve ("Human Rights and Qualitative Health Inquiry: On Biofacism and the Importance of *Parrhesia*"), Geneviève Rail, Stuart J. Murray, and Dave Holmes take up the effects of biomedical, bioeconomic, and biocultural discourses on qualitative health inquiry as related to both evidence-based health sciences and medical ghostwriting (i.e., the practice of scholars accepting money to put their names on and publish a pharmaceutical company's own research and passing it off under the guise of independent research). Additionally, they argue that qualitative researchers, what Foucault would called "specific intellectuals," have a duty to be engaged in the practice of "fearless speech" that "questions the manifold of authority and power, despite the risks and dangers," especially in the face of the ever-increasing corporatization of the university.

The volume concludes with a Coda on meaningful research, aging, and positive transformation, which was first delivered as a plenary roundtable organized by Carolyn Ellis at the 2009 International Congress of Qualitative Inquiry. Ellis is joined by Laurel Richardson, Mary Gergen, Kenneth Gergen, Norman Denzin, and Arthur Bochner, as they each recount stories about moments in which they felt their research was "meaningful," and how their research and research perspectives have transformed over time.

By Way of a Conclusion

Qualitative Inquiry and Human Rights marks the fifth[10] entry in our series on qualitative research in the historical present. Each of these five volumes has found its genesis in and come out of our parallel involvement with organizing the annual International Congress of Qualitative Inquiry at the University of Illinois, Urbana-Champaign. The first, titled *Qualitative Inquiry and the Conservative Challenge: Confronting Methodological Fundamentalism* (2006b), sought to actively contest the right-wing/neoconservative-dominated direction of regulatory policy governing scientific inquiry. Such regulatory efforts—primarily those obsessed with enforcing scientifically based, biomedical models of research—raise fundamental philosophical, epistemological, and ontological issues for scholarship and freedom of speech in the academy.

Our second volume, *Ethical Futures in Qualitative Research: Decolonizing the Politics of Knowledge* (2007), charted a radical path for a future in which ethical considerations transcend the Belmont Principles (which focus almost exclusively on the problems associated with betrayal, deception, and harm), calling for a collaborative, performative social science research model that makes the researcher responsible not to a removed discipline or institution, but to those he or she studies. In so doing, personal accountability, the value of expressiveness, the capacity for empathy, and the sharing of emotionality are stressed. Scholars were directed to take up moral projects that decolonize, honor, and reclaim (indigenous) cultural practices, where healing leads to multiple forms of transformation at the personal and social levels, and where these collective actions can help persons realize a radical politics of possibility, hope, love, care, and equality for all humanity.

In our third volume *Qualitative Inquiry and the Politics of Evidence* (2008), our authors challenged the very ground on which evidence has been given cultural and canonical purchase: What is truth? What is evidence? What counts as evidence? How is evidence evaluated? How can evidence—or facts—be "fixed" to fit policy? What kind of evidence-based research should inform this process? How is evidence to be represented? How is evidence to be discounted or judged to be unreliable, false, or incorrect?

And in our fourth volume, *Qualitative Inquiry and Social Justice: Toward a Politics of Hope* (2009), our authors took on and advocated for a more activist-minded role for scholarship and research in the academy, of making a space for critical, humane discourses that create sacred and spiritual spaces for persons and their moral communities—spaces where people can express and give meaning to the world around them. A project organized around moral clarity and political intervention (i.e., a focus on the personal and the biographical, the launching of critical discourse at the level of the media and the ideological, the fostering of a critical international conversation that helps us develop a contextual theory of radical politics and social justice and democracy, and the enacting of critical interpretive methodologies that can help us make sense of life in an age of the hyperreal, the simulacra, TV wars, staged media events, and the like). Such a project, then, embraced a public intellectualism on the order of Noam Chomsky's 1967 article "The Responsibility of Intellectuals," in which he argues that we (i.e., all of us) have a moral and professional obligation to speak the truth, expose lies, and see events in their historical perspective (see also Denzin & Giardina, 2006a).

Here, with our fifth volume, our attention has been turned to that of human rights. As the proem to this Introduction outlined, the last several years have witnessed unspeakable assaults on human rights by governments and corporations: Poverty. Homelessness. Racial, sexual, and religious discrimination. Political persecution. Torture, pain, and suffering. These are the topics on display, the topics we challenge those working in the field of qualitative inquiry to focus on.

Taken together, all five volumes work in tandem to address a fundamental question: *How are we as qualitative researchers to move forward in this new paradigm?* Scholars who share the values of excellence, leadership, and advocacy need venues to engage in debate, frame public policy discourse, and disseminate research findings. We need a community that honors and celebrates paradigms and methodological diversity, and showcases scholarship from around world. As fellow travelers, we need research agendas that advance human rights and social justice through qualitative research. If we can do this the rewards will be "plentiful and the opportunity for professional [and societal] impact unsurpassed" (Guba, 1990, p. 378).

ooooo

Qualitative research scholars have an obligation to change the world, to engage in ethical work what makes a positive difference. We are challenged to confront the facts of injustice, to make the injustices of history visible and hence open to change and transformation. We write always against history, offering reactions to, not records of, history. As critical scholars our task is to make history present, to make the future present, to undo the present, by making the unreal present (Smith, 2004, p. xvi).

Writing in *Le Monde Diplomatique* during the height of the (second) U.S.-Iraq War, the radical American historian, Howard Zinn (who left this world all too early in January 2010), asked and answered a particularly relevant question to our aims as qualitative researchers. "What is our job?" he wrote. The answer?

> To point all this out. [...] We need to engage in whatever actions appeal to us. There is no act too small, no act too bold. The history of social change is the history of millions of actions, small and large, coming together at points in history and creating a power that governments cannot suppress. (Zinn 2005)

We have a job to do. Let's get to it.

Notes

1. Portions of this chapter are drawn from Denzin, 2010 (especially Chapter 7).

2. Carlin (2008) offers a compelling statement on the matter: "There's no such thing as rights ... rights are an idea, they're just imaginary ... and fictional. [...] Rights aren't rights if someone can take them away. [...] Either we have unlimited rights, or we have no rights at all."

3. In March 2009, the American public finally learned the truth concerning the extent to which the Bush administration *actively* sought to curtail civil liberties, most especially through a series of memos written by John Yoo from his post in the Office of Legal Counsel at the Justice Department. In short, Yoo's memos effectively created a legal opinion that understood the president to have the *inherent power* to suspend both the First and Fourth Amendments. As Jack Balkin (2009) of Yale Law School stated, the memos, "sought, in secret, to justify a theory of Presidential dictatorship." For more, see Glenn Greenwald's (2009) essay "The Newly Released Secret Laws of the Bush Administration."

4. For more information, see the ongoing (2009–2010) federal investigation of Jay Bybee by the Justice Department's Office of Professional Responsibility. Bybee, who is now a federal judge on the Ninth Circuit Court of Appeals, authored the legal memorandum known as the "Bybee Memo" (or, colloquially, the "Torture Memo") while serving as the assistant attorney general for the Office of Legal Counsel in the U.S. Justice Department (2001–2003) during the Bush administration. The memo in question effectively defined "enhanced interrogation techniques" in ways that are regarded as torture by the current Justice Department, Amnesty International, Human Rights Watch, medical experts, and so forth. Bybee is also the subject of a war crimes investigation in Spain (along with Alberto Gonzales, John Yoo, Douglas Feith, William Haynes II, and David Addington, who are collectively known as "The Bush Six"). For more details, see especially Andrew Sullivan's reporting on torture in *The Atlantic Monthly* magazine and on his blog, *The Daily Dish*, especially Sullivan, 2009; see also Jeffrey Toobin, 2009; Karen J. Greenberg and Joshua L. Dratel, 2005; and Seymour Hersh's (2005) magisterial exposé of Abu Ghraib torture.

5. Here are the numbers from the first five congresses: **2005**: Over 700 delegates; 40 nations; 150 sessions; **2006**: 800 delegates; 42 nations; 186 sessions; **2007**: 900 delegates; 42 nations, 203 sessions (including a Day in Turkish, and the Couch-Stone SSSI Symposium; 850 papers; **2008**: 975 delegates; 41 nations; 230 sessions (including a Day in Turkish, a Day in Spanish, A Day in Technology, and the Couch-Stone SSSI Symposium; 850 papers; **2009**: 1100 delegates, 40 nations; 250 sessions including a Day in Turkish, a Day in Spanish, and the Couch-Stone SSSI Symposium).

6. The next five congresses engaged these topics: "Ethics, Politics and Human Subject Research in the New Millennium (2006); Qualitative Inquiry and the Politics of Evidence" (2007); "Ethics, Evidence and Social Justice" (2008); "Advancing Human Rights through Qualitative Research" (2009); and "Qualitative Inquiry for a Global Community in Crisis" (2010). See Denzin and Giardina, 2006b, 2007, 2008, 2009 for the edited volumes, which contain the keynote addresses and plenary sessions at these congresses.

7. See Atkinson and Delamont (2006, p. 753) for a list of journals, many published by Sage: *Qualitative Inquiry, Qualitative Health Research, Qualitative Research, Qualitative Social Work, Cultural Studies ↔ Critical Methodologies, Journal of Contemporary Ethnography, Discourse Studies, Discourse and Society, Ethnography, Field Methods, Ethnography and Education, International Journal of Qualitative Studies in Education, Anthropology and Education, Communication and Critical/Cultural Studies, Text and Performance Quarterly,* and *International Review of Qualitative Research.* Thanks to Left Coast Press, Sage, and Routledge, the borders and boundaries between nation states, scholars, and journals have truly collapsed.

8. This play appears in slightly altered format in Denzin, 2010, Chapter 7.

9. Portions of this section rework pp. 429–438 in Denzin, Lincoln, and Smith (2008).

10. Or it is the sixth, if you count our contextually related volume *Contesting Empire, Globalizing Dissent: Cultural Studies after 9/11* (Denzin & Giardina, 2006a).

References

Atkinson, P., & Delamont, S. (2006). In the roiling smoke: Qualitative inquiry and contested fields. *International Journal of Qualitative Studies in Education, 19*, 6, 747–755.

Balkin, J. (2009). The end of the Yoo doctrine. *Balkinization* March 3. http://balkin.blogspot.com/2009/03/end-of-yoo-doctrine.html (accessed August 12, 2009).

Begaye, T. (2008). Modern democracy: The complexities beyond appropriating indigenous models of governance and implementation. In K. Denzin, Y. S. Lincoln, and L. T. Smith (Eds.), *Handbook of critical and indigenous methodologies* (pp. 459–469). Thousand Oaks, CA: Sage.

Bishop, R. (2005). Freeing ourselves from neo-colonial domination in research: A Kaupapa Maori approach to creating knowledge. In N. K. Denzin and Y. S. Lincoln (Eds.), *Handbook of qualitative research* (3rd ed., pp. 109–138). Thousand Oaks, CA: Sage.

Bloom, L. R. (2009). Introduction: Global perspectives on poverty and social justice. *International Journal of Qualitative Studies in Education, 22,* 3, 253–261.

Bloom. L. R., & Sawin, P. (2009). Ethical responsibilities in feminist research: Challenging ourselves to do activist research with women in poverty. *International Studies of Qualitative Studies in Education, 22,* 3, 333–351.

Carlin, G. (2008). *It's bad for ya.* Orland Park, IL: MPI Home Video.

Chomsky, N. (1967). The responsibility of intellectuals. *The New York Review of Books,* February 23. http://www.nybooks.com/articles/12172 (accessed February 4, 2010).

Denzin, N. K. (2010). *The qualitative manifesto: A call to arms.* Walnut Creek, CA: Left Coast Press.

Denzin, N. K., & Giardina, M. D. (2006a). Introduction: Cultural studies after 9/11/01. In N. K. Denzin and M. D. Giardina (Eds.), *Contesting empire/globalizing dissent: Cultural studies after 9/11* (pp. 1–21). Boulder, CO: Paradigm.

Denzin, N. K, & Giardina, M. D. (Eds.). (2006b). *Qualitative inquiry and the conservative challenge: Confronting methodological fundamentalism.* Walnut Creek, CA: Left Coast Press.

Denzin, N. K., & Giardina, M. D. (2007). Introduction: Ethical futures in qualitative research. In N. K. Denzin and M. D. Giardina (Eds.), *Ethical futures in qualitative research: Decolonizing the politics of knowledge* (pp. 9–44). Walnut Creek, CA: Left Coast Press.

Denzin, N. K., & Giardina, M. D. (2008). Introduction: The elephant in the living room, OR Advancing the conversation about the politics of evidence. In N. K. Denzin and M. D. Giardina (Eds.), *Qualitative inquiry and the politics of evidence* (pp. 9–52). Walnut Creek, CA: Left Coast Press.

Denzin, N. K., & Giardina, M. D. (2009). Introduction: Qualitative inquiry and social justice: Toward a politics of hope. In N. K. Denzin and M. D. Giardina (Eds.), *Qualitative inquiry and social justice: Toward a politics of hope* (pp. 11–50). Walnut Creek, CA: Left Coast Press.

Denzin, N. K., Lincoln, Y. S., & Smith, L. T. (Eds.). (2008). *Handbook of critical and indigenous methodologies* (pp. 563–571). Thousand Oaks, CA: Sage.

Diversi, M., & Moreira, C. (2009). *Betweener talk: Decolonizing knowledge production, pedagogy and praxis.* Walnut Creek, CA: Left Coast Press.

Freire, P. (1999 [1992]). *Pedagogy of hope* (R. R. Barr, Trans.). New York: Continuum.

Garoian, C. R., & Gaudelius, Y. M. (2008). *Spectacle pedagogy: Art, politics and visual culture.* Albany: State University of New York Press.

Greenberg, K. J., & Dratel, J. L. (Eds.). (2005). *The torture papers: The road to Abu Ghraib*. Cambridge: Cambridge University Press.

Greenwald, G. (2009). The newly released secret laws of the Bush administration. *Salon*, March 3. http://www.salon.com/opinion/greenwald/2009/03/03/yoo (accessed August 12, 2009).

Guba. E. (1990). Carrying on the dialog. In E. Guba (Ed.), *The paradigm dialog* (pp. 368–378). Thousand Oaks, CA: Sage.

Hammersley, M. (2008). *Questioning qualitative inquiry: Critical essays*. London: Sage.

Hersh, S. (2005). *Chain of command: The road from 9/11 to Abu Ghraib*. New York: HarperCollins.

Jones, A., & Jenkins, K. (2008). Rethinking collaboration: Working the indigene-colonizer hyphen. In N. K. Denzin, Y. S. Lincoln, and L. T. Smith (Eds.), *Handbook of critical and indigenous methodologies* (pp. 47–486). Thousand Oaks, CA: Sage.

Kaufman, M. (2001). *The Laramie Project: A Play of Moises Kaufman and the members of the Tectonic Theater Project*. New York: Vintage Books.

Keifer-Boyd, K. (2009). Arts-based research as social justice activism: Insight, inquiry, imagination, embodiment, and relationality. Unpublished manuscript.

Kennedy, R. F. (1966). Day of Affirmation address. University of Cape Town. Cape Town, South Africa, June 6. http://www.jfklibrary.org/Historical+Resources/Archives/Reference+Desk/Speeches/RFK/Day+of+Affirmation+Address+News+Release.htm (accessed December 20, 2009).

Krog, A., Mpolweni-Zantsi, N., & Ratele, K. (2008). The South African Truth and Reconciliation Commission (TRC): Ways of knowing Mrs. Konile. In N. K. Denzin, Y. S. Lincoln, and L. T. Smith (Eds.), *Handbook of critical and indigenous methodologies* (pp. 531–546). Thousand Oaks, CA: Sage.

Lincoln, Y. S., & Denzin, N. K. (2008). Epilogue: The lions speak. In N. K. Denzin, Y. S. Lincoln, and L. T. Smith (Eds.), *Handbook of critical and indigenous methodologies* (pp. 563–571). Thousand Oaks, CA: Sage.

Madison, D. S. (2005). *Critical ethnography*. Thousand Oaks, CA: Sage.

Madison, D. S., & Hamera, J. (2006). Performance studies at the intersection. In D. S. Madison and J. Hamera (Eds.), *The Sage handbook of performance studies* (pp. xi–xxv). Thousand Oaks, CA: Sage.

Martinez-Salgado, C. (2009). Qualitative inquiry with women in poverty in Mexico City: Reflections on the emotional responses of a research team. *International Journal of Qualitative Studies in Education, 22*, 3, 297–314.

McCaslin, W. & Breton, D. C. (2008). Justice as healing: Going outside the colonizer's cage. In N. K. Denzin, Y. S. Lincoln, and L. T. Smith (Eds.), *Handbook of critical and indigenous methodologies* (pp. 511–530). Thousand Oaks, CA: Sage.

Mertens, D. M., Holmes, H., & Harris, R. (2009). Transformative research and ethics. In D. M. Mertens and P. E. Ginsberg (Eds.), *Handbook of social research ethics* (pp. 85–101). Thousand Oaks, CA: Sage.

Schwandt, T. (2006). Opposition redirected. *International Journal of Qualitative Studies in Education, 19*, 6, 803–810.

Sinclair, U. (1906). *The jungle.* New York: Doubleday.

Smith, A. D. (2004). *House arrest and piano.* New York: Anchor.

Stanfield, J. H., II. (2006). The possible restorative justice functions of qualitative research. *International Journal of Qualitative Studies in Education, 19*, 6, 723–727.

Sullivan, A. (2009). Yoo, Bybee, Bradbury: Tick tock. *The Daily Dish*, February 15. http://andrewsullivan.theatlantic.com/the_daily_dish/2009/02/yoo-bybee-bradb.html (accessed December 20, 2009).

Toobin, J. (2009). Hiding Jay Bybee. *The New Yorker*, April 16. from http://www.newyorker.com/online/blogs/newsdesk/2009/04/jeffrey-toobin-hiding-bybee.html (accessed December 19, 2009).

Yellow Bird, M. (2005). Tribal critical thinking centers. In W. A. Wilson and M. Yellow Bird (Eds.), *For indigenous eyes only: A decolonizing handbook* (pp. 9–30). Santa Fe, NM: School of American Research.

Zinn, H. (2005). Occupied zones. *Le Monde Diplomatique.* http://mondediplo.com/2005/08/04iraq (accessed February 4, 2010).

Section 1: Theory

1. Theories for a Global Ethics

Clifford G. Christians

The urgent need for a global media ethics that matches the scope and muscle of today's communication technologies has become obvious. In light of the power of transnational media corporations and worldwide high-speed electronic technologies, it is imperative that communication ethics become broad enough and strong enough to match the media's international impact. Human rights are a global concern also. Without universal principles to deal with them, we are stuck with a subservient ethics that echoes the status quo. Ethical theories rooted in Enlightenment rationalism have been exposed as imperialistic. The primary issue is identifying a different kind of universal, one that honors the splendid variety of human life while articulating cross-cultural norms. Rather than presuming the modernist logic of abstraction, social justice requires normative models that can be advocated and empower us to action.

Scientific Theories

Ethical rationalism has served as the prevailing paradigm in Western communication ethics. Consistent with mainstream philosophical ethics generally, media ethics has presumed that rationality marks all legitimate claims about moral obligations, so that the truth of those claims can be settled by formal examination of their logical structure. This is the unilateral model rooted in René Descartes (1596–1690), the architect of the Enlightenment mind.

Descartes insisted on the noncontingency of starting points, unconditioned by circumstance. His *Meditations II* presumes clear and distinct ideas, objective and neutral. And his *Discourse on Method* (1998 [1637]) elaborates this objectivist notion in more detail. Genuine knowledge is built up in linear fashion, with pure mathematics the least touched by circumstances. The equation 2 + 2 = 4 is lucid and testable, and all valid knowledge in Descartes' view should be as cognitively clean as arithmetic.

As the eighteenth century heated up around Cartesian rationality, Kant (1724–1804) was schooled in Descartes, mathematics, and Newtonian physics. Kant's first major book, *Universal History of the Nature and Theory of the Heavens* (2009 [1755]), explained the structure of the universe exclusively in terms of Newtonian cosmology. Then, in the *Groundwork of the Metaphysic of Morals* (1964 [1785]) and *Critique of Practical Reason* (1997 [1788]), Kant assimilated ethics into logic. He demanded that moral laws be universally applicable and free from inner contradiction. Society was presumed to have a fundamental moral structure embedded in human nature as basic as atoms in physics, with the moral law the analog of the unchanging laws of gravity. Through the mental calculus of willing an individual's action to be universalized, imperatives are understood to emerge unconditioned by circumstances. Moral absolutes are identified precisely in the rational way syllogisms are divided into valid and invalid.

This is a correspondence view of truth, with an extremely narrow definition of what counts as ethics. Instead of prizing care and reciprocity, for example, moral understanding becomes prescriptivist, arid, and absolutist. For the ethical rationalism of single-strand theorizing, the truth of all legitimate claims about moral obligation can be settled by formally examining their logical structure. Humans act against moral obligations only if they are willing to endure the illogic of self-contradiction. In contrast to the tri-level ethics introduced here, modernity's confidence in the power of reason produces ethical principles that are considered the same for all thinking subjects, every nation, all epochs, and every culture.

This ethical formalism has been the dominant paradigm in communication ethics. In mainstream professional ethics, an apparatus of neutral standards is constructed in terms of the major issues practitioners face in their everyday routines. The influential theory—utilitarianism, for example—presumes one set of calculations that is applied consistently and self-consciously to every choice. As a single-consideration theory, it not only demands that we maximize general happiness but considers irrelevant other moral imperatives that conflict with it, such as equal distribution. Since the origins of this model from Mill (1888 [1843], 1975 [1859], 1979 [1861]), neutrality is seen as necessary to guarantee individual autonomy; and through autonomous reason, principles and prescriptions established as the arbiters of moral disputes. This commitment to neutrality made utilitarian ethics attractive for its compatibility with the canons of rational calculation. Cognitive processes create basic rule of ethics that everyone is obliged to follow and against which all failures in moral duty can be measured.

Alternative Theories of Universals

Several anti-Enlightenment models of ethics have been developed or are under way. The Eurocentric ethical canon—essentially a monocultural, parochial, and patriarchal one—is being replaced by transnational frameworks. In recovering the idea of moral universals, they recognize that this must be done without presuming first foundations, without the luxury of an objective reality from which to begin.

Seyla Benhabib (1992, and see 2002) has developed the principle of interactive universalism, not subject to Lyotard's objection that grand narratives are no longer possible. She takes seriously the contributions of feminism and communitarianism. Her idea of interactive, dialogic rationality keeps ethics close to human everyday experience. Diversity in culture is recognized rather than burying differences under an abstract metaphysics.

Cees Hamelink (2000) appeals to international human rights for moral guidance. Human rights provide the only universally available principles for the dignity and integrity of all human beings. The world political community has recognized the existence of human rights since the adoption of the UN Charter in 1945 and has accepted international legal machinery for their enforcement. Core human rights include the rights to life, food, health care, the due process of law, education, freedom of expression, and political participation.

Martha Nussbaum (2000, and see 2006) uses extensive research into the daily lives of women in the nonindustrial world to argue for overlapping capabilities that are true of humans universally as they work out their existence in the world. The common values that emerge from people's daily struggles are bodily health, affiliations of compassion, recreation, education, employment, and political participation. All human beings are fully capable of all these functions and the countless ways of doing them overlap and establish the possibilities of universals.

Kwasi Wiredu (1996) writes from an African philosophical perspective. The human species lives by language. All languages are similar in their phonemic complexity and all serve not merely functional roles but cultural formation. Languages everywhere are communal and give peoples their identity. Through the commonness we share as lingual beings we can believe that there are universals at the same time as we live in our particular communities.

In a study of ethical principles in thirteen countries on four continents, the sacredness of human life is consistently affirmed as a universal value (Christians & Traber, 1997). The rationale for human action is reverence for life on Earth. The scientific view of the natural world cannot account for the purposiveness of life itself. Living nature reproduces itself in terms of its very character. Therefore, within natural reality is a moral claim on us for its own sake and in its own right. Reverence for life on Earth is a pretheoretical given that makes the moral order possible. The veneration of human life represents a universalism from the ground up. Various societies articulate this protonorm in different terms and illustrate it locally, but the primal sacredness of life binds humans into a common oneness.

What theory of knowledge is entailed by these efforts to establish credible universal models and is it defensible? What they presume is a presuppositional epistemology. Each of the theoretical models is grounded in first beliefs, not in objectivist absolutes.

Universalist theories have discredited themselves over history by breeding totalitarianism. Those who claim knowledge of universal truth typically use it to control or convert dissenters. In light of this objection, it must be reiterated that the universalist appeals from Benhabib through Traber and Christians are not foundational *a prioras*. Interactive universalism, international human rights, overlapping capabilities, lingual commonality, and the sacredness of life in the alternative models are not metaphysical givens but core beliefs about human existence. They are presuppositions to which we are committed inescapably; one cannot proceed intellectually without taking something as given.

Cartesian rationalism and Kant's formalism presumed noncontingent starting points. These five theories do not. They are interpretive schemes that arise from and explicate our fundamental beliefs about the world. As Michael Polanyi (1968) made obvious, all our knowledge cannot be formalized. Any series of explicit operations presupposes a fund of inexplicit beliefs. It is our reliance on these primordial generalities that makes comprehension possible. A faith commitment is the very condition through which human cognition is intelligible.

In communication ethics, we articulate practices and moral claims to the normative theory they imply, and such normative claims to the worldview or presuppositions on which they are based. Humans live by interpretations. Systems of meaning and value are produced as a creative process. We are born into an intelligible and interpreted universe, and we use these interpretations creatively for making sense of our lives and institutions. The researcher's primary obligation is getting inside the way humans arbitrate their presence in the world; therefore, the presuppositions of human existence are the centerpiece of interpretive research.

The connection between intellectual work and descriptive accounts cannot be understood in one-dimensional terms. Plato has convinced us apparently that if B depends on A or its existence, then B is inferior. In Platonic terms, generic knowledge is superior to particular knowledge. In the alternative models summarized here, though, the theory-practice relationship is not linear but dialectical. Theories are embedded existentially, and they integrate and interpret knowledge without jettisoning natural settings. Philosophical proclivity toward reason presumes an objective, ahistorical foundation of knowledge. However, an epistemology of first beliefs is grounded theory. These theories yield meaningful portraits, not statistically precise formulations derived from artificially fixed conditions. Theorizing is redefined not as an examination of external events but as the power of the imagination to give us an inside perspective on reality. Thomas Kuhn (1996) calls this revolutionary science—the construction of paradigms—rather than the normal science of verifying that propositions are externally and internally valid.

This perspective situates normative phenomena within culture and history. As an intellectual strategy, it shifts transcendental criteria from a metphysical and vertical plane to horizons of community and being, but universal norms they remain nonetheless. Our common humanity is not inscribed, first of all, in politics or economics, or in overcoming national boundaries by the transportation of data. Human beings resonate cross-culturally through their moral imagination with one another. Our mutual humanness is actually an ethical commitment rooted in the moral domain all humans share.

Three-Level Theory

Learning from the alternative models described here, I propose a three-dimensional theory for global media ethics—that is, one composed of presuppositions, principles, and precepts. It is opposed explicitly to single-strand Enlightenment universals. Its integration of the three levels makes it more sophisticated than the existing schemes, and it privileges social justice to an extent the others do not.

In the tripartite moral theory proposed here, on the presuppositional level, the human species is not simply a biological or psychological entity, but understood as lingual beings who seek expression within the physical and cultural world. For Hans Georg Gadamer (1989 [1975]), theory construction is embedded within everyday life and is borne along by it. In the tri-level alternative, our theorizing seeks to disclose the fundamental conditions of our mode of existence (Shin 1994). Gadamer calls this broad inquiry "ontological." Language situates our human beingness in the world. Theories do not exist without starting points or what is typically labeled "worldviews." Worldviews as pre-principial conditions of knowledge are ineluctable, not accidental, fundamental though not foundational. Worldviews are the gyroscopes around which thinking and experience revolve, our ultimate commitments at the core of our being. They are sine qua non in theory building.

Various philosophies and religions will disagree fundamentally on their presuppositions about the human, reality, and knowing. But consensus on principles may be possible around such universal norms as the sacredness of human life, Benhabib's dialogic mutuality, core human rights, overlapping capabilities, or authenticity in communication (Cooper, 1998). Such principles are not abstract theorems, noncontingent and decontextual. Triangular theory situates principles as normative phenomena within culture and history. They are protonorms that hold our conceptual world together.

On another level, such precepts as justice, human dignity, and nonviolence are entailed by the presuppositions and principles. Precepts are not a linear next step, that is, application, but one constituent of a composite whole. One can enter the hermeneutic circle through these precepts and solve the universal problem on this level too. We can reach transnational agreement on a precept such as human dignity, for example, despite differences over presuppositions and the principial. In monotheism, humans are created in the image of God and are therefore sacred. The Universal Declaration of Human Rights by the United Nations General Assembly in 1948 recognizes the "inherent dignity and inalienable rights of all members of the human family." In Latin America, insisting on cultural identity is an affirmation of the unique worth of the human species.

This triangular theory does not fall prey to the fallacy of rationalistic ethics, where reason determines both the genesis and the conclusion. In a normative ethics of this sort, the domain of the good is not extrinsic, calibrated by formal rules that autonomous moral agents must apply consistently and self-consciously to every choice.

For universals to be credible as theory, the three dimensions need to be integrated into a coherent whole. Therefore, the theory of global media ethics that I propose has holistic humans as its presupposition, the universal sacredness of life understood as the golden rule for its principle, and the precept of justice entailed by the principle and presupposition while feeding back into them.

As a presupposition, humans are understood in this theory to be an indivisible, organic unity with multisided moral, mental, and physical capabilities. Deeper than technical strategies for teaching moral codes to professionals is the profound educational need to awaken our inner being to the higher vision. This is a way of knowing that is nonconceptual or preconceptual, one in which the inner powers of our basic humanity are released. In Taoism, this is Tian—an unseen power that leads the world's creatures in a harmonious way. People belong to a supersensible world of soul and spirit that always surrounds them while animating them. Morality is rooted in our whole being—body, mind, and spirit. Ethics' vitality depends on the interconnectedness of life and ultimately exposes us to the larger vision of what it means to be humans inhabiting the cosmos.

Holistic humans as beings-in-relation live within and bring to expression the sacredness of life, elaborated as a norm in terms of the golden rule. From a religious perspective, almost all discussions of a common ethics refer to the golden rule as a guide for morally appropriate action. Küng (1991, chap. 5) is one prominent scholar who believes that all the great religions require observance of something like, "Do to others as you would have them do to you." In monotheistic religions it becomes "love your neighbor as yourself." In Confucianism, others are encouraged to go the way we would ourselves desire (Waley, 1989). Acting toward others as we wish others to treat us is clear, unarguable, and the intuitive way to live harmoniously in the human world. It proceeds from an understanding of human dignity—we regard others basically like ourselves. Its secret is avoiding a list of prohibited acts and providing a way to think about the common good. Its brevity and simplicity obscure its radical implications for acting principially in the face of complex situations. When followed as a normative strategy, it produces a community of good will.

Precepts in formal terms include all duties to self, to others, and to human institutions. In this coherent theory of global media ethics, the presupposition of holistic humans and the golden rule as principle yield the precept of justice. They are entailed by reflective equilibrium, and even as the presupposition and principle invoke justice and are inscribed in it, the precept feeds into the whole. Justice is rooted in holistic humanness and the golden rule. Humans-in-dialog require that justice be normative. The golden rule presumes justice in its formulation and execution. Without the presumption of justice, the moral dimension of society is inconceivable. Undergirded by holistic humanness and the reciprocity of the golden rule, social justice becomes a compelling constituent of a global media ethics.

Justice

In the traditional understanding of modernist ethics, "justice means the consistent and continuous application of the same norms and rules to each and every member of the social cluster to which the norms and rules apply" (Heller, 1987a, p. 5). But this formal concept presumes a discredited quasi-scientific functionalist view of society, and it does not ensure that the rules being applied correctly are themselves just. Nor does it calibrate the extent to which social causes make the equal application of rules inequitable.

Moreover, static modernist justice has been emaciated by the crises of contemporary life. Only remnants of distributive justice remain. It is haunted by its inability to determine criteria for inequality, its struggles over which kind of inequalities beyond income matter, and how far inequalities should go. In John Rawls's theory of justice, "what is approved of is 'fairness,' the shabby remnant of the 'sum total of virtues' that once was called 'justice.'... In the place of sociopolitical justice, only *minima moralis* remains" (Heller, 1987a, p. 93). Instead of the thin version of modernity, triangular theory produces a dynamic justice with three emphases: universal access, cultural continuity, and principled politics.

Universal Access

The first question of justice is accessibility. In terms of distributive justice in a global ethics, media access is allocated to everyone according to essential needs, regardless of income or geographical location. Comprehensive information ought to be ensured to all parties without discrimination. In contrast, the standard conception among privately owned media is allocating to each according to ability to pay. The open marketplace of supply and demand determines who obtains the service. From this perspective, commercial companies are not considered charitable organizations and therefore have no obligation to subsidize the information poor.

An ethics of justice where distribution is based on need offers a radical alternative to the conventional view. Fundamental human needs are related to survival or subsistence. They are not frivolous wants or individual whims. Agreement is rather uniform on a list of most human necessities—food, housing, safety, and medical care. Everyone is entitled without regard for individual success to that which permits them to live humanely.

The electronic superhighway cannot be envisioned except as a necessity. Communications networks make the global economy run; they give us access to agricultural and health care information; they organize world trade; they are the channels through which the United Nations and political discussion flow; through them we monitor war and peace. Therefore, as a necessity of life in a global order, the information system ought to be distributed impartially, regardless of income, race, religion, or merit.

But there is no reasonable likelihood that need-based distribution will ever be fulfilled by the marketplace itself. In some African nations, only 5% have regular access to telephones—and telephony is a minimal tool of the information highway. In industrialized societies, digital networks tend to reach their maximum power and profitability at 25% of the gross population, making universal access driven by profits unlikely. An ethics of justice requires that we intervene through legislation, government policy, and public ownership to implement open accessibility. Our approach to media institutions should be modeled after schools, which we accept as our common responsibility, rather than determined by engineers or by profits alone.

Given the realities of international politics and limited resources, the need-based principle of justice must be supplemented by the similar treatment formula. In the actual distribution of services under suboptimal conditions, the principle of similar treatment for similar cases calls us to honor the equal distribution of limited services for all. If providing an entire range of expensive technologies for everyone is impossible, it is unjust for a few to be equipped with sophisticated systems and the rest given only minimal service or none at all. If we accept the case for equal access, it is more just to discriminate in terms of categories of service rather than between the information rich and poor. All homes, for instance, could have fire and police view-data communications capability, rather than some being served by every convenience and others receiving no benefits. The formula of similar treatment for similar cases modifies the application of a need-conception of justice to address the real world of constraints. But the goal of equal access to essential services remains because of its moral significance. To realize it only in part is better than jettisoning the formula because of difficulties in implementing it within an environment characterized by resource limitations.

Obviously our conceptual world at this stage must be distinctively global rather than nation-state in orientation. Distributive justice earlier produced a social responsibility framework for broadcasting and a professional ethics of social responsibility for newspapers and magazines. The guideline was informed citizenship, a public learning the day's events in a context of meaning. For telecommunications, the just distribution principle yields the norm of equitable access, with data transmission, telephony, and legal and postal services available to everyone following equivalent standards.

But social responsibility for broadcasting and journalism and equitable access for telecommunications are guidelines in a national setting. They presume and serve explicit political entities. In the digital age—rooted in computers, the Internet, satellites, and the World-Wide Web—ideally all types of persons will use all types of media services for all types of audiences. Therefore, the normative guideline ought to be universal access, based on need. And universal service is the Achilles heel of new technologies driven by invention, engineering, and markets. As the economic disparity between rich and poor continues to grow, a structurally defined information underclass is excluded from an important pathway to equality. Without intervention into the commercial system on behalf of distributive justice, we will continue to divide the world into the technologically elite and those without adequate means to participate.

Cultural Continuity

The second question of justice as a precept is cultural continuity. The global media as agents of enculturation ought to be judged by the norm of cultural continuity. Cultures are patterns of belief and behavior that orient life and provide it significance. They constitute the human kingdom by organizing reality and indicating what we ought to do and avoid. Cultures are stitched together to direct societal practice. Max Weber called them the "webs of significance" within which the human race uniquely lives. Without the inheritance and transmission of cultural forms, we cannot exist as a species. I speak of the natural order—all humans are cultural beings.

To put this dimension of justice in more technical language, note the formal criterion: Technological products are legitimate if and only if they maintain cultural continuity. This value-laden enterprise we call media technology, to be set in a normative direction, must comport well with cultural continuity.[1] The viability of historically and geographically constituted peoples ought to be nonnegotiable. Given culture's centrality in our humanness, its continuity warrants a distinctive emphasis.

I am suggesting that our technological activities must comport well with the norm of cultural continuity, "comport well" carrying with it a creative ambiguity. One the one hand, it asks for a strong relationship, one rooted in cultural continuity. On the other hand, it does not specify this relationship precisely. "Comport well" suggests that not all technological activities are detailed in the principle and that they cannot be deduced directly from it.

I am not proposing a truncated view of continuity without discontinuity; that, at best, represents an ancient Greek cyclical view of history. But I choose to emphasize continuity so as to contradict notions of blind evolutionary progress that undervalue continuity altogether. Also, continuity undercuts the modernization schemes perpetrated by transnational companies to strengthen their hegemony. Perhaps oscillation conveys the appropriate image of a dialectic between continuity and discontinuity, with the overall pattern one of cultural formation rather than rejection.

Clearly, opposites are at work here—differentiation and integration, centralization and decentralization, large scale and small scale, uniformity, and pluriformity. And difficult choices must often be made between these opposites. But the prevailing direction is always toward differentials, decentralization, small scale, and pluriformity. Sometimes that results in a break with past practices (discontinuity), but such disruptions are made more gradually and by smaller steps when controlled by continuity as the master principle. The point is to place a final decision about the mix in the hands of natives who speak in their own interests for those technological innovations that most appropriately serve their local cultures.

Ivan Illich (1973) calls for convivial tools—those responsibly limited and thereby empowering. Convivial technology respects the dignity of human work, needs little specialized training to operate, and is generally accessible. Convivial tools with a human face are interactive and maintain a kind of open-ended conversation with their users. Because of their simplicity and transparency, they cannot be mystified and do not give rise to professional monopolies of knowledge.

Opposition to the autocratic leadership of Iran has been effectively organized by alternative media—iPods, Facebook, laptops, cell phones, photocopiers, and digital cameras. Independent film companies, underground presses, community radio, and popular theater can go for the mass media's jugular and provide a competitive communication system from below. In the people's tongue they nurture communities of authentic being in local settings. TV Globo has a virtual monopoly in Brazil, for example. But locally owned video cameras provide a convivial alternative; backyard groups use them as a tool for social change. The Metalworkers Union of São Bernardo has developed a training project called Workers' TV. The diffusion of video among union locals gives a voice to audiences outside government control.

In Toronto, videos in schools, churches, and community forums are used to help Latin American immigrants settle into a new way of life in Canada. Programs produced and distributed by immigrants themselves encourage the cultural authenticity that is marginalized by the corporate and technological constraints of the traditional media.

In June 1989, the government of the People's Republic of China brutally crushed the student-led pro-democracy movement at Tiananmen Square. The government issued massive disinformation and slapped restrictions on the foreign reporters in China for the Sino-Soviet Summit. But Chinese students within the country set the record straight by using personal electronic media—fax, radio, cassettes, instamatic cameras, and mobile phones—to communicate to the world.

We can weave together an alternative media system following the norm of cultural continuity—one that is close to the ground and participatory in character, at the fissures in political and economic institutions where some wiggle-room is possible. Manifestoes, pamphlets, websites, educational materials, smartphones (BlackBerrys, iPhones, etc.), discussion guides, online journalism, films—all in the vernacular tongue—help people's movements gain their own voice and nurture appropriate options for social change. History provides indisputable evidence that the word is mightier than the sword—that it can cut deeply into our consciences if operating in everyday language out of cultural authenticity.

Principled Politics

In terms of principled politics as described by Agnes Heller,[2] social change is not limited to economic and political reforms, but, instead, involves our entire way of life—human interpersonal relationships included. Justice is not only concerned with poverty, "but with the eradication of human degradation, dependency and lack of dignity" (Murphy, 1994, p. 171). Rather than a formal righteousness of complying with the established rules, the virtues of the good life are promoted: Turning one's endowments into talents, vigorous involvement in public affairs, and the formation of close personal attachments that enhance the well-being of others (Heller, 1987a, pp. 313–320).

A sociopolitical world characterized by principled politics offers optimal possibilities for developing natural capacities to the maximum. In the best possible political system, "no way of life involves domination; ... there cannot exist any endowment the development of which into a talent would not be permitted. ... Different ways of life enhance different talents; and a person is free to relinquish one way of life and take up another" (Heller, 1987a, p. 313). In modern functionalist societies, talents for the market have increased and it is easier "to maneuver well within rationalized institutions" (Heller, 1987a, p. 309). However, liberal egalitarianism is not radical enough to foster human growth as a whole. It may have the "best interests of ordinary people at heart, but it is a model that favors ... the capitalist model of 'merit' as profit maximization"; those with a "formidable talent for poetry and a lesser talent for learning legal case studies would rarely be encouraged to develop the former in favor of the latter" (Tormey, 2001, p. 140). Consistent with the presupposition of organic humans on which this precept is based, the process of developing our endowments is understood as the holistic construction of the self—moral, intellectual, artistic, and personal.

This dimension of justice also means control over one's affairs through active involvement in politics. Good citizens interpret their rights as responsibilities. They are "concerned with matters of justice and injustice in the state and participate in acts which aim to remedy injustice" (Heller, 1990a, pp. 124, 147). Good citizens share the conviction that justice is the supreme public good and show a commitment to social institutions and the flourishing of the citizenry.

Dynamic justice is affirmed and sustained cross-culturally. When principled politics comes into its own, we live in a "pluralistic cultural universe in which each culture is tied to every other culture by the bonds of symmetric reciprocity" (Heller, 1987a, p. 323). There is no attempt to legislate a single way of life. Various value systems can exist without destroying each other. Principled politics respects heterogeneity and multiculturalism and defends a multiplicity of customs, individual options, and cultural traditions.

But the challenge of cultural diversity raises the stakes and makes easy solutions impossible. One of the most urgent and vexing issues on the democratic agenda at present is recognizing explicit cultural groups politically. However, liberal proceduralism cannot meet this vital human need. Emphasizing equal rights, with no particular substantive view of the good life, "gives only a very restricted acknowledgement of distinct cultural identities" (Taylor et al., 1994, p. 26). Insisting on neutrality and living without collective aspirations, produce at best only personal freedom, safety, and economic security. Unlike liberalism, the primary concern of principled politics is not simply expanding the sphere of private choice, but "eradicating those kinds of asymmetrical human relationships where one person can impose and direct the will of another person" (Murphy, 1994, p. 171). With holistic humans as the presupposition and the golden rule as principle, the flourishing of particular cultures, religions, and citizen-groups is the substantive precept to which we are morally committed as human beings.

Conclusion

Social justice as universal access, cultural continuity, and principled politics establishes the ethics framework in which human rights can be theorized and practiced. This model of justice leads to resistance and empowers the interactive self and others to action. Although a transnational concept, it enables the humane transformation of the multiple spheres of community life locally—religion, politics, ethnicity, gender, and education. As a precept within a universal presupposition and principle, justice refuses to deal with power in cognitive terms only. With its political-institutional bearing, although committed to the dialogic spaces of everyday life, the issue is how we can empower people instead. Otherwise there is only acquiescence in the status quo.

Given its struggles over citizenship, access, and cultural continuity, dynamic justice steadfastly refuses to decouple the rational and radical, and thus contributes an extraordinary understanding of emancipatory praxis to global media ethics.

For both theory and practice, justice—defined here as a precept—advocates a process of moral reasoning. But how can we recognize such moral discourse when it occurs and prevent its distortions and contradictions? Agnes Heller (1994) answers the question this way: Morality belongs to the human condition; there are immoral but no amoral persons. The existential choice of humans for justice is the basis for claiming that righteous persons are possible. Thus, as Heller describes her work in *A Philosophy of Morals* (1990a), she did not build a system, but observed decent persons in their lives. "I gave a report of their predicaments and noted how they dealt with them" (Heller, 1995, p. 308). Exceptional acts of responsibility under duress and predicaments, each in their own way, are especially "worthy of theoretical interest" (Heller, 1995, p. 3). Accumulated wisdom from human struggles and moral meaning from choices of justice together produce a comprehensive, nonabsolutist, but principled concept of morality.

Persons understand justice if they prefer to suffer wrong rather than to wrong others (Heller, 1988, p. 174). In formal terms, "The righteous person is the person who prefers suffering injustice (being wronged) to committing injustice (doing wrong), where committing injustice means infringing moral norms in direct relation to other people" (Heller, 1987a, p. 279). Heller recognizes that it is impossible to prove that suffering injustice is better than committing it. In fact, it often seems irrational "to opt for honesty and goodness even though these qualities may not bring obvious benefits" (Camps, 1994, p. 239). But this affirmation is the cornerstone of justice as an ethical precept nonetheless. Trying to answer the question why some people prefer justice is unproductive. The primary ingredient of the good life is righteousness—that is, preferring good rather than evil. "Certainly there are persons who demonstrate their moral autonomy in this way," whether we know why or not (Camps, 1994, p. 240). A physician trained in the Royal College of Surgeons chooses a leper colony near Cairo rather than practice medicine among the wealthy in London. A person suffers slander in order to not betray the confidence of a friend (Heller, 1987a, p. 319). The Holocaust as a defining evil of the twentieth century cannot be understood only in terms of Hitler. One must account for Oscar Schindler and the benefactors of Anne Frank. "No matter where we look, we shall always find righteous people. Whether such people are few or many is irrelevant. They exist" (Heller, 1987a, p. 281).

In resolving the central question of how persons acting justly are possible, the theory of global ethics presented here appeals to the human context rather than to essentialist human nature. Through Heller, the aspect of the human condition on which the theory focuses is that of contingency. She sees us as "the first generation who knows of the absence of its existential foundations." This is not a temporary absence or a nuisance to be overcome, but an "absence which one needs to accept as a fate" (Bauman, 1994, p. 116). We live with Dostoyevsky's warning, "If there is not God, everything is permissible" and with Durkheim's premonition that "if the normative grip of society slackens, the moral order will collapse." Heller calls us to "make the fate of contingency into a consciously embraced destiny" (Bauman, 1994, p. 116). Justice, not as an isolated imperative but the perceptual component of a triangular ethics, equips us to make contingency a conscious choice and life-building principle.

The three-tiered theory introduced here points us to a new model of universals in communication ethics. Rather than searching for neutral principles to which all parties can appeal, this global media ethics is rooted in a complex view of moral judgments as integrating presuppositions, principles, and precepts in terms of human wholeness. It escapes the reductionist and static view of humans as rational beings, while bringing a dynamic justice decisively into the public arena. Moral theory in three dimensions enables a new generation of communication ethics, one that is philosophically credible, transnational, intercultural, gender inclusive, and ethnically diverse. Instead of single-strand modernist theories that are considered neutral and entail a correspondence view of reality, this normative model inspires our passion for human rights.

Notes

1. For an expanded version of this principle, see Christians (2007).
2. Agnes Heller is the Hannah Arendt Professor of Philosophy emerita at the New School for Social Research. She was a star student of Hungarian Georg Lukás, and professor with him at the University of Budapest and at the Institute of Sociology until her dismissal in 1973. As Martin Jay observes,

> There have been few more strikingly appropriate academic honors than the selection of Agnes Heller as the New School's Hannah Arendt Professor of Philosophy (in 1986). For the holder of the chair and the thinker after whom it is named are inextricably linked in a myriad of important ways. ... Born a generation apart, both were products of that remarkably creative, if often restlessly tormented ... Central European Jewry. (1994, p. 41)

For two examples of how their work intersects, see Heller's inaugural address (1990b) and an essay of hers devoted to Arendt's final work (1987b).

References

Bauman, Z. (1994). Narrating modernity. In J. Burnheim (Ed.), *The social philosophy of Agnes Heller* (pp. 57–77). Amsterdam, the Netherlands and Atlanta: Rodopi.

Benhabib, S. (1992). *Situating the self: Gender, community, and postmodernism in contemporary ethics.* New York: Routledge.

Benhabib, S. (2002). *The claims of culture: Equality and diversity in the global era.* Princeton, NJ: Princeton University Press.

Camps, V. (1994). The good life: A moral gesture. In J. Burnheim (Ed.), The social philosophy of Agnes Heller (pp. 239–248). Amsterdam, The Netherlands, and Atlanta: Rodopi.

Christians, C. (2007). Cultural continuity as an ethical imperative. *Qualitative Inquiry*, 13, 3, 437–444.

Christians, C., & Traber, M. (1997). *Communication ethics and universal values.* Thousand Oaks, CA: Sage.

Cooper, T. (1998). *A time before deception: Truth in communication, culture and ethics.* Santa Fe, NM: Clear Light Publishers.

Descartes, R. (1998 [1637]). *Discourse on method* (D. A. Cress, Trans.). Indianapolis: Hackett Publishing Co.

Gadamer, H. D. (1989 [1975]). *Truth and method. [Wahrheit und methode: Grunzuge einer philosophischen hermeneutic]* (J. Weinsheimer and D. G. Marshall, Trans.) (2nd ed.) New York: Seabury Press.

Hamelink, C. (2000). *The ethics of cyberspace.* Thousand Oaks, CA: Sage. (Originally published as *Digital fasoen,* Amsterdam, the Netherlands: Uitgeverij Boom, 1999.)

Heller, A. (1987a). *Beyond justice.* Oxford, UK: Basil Blackwell.

Heller, A. (1987b). Hannah Arendt on the "Vita Contemplative." *Philosophy and Social Criticism,* 12, 4, 281–296.

Heller, A. (1988). *General ethics.* Oxford, UK: Basil Blackwell.

Heller, A. (1990a). *A philosophy of morals.* Oxford, UK: Basil Blackwell.

Heller, A. (1990b). The concept of the political revisited. In A. Heller (Ed.), *Can modernity survive?* (pp. 112–127). Cambridge, UK: Polity.

Heller, A. (1995). *An ethics of personality.* Oxford, UK: Basil Blackwell.

Illich, I. (1973). *Tools for conviviality.* New York: Harper Colophon.

Jay, M. (1994). Women in dark times: Agnes Heller and Hannah Arendt." In J. Burnheim (Ed.), *The social philosophy of Agnes Heller* (pp. 41–55). Amsterdam, the Netherlands and Atlanta: Rodopi.

Kant, I. (2009 [1755]). *Universal history of the nature and theory of the heaven.* (I. Johnston, Trans.). Arlington, VA: Richer.

Kant, I. (1964 [1785]). *Groundwork of the metaphysic of morals* (M. Gregor, Trans.). Cambridge, UK: Cambridge University Press.

Kant, I. (1997 [1788]). *Critique of practical reason* (M. Gregor, Trans.). Cambridge, UK: Cambridge University Press.

Kuhn, T. (1996). *The structure of scientific revolutions* (3rd ed.). Chicago: University of Chicago Press.

Küng, H. (1991). *Global responsibility: In search of a new world ethic* (J. Bowden, Trans.). London: SCM Press.

Mill, J. S. (1888 [1843]). *A system of logic, ratiocinative and inductive: Being a connected view of the principles of evidence and the methods of scientific investigation* (8th ed.). New York: Harper and Brothers.

Mill, J. S. (1975 [1859]). *On liberty.* New York: Norton.

Mill, J. S. (1979 [1861]). *Utilitarianism.* Indianapolis: Hackett.

Murphy, P. (1994). Civility and radicalism. Pluralism and politics. In J. Burnheim (Ed.), *The social philosophy of Agnes Heller* (pp. 170–192, 194–238). Amsterdam, the Netherlands and Atlanta: Rodopi.

Nussbaum, M. (2000). *Women and human development: The capabilities approach.* Cambridge: Cambridge University Press.

Nussbaum, M. (2006). *Frontiers of justice: Disability, nationality, species membership.* Cambridge, MA: Harvard University Press.

Polanyi, M. (1968). *The tacit dimension.* Garden City, NY: Doubleday.

Shin, K. (1994). *A hermeneutic utopia: H. G. Gadamer's philosophy of culture.* Toronto: Two for Tea Press.

Taylor, C., Appiah, K. A., Habermas, J., Rockefeller, S. C., Walzer, M., & Wolf, S. (1994). *Multiculturalism: Examining the politics of recognition.* Princeton, NJ: Princeton University Press.

Tormey, S. (2001). *Agnes Heller: Socialism, autonomy and the postmodern.* Manchester, UK: Manchester University Press.

Waley, A. (1989). *The analects of Confucius.* New York: Vintage.

Wiredu, K. (1996). *Cultural universals and particulars: An African perspective.* Bloomington: Indiana University Press.

2. Human Rights Theory
Criteria, Boundaries, and Complexities

A. Belden Fields

Introduction

At the beginning of our century, the subject of human rights was largely dealt with by activists and scholars in political science (both international relations and political theory) and law. Since that time, it has been dealt with by a much wider array of disciplines, including those in the humanities. I applaud that scholarly diffusion. At the same time, as a political theorist, I have become a bit uneasy that perhaps those words "human rights" are being used without some kind of theoretical grounding as to what they really mean.

In certain cases, I suppose it does not matter very much. There was a very interesting conference held at the University of Illinois this past winter that focused on human rights in literature and film. The expression "human rights literature" was used when some of the subjects dealt with were obvious human rights violations. But when we move beyond the imaginary of literary fiction and film, more theoretical grounding of the words is called for. This obviously does not mean that we all have to agree on a particular grounding. But I think that we should be aware of at least some of the theoretical approaches that have been taken to ground human rights.

In this chapter, I am going to do five things. First, I am going to very briefly present three arguments as to why human rights really cannot be adequately grounded because it is a species of a genus, rights, that is itself suspect. In other words, human rights are a derivative of a concept that is socially and politically toxic. Second, I am going to discuss some of the criteria used by people who accept the concept of human rights as a valid one but attempt to constrain its scope. Third, I am going to refer very briefly to criteria used by a number of scholars who have attempted to ground human rights. Fourth, I am going to present an outline of my own "holistic" theory of human rights as a set of social practices. Finally, I am going to point to some of the perhaps disquieting complexities that inhere in such a holistic theoretical understanding.

Human Rights as Null and Void

The first two rejections of human rights are rejections of liberalism as such. Of course, one of the defining characteristics of Western liberalism was the reversal of the priority given to political obligation over individual rights claims. We see that manifested very clearly in the writing and speeches of the philosopher and politician Edmund Burke (1790). For Burke, society, including its political manifestations, is an organic process. It unfolds over time and its traditions are an important glue holding it together. Society can change, but that change must be gradual. Calls for change based on radical and utopian ideals or revolutionary experiences outside of a given particular society are a threat to the society itself. Thus, Burke was appalled both by the French Revolution, which broke completely with the prior tradition in France (as opposed to the American Revolution), and by the universalistic and egalitarian statements in the 1789 French Declaration of the Rights of Man and Citizen. For Burke, hierarchies that he judges to be not oppressive, such as the French monarchy, were important both as positive examples of appropriate conduct and culture and as a barrier to the excesses of the "swinish multitude." For Burke, then, it came as no surprise that the initial revolution and the Declaration of Rights were followed by the Terror and the guillotine as the oppressed took their revenge under the cloak of natural or universal rights that transcend any society.

The second rejection of rights that is also a rejection of liberalism is Marxism. Marx takes on the issue of individual rights as it is articulated by liberals in his essay, *On the Jewish Question* (1844). Here Marx argues, as many contemporary conservatives do, that the rights of individuals are intrinsically tied to the right to private property. Thus, for Marx, the "rights of man" are in fact an ideological cloak for the rights of individualistic, self-interested monads. The universalism of the rights of man hides a particularistic class interest. It is an ideological veil that leads us to believe that we can attain a good society without examining the role that property plays in estranging individuals from one another, as well as from oneself and in perpetuating the rule of one class of people over the other. Rights discourse, whether civil or individual, thus perpetuates an idealism that is counterproductive if the goal is human emancipation.

Not all contemporary Marxists agree with this assessment. For example, Levine (1981), although agreeing with Marx's analytical point that there can be no rational grounding for human rights if one is really interested in human dignity, also argues that at the present ideological and institutional moment there is no other device that can serve as such an effective reference point for criticism of the political and economic effects of contemporary dominant institutions. So Levine accepts human rights as a strategic necessity, even if an ungroundable concept (1981).

A third rejection of rights ironically emerged within liberalism itself. This is the utilitarianism of Jeremy Bentham and James Mill. This kind of liberalism has similarities with the thinking of both Burkean conservatism and Marxism. Like Burke, Bentham (1781) argued against any universal values that can be applied a priori to a given society. And, like Marx, he argued that rights thinking, because it is abstract and deontological, is necessarily separated from the relations of real people. Bentham argues instead for a consequentialist approach to political and juridical evaluation. That is to say, the criterion for the public good should be whatever produces the greatest happiness in a society. Although that calculation has a number of quantifiable dimensions to it, there can be no other extraneous qualitative value or criterion that can override it, values such as equality, freedom, or human rights. The idea is that good legislation reflects the calculation of legislators as to what maximizes general happiness and that no rights can be legitimately accepted that are outside of what those good laws would grant. Therefore, the only valid rights are legal rights, not natural rights, not universal rights, not human rights. Although their political values are very different, both Burke and Bentham accept a relativistic conception of rights specific to the society in question.

Human Rights Constrained

A second set of views on human rights values them but argues that if they are to be meaningful and/or effective, they must be circumscribed. Political theorist Cranston (1989) feared that if the list of human rights were too long they would simply not be taken seriously. Indeed, there is some merit to this argument. If every specific claim to a human right or its violation is a priori acknowledged as valid, or if every public policy that one favors is given the status of a human right, then the concept does become meaningless. There have to be criteria established. One way of doing this, which Cranston favors, is to limit valid human rights claims to those made against states for which the remedy would be that the government simply cease and desist from the offending action or policy. So, a government that suppresses free speech could stop such suppression and a government that tortures could stop the torturing. Given the wide liberal consensus that such actions violate the dignity of the person and are inconsistent with a modern democratic society, this makes the conception of human rights very clear-cut and easy to apply in specific cases.

Another criterion, to which Cranston also adheres, is that only political and civil rights should be considered to be human rights. Political and civil rights often overlap, that is to say they are recognized internationally but must usually be implemented within given states. The rights to vote or to petition a government are treated as both political and civil rights in the UN General Assembly's 1948 Declaration of Human Rights and in the subsequent International (1966) Covenant on Civil and Political Rights, which gives legal treaty status to much of what is in the 1948 declaration. But there can be political rights demanded of and/or granted by a state that might not be human rights, but might well be more humane policy. For example, citizens of a country have a right to vote. That is considered to be both a human and a civil right. Noncitizens do not have such a human right. But states could offer noncitizen residents the right to vote, as France has done in some local elections. A state could thus grant such a civil right without it being recognized as a human right, *at least at this point in time.*

More importantly, however, is that this view of human rights being only political/civil excludes two other kinds of rights that have been asserted and internationally accepted as human rights (i.e., economic and social rights). There is a history behind this. The 1948 declaration, which showed echoes of the Roosevelt administration (especially by Eleanor Roosevelt who was appointed by Truman to the first UN Commission on Human Rights and chaired it) included a wide array of economic human rights. But during the process of putting the declaration into legally binding treaties, the Cold War had broken out and there were severe differences between the communist world, the rising Third World, and the Western nations over the status of the economic and social claims that were made in the declaration. The way this was resolved was to draft two separate covenants, one for civil and political rights, and the other for economic and social rights. Eleven years after its drafting, in 1977, President Carter did sign the latter covenant but it was never ratified by the Senate. Hence, the United States is not a party to it.

A combination of ideological and philosophical positions has served to block the U.S. government's acceptance of this covenant. It is seen by some as diluting the clarity and force of human rights by going beyond the political. It is seen as asking too much of governments, especially poor ones, by demanding that they act positively in certain specific directions in economic and social policy. And it is seen as validating a socialist position, even if a democratic one when coupled with the covenant on political and civil rights, that has been an anathema to many in the West, especially in the United States. All of this could be avoided, it is argued by some, if we just remained within the boundaries of political and civil rights in our considerations of human rights.

A third boundary is the one around individual rights, excluding group rights. This is a position that has been advanced by Donnelly in his widely read text, *Universal Human Rights in*

Theory and Practice (1989). Although it shifted slightly between the first and second editions of his book, the argument is basically that when we think about human rights violations against a group, we should think of them as violations against each member of the group rather than against the whole.

There are five reasons for setting the boundaries of human rights around individuals. We have already discussed one, keeping human rights simple. A second is that because groups are by definition partial and are very different from each other, setting the boundaries of human rights around individuals is more consistent with universalism. A third reason is that liberal thinkers often view the historical narrative of development of rights in the West as the struggle for individual autonomy against political and social structures that confined individuals to positions in the old hierarchical orders. The struggle for rights is seen, then, as a struggle for individualism, often in both the economic and political domains. A fourth reason is that the seminal human rights documents in the West, the U.S. Declaration of Independence and the French Declaration of the Rights of Man and Citizens, do not recognize group rights; more on this below. Finally, as groups are never really homogeneous, there is the fear that the concept of group rights is antagonistic to individual rights, that individuals can be crushed as dominant elements within groups manifest their rights to, for example, self-determination.[1]

Some Previous Approaches to Grounding Human Rights

It is difficult simply to choose a position on the boundaries of human rights unless one has an underlying conceptual grounding for doing so. There are a large number of attempts to ground human rights. In my book, *Rethinking Human Rights for the New Millennium* (see Fields, 2003), I distinguish between nonrationalist and rationalist grounds. Among the former is Rorty's (1993) reliance on moral sentiment (the capacity to feel the suffering of those one does not even know or share a common culture with), Donnelly's (1989) reliance on consensus at the international level as reflected in international human rights documents, and the above-mentioned Levine (1981), who believes that there can be no rational grounding for human rights but that it is the most effective ideological tool available to counter the most inhumane practices, especially those of international capitalism and imperialism.

Among those writers who attempt to rationally ground human rights, the propensity is to look for a single value or characteristic as the basis of such a grounding. Many of the human rights documents contain the Kantian "dignity." Gewirth (1982), finding that word too vague to give much theoretical purchase, argues for freedom and agency that he thinks offers a deeper ontological basis. Dworkin (1977), the legal philosopher, argues for equality in the sense of the right to treatment as an equal under the law. Writers such as Bay (1965), Shue (1980), and Galtung (1994) look to the concept of needs. Then there is Habermas's (1996) discursive inclusiveness, which turns out to be another form equally similar to Dworkin's approach but surprisingly even more bound to legalism than Dworkin's. I refer those interested in my critique of each of the above attempts to the second chapter of my book.

A Holistic Approach to Grounding Human Rights

My holistic approach does not look for a single value on which to ground human rights. I think that such an approach entails an unjustifiable abstraction from the realm of concrete human experience over time. What follows below is a very schematic outline of a more elaborated argument contained in my book.

I look at human rights as a set of historical practices that has an ongoing history. I begin with the observation that all human beings have the potential for development. The realm of that development extends to the intellectual or cognitive, the moral, the creative, and the affective. This is a minimalist commitment to a conception of what it means to be a human being beyond the physical body.

This development is not a purely internal one, as is suggested by the expression "a self-made man or woman." That is a pure fiction, which lends support to a selfish egoist view of the world.

Human potentialities are always developed within webs of cultural, economic, and social relationships that are both facilitating and constraining of such development. Stated a little differently, such development entails a process of "co- and self-determination."

Even the most supposedly self-made people grew up within an intimate set of relationships called the family, which had a crucial impact on their development in the years of infancy, childhood, and young adulthood. In all but the poorest areas of the world, these so-called self-made people went to schools in which teachers and age-peers played an important role in their development. And then there were relationships entailing work, friendship, religious affiliation, and possibly civic engagement that all played a role in the process of co- and self-determination.

Although development is part of the experience of being human, the possibilities and directions of such development are materially and culturally conditioned. Thus, the developmental possibilities open to a nomad in the Sahara Desert are quite different from those open to a middle- or upper-class person in a highly industrialized or technologically advanced country.

History is also crucial. Historical phenomena of a grand scale do not occur accidentally, if we mean by that unrelated to other phenomena. There was no conception of, or discourse about, human rights among the Greeks, Romans, or feudal Europeans. In the latter, one's developmental possibilities were fixed by one's status in the society (which, in turn, was determined by the status of one's parents). Although there were earlier expressions, especially in the seventeenth and early eighteenth centuries, that all people enjoyed certain rights just by virtue of being human beings, it was at the end of the eighteenth century, with the political and economic dynamics that led to the American and French Revolutions and the advent of the modern constitutional state, that human rights gained significant force as a legitimate conception and justification for political struggle.

But, although these revolutions opened up developmental possibilities for some white males in the Western world, they excluded women, slaves, indentured servants, Native Americans, and people outside of Europe and the early American states.

Here we have revealed the clue to the unfolding over time of the social practice that we call "human rights." Since the

American and the French Revolutions, it has been precisely this exclusion, and the developmental possibilities and aspirations of the excluded, that provide the dynamic for the practice of human rights. When structures, institutions, and practices are outpaced by developmental possibilities and aspirations, we have "domination." In other words, domination is the exercise of power that frustrates the development of individuals, segments of societies, or entire societies. It manifests itself through a combination of raw force, complex institutional practices, and ideological justification in which the dominated Other is characterized as somehow inferior (i.e., having a low potential for development), or morally deserving of domination, whereas the dominator is deserving of the benefits.

The struggle for human rights is thus a struggle against domination. It is a struggle for new structures, institutions, and practices that will open up the developmental possibilities for the dominated. Although some view any kind of violence against human beings as a human rights violation, in the grand scheme of history the struggle against domination has almost always entailed violence from one side or the other. Moreover, because domination is almost always protected by law, the struggle against domination almost always violates law. Thus, civil disobedience, if not outright rebellion or revolution, have historically been a key ingredient in the advancement of human rights. The risk, particularly in the case of revolution, is that struggles against one set of dominating practices and dominators, can lead to a new set of dominators and practices. The Terror after the French Revolution and the persecution of loyalists after the American Revolution are cases in point.

Rather than being a priori determined by a theorist, the core values of human rights emerge out of the concrete struggles for human rights. The battle cry of the French Revolution—*liberté, égalité, fraternité*—gave us the historically new legitimizing values that encapsulate the developmental aspirations of people who were dominated as subjects rather than being citizens under the *ancien régime*. We are left with the problem of interpreting and practically implementing these values is such a way that they are complementary. A particular reading of any one of them could nullify the others. Excessive measures to ensure equality or solidarity have led to a totalization and hyperpatriotism that stifle critical thinking and expression. Excessive measures to ensure liberty have led to economic domination and an egoism that makes solidarity impossible. Some conceptions of solidarity have led to an exclusiveness based on racial, religious, ethnic, or national ties that have called into question liberty and equality and undercut the universality of human rights.

The difficulties in reconciling the three values notwithstanding, in virtually all emancipatory struggles against domination since the American and French Revolutions, these values have been used as the legitimizing basis of the struggles. They have arisen out of concrete experiences of people who have felt dominated; that is to say, their potentiality for development has not been recognized and has been impeded in fundamental ways by the dominant institutions and practices under which they lived. The underlying values of human rights are articulated in the struggles to attain recognition of those rights in concrete situations as well as in the formal national and international documents and juridical processes that give constitutional and legal legitimacy to such rights claims and struggles. These constitute the social practices of human rights as they have unfolded, and continue to unfold, historically.

A crucial, if contentious, point is that groups and collectivities are legitimate claimants for recognition as human rights holders. This point is contentious because it runs up against the strong individualism of Western liberalism, especially the Anglo American variants of that liberalism, as well as against the individualism of American culture and economy. In contending this, I do not mean to deny that there are not some human rights that are held just by individuals or that there are some human rights— I would argue most—that are simultaneously individual and collective rights. An example of an exclusively individual human right would be the right to habeas corpus. An example of a human right that is both individual and collective is the right of a racial or ethnic group to be treated equally. Another would be the right of free expression; as John Stuart Mill (1851 [1989]) pointed out in *On Liberty*, that is as much a right of the larger society to hear the expression as it is the right of the individual to express it. Arguments to the contrary notwithstanding, the rights claims to self-determination by the French and American revolutionists were certainly of this category of both individual and group rights.

It is thus surprising that so many theorists and writers on human rights, especially in the United States and Britain, attempt to draw the boundary around human rights in such a way that only individual rights can be considered to be human rights. Of greater, but certainly not universal, acceptance in the Anglo-American contexts, is the conception of human rights as including social rights and economic rights beyond the right to private property, as well as political rights. But if we are conceiving of human rights claims as those entailing the potential for development, it makes as little sense to exclude these realms as it does to exclude group rights. The only way of doing this is through some a priori assumption based on a particularly individualistic or monadic approach to economic morality—one that ironically treats the privatized group called the corporation as an individual with individualized legal rights.

Complexities

A number of complexities enter into the picture when one takes such an expanded view of human rights as I have proposed. Here I just want to raise three of them that I think are the most challenging:

One is the temporal dimension. If human rights are a set of relational social practices, they are not going to be static over time. In other words, over time people are going to resist forms of domination and demand that the structures and practices be recognized as human rights violations, in ways that previous generations have not. The history of the women's movement in the West (French women did not get the ballot until after World War II) and the history of the gay, lesbian, and transsexual movement are cases in point. As the legitimacy of specific forms of cultural, economic, and political practices is called into question by groups or collectivities feeling dominated, the extension of the list of human rights so feared by Cranston is going to occur. No arbitrary maximum can be placed on it simply to constrain. Nonarbitrariness can be attained only though an assessment of the validity of the claims to domination, an assessment of the balance between the values of liberty, equality, and solidarity and other values or needs that might enter into the specific situation—especially security and subsistence that Shue (1980) sees as underlying conditions for the realization of any other rights.

The second is the cultural dimension. The temporal dimension discussed above notwithstanding, human rights are supposed to be universals in some sense of that term. Yet, when I referred to the woman's movement in the above paragraph, I was careful to say "in the West." Alas, the problem of how to handle the attack on human rights from a cultural relativist perspective is present whether we conceive of human rights as being only individual rights or if we conceive of them holistically. Indeed, there is even more suspicion within non-Western cultures of individualistic rights claims than there is of group claims. However, the question is, at any given point in history, can there be a set of human rights norms that can be applied across cultural identities such that the determinations are not arbitrary or self-serving intrusions of more powerful outsiders? Put a little differently, can determinations be made about the validity of claims to domination in whatever context within a given point of time? We can go back to the issue of women, and note their condition under the Taliban or in the Swat region of Pakistan. Or, as I was writing this paper, about the murder of gays by both disgraced family members and armed gangs in the newly liberated Iraq. These murders appear to have been legitimized by a 2005 religious decree by the Shiite Grand Ayatollah Ali al-Sistani, only he advocated a more painful way of killing than mere shooting (*New York Times*, April 8, 2009). Can people or institutions like the UN or nongovernmental human rights organizations condemn such practices without being arbitrarily dismissive of specific cultural or religious practices? (I use the two examples not because I want to select out some practices in Islamic countries, but because they are posing very practical human rights problems in areas in which the U.S. government has intruded itself, however one judges the legitimacy of the intrusion.)

What perhaps mitigates the difficulty for my holistic approach is that, whereas it recognizes the validity of group or collective rights, it refuses to treat groups as monolithic wholes. There are always differences within groups, and often these differences can entail intra-group domination. This is why it is important to recognize that although individual rights and rights violations can sometimes stand alone, when we talk about group or collective rights violations we recognize that they entail simultaneously both individual and collective rights. We cannot sacrifice one for the other. To sacrifice individual rights in the name of group rights is, in fact, to serve the interests of the most powerful within the culture or the society. This would be a perversion of human rights, the function of which in my holistic approach is precisely to counter domination.

Moreover, in the modern world of international communication, media, travel, business, and educational exchanges there is a process of mutual learning going on. No culture is hermetically sealed off anymore. There is no reason to accept the argument made by those in power in a given country that people who challenge the dominant customs or practices, such as women's rights activists in the South, are an illegitimate contaminant because they have been influenced by or in contact with rights advocates and activists elsewhere.

I do not mean to contend that there are not problems remaining in a cross-cultural understanding of human rights even if one accepts my holistic approach, although this approach does have more of a resonance in societies with strong collectivist traditions than does a completely individualistic one. But I do not think that those problems should lead us to either give up on a holistic approach to human rights (the exclusively individual rights approach is even further from resolving them), nor lead us to a completely relativistic position that precludes any conception of human rights.

Third, whether one accepts my view of human rights as struggles against domination or not, we tend to think of a human rights violation as a clear case of one offended party with a clear case against another offending party. Especially in instances where one group declares a right to self-determination, this is often not the case. This is especially so when the form of self-determination entails secession. Claims to secession by a group can entail harm others, such as when a sectional group in one resource-rich part of a state wants to secede in order to become the sole beneficiaries of that wealth. Or a section that is the only one on the coast wants to secede, thus possibly blocking access to the sea of the rest. Or a residual minority or minorities in the newly created state risk falling under the domination of, or expulsion by, the new majority group.

Although some theorists argue that the collective right to self-determination in the form of secession should be accepted as an inherent democratic right, others have argued that it should only be a remedial right, that those who are seeking independence must be obliged to demonstrate that they have indeed been dominated, discriminated against, or otherwise unfairly treated by the state they want to break away from. Even then, the maximal resolution of the case in terms of the rights of both sides might be better served by mechanisms short of the zero-sum resolution of total loss of territory, resources, and population on one side, and total gain on the other. Perhaps with international mediation or adjudication, the state can be convinced to change its behavior and the resolution can be regional autonomy rather than complete independence.

The point is that Cranston is right when he says that if we limit human rights to those things that states do to individuals, like preventing them from speaking or torturing them, our considerations of human right are less complicated than when we bring group rights into the picture. But social reality has a way of complicating matters whether we like it or not. Then, as scholars, the question becomes the sufficiency of our analytical tools to understand and elucidate these complexities. The much harder task is for human rights activists, international organizations, and powerful nations to act in nonarbitrary and reflective ways in this complex real world in which domination exists, but castigations of "evil" directed toward one side and attempts at zero-sum resolutions (as in Iraq) can often be counterproductive to the advancement of human rights.

Note

1. "All peoples have the right of self-determination. By virtue of that right they freely determine their political status and freely pursue their economic, social, and cultural development" (International Covenant on Civil and Political Rights [1966], Part I, Article 1, [1]).

References

Bay, C. (1965). *The structure of freedom*. New York: Atheneum.

Bentham, J. (1781 [1988]). *An introduction to the principles of morals and legislation*. New York: Prometheus Books.

Burke, E. (1790 [2009]). *Reflections on the revolution in France*. New York: Oxford University Press.

Cranston, M. (1989). Human rights real and supposed. In M. E. Winston (Ed.), *The philosophy of human rights* (pp. 121–128). Belmont, CA: Wadsworth.

Donnelly, J. (1989). *Universal human rights in theory and practice*. Ithaca, NY: Cornell University Press.

Dworkin, R. (1977). *Taking rights seriously*. Cambridge, MA: Harvard University Press.

Fields, A. B. (2003). *Rethinking human rights for the new millennium*. New York: Palgrave-Macmillan.

Galtung, J. (1994). *Human rights in another key*. London: Polity Press.

Gewirth, A. (1982). *Human rights: Essays on justification and applications*. Chicago: University of Chicago Press.

Habermas, J. (1996). *Between facts and norms* (W. Rehg, Trans.). Cambridge, MA: MIT Press.

International Covenant of Civil and Political Rights. (1966). International Treaty. Geneva, Switzerland: Office of the United Nations High Commissioner for Human Rights.

Levine, A. (1981). *Liberal democracy: A critique of its theory*. New York: Columbia University Press.

Marx, K. (1844 [1975]). On the Jewish question. First published as "Zur Judenfrage" in the newspaper *Deutsch-Französische Jahrbücher*. http://boston.marxists.org/archive/marx/works/1844/jewish-question/ (accessed February 4, 2010).

Mill, J. S. (1851 [1989]). *On liberty*. Cambridge: Cambridge University Press.

New York Times (2009), April 8, p. A10.

Rorty, R. (1993). Human rights, rationality, and sentimentality. In S. Shute and S. Hurley (Eds.), *On human rights: The Oxford Amnesty Lectures 1993* (pp. 111–134). New York: Basic Books.

Shue, H. (1980). *Basic rights: Subsistence, affluence, and U.S. foreign policy* Princeton, NJ: Princeton University Press.

3. Human Vulnerabilities

Toward a Theory of Rights for Qualitative Researchers

Svend Brinkmann

That we do not normally treat other people as objects, as things, is perhaps the fundamental fact in human life and ought to be foundational for the human and social sciences (Polkinghorne, 2004). Almost all our attitudes toward human beings, and our practices with them, are different from our practices and attitudes with and toward things. Alas, it is also the case that from time to time in the history of humanity, the human reactive attitudes have been subdued (e.g., during times of slavery, wars, and genocides). This nearly always presupposes significant dehumanizing work. For example, in the Nazi concentration camps, the humanity of Jews, communists, and others hated by the Nazis had to be subdued by giving individuals numbers rather than names, providing them with identical clothes or stripping off their clothes entirely, shaving their heads, and transporting them in carriages as if they were cattle. When we describe such moral transgressions, we say that people's human rights have been violated.

Sadly, such horrendous acts have been committed many times since the Holocaust. Rorty (1998) gives an example from Bosnia and the war that took place in the former Yugoslavia. He cites a horrifying description of a Muslim man being forced by the Serbs to bite off the penis of a fellow Muslim. The moral to be drawn from this and similar accounts, Rorty says, is that the murderers, torturers, and rapists involved do not think of themselves as violating human rights, for they do not see themselves as doing these things to other human beings, but (in this case) to *Muslims*. The dehumanizing acts involved are in a perverse sense functional for the perpetrators who strive to become convinced that they are not, in Rorty's words, "being inhuman, but rather are discriminating between true humans and pseudo-humans" (p. 167).

One of the most important things a human being can learn is, if I may use rather grandiose and sweeping terms, to see through acts of dehumanization and recognize vulnerable human beings *as* human beings, especially when people's humanity is difficult to perceive because of strangeness, difference, or situational complexity. And one of the most important things qualitative human and social science can do is to help us recognize people as fellow human beings with the all-too-human powers and vulnerabilities that characterize our species. The argument I make here implies that this involves recognizing duties and rights. There is still not, however, consensus among qualitative researchers that the advancement of human rights is a legitimate goal for our research practices. Some question this goal because they advocate a morally and politically neutral stance for research; others reject the idea because they are suspicious of rights talk in general as too firmly tied to neoliberal individualism. In this chapter, I attempt to tackle both of these objections.

Rights and the Generative Aims of Social Science

In some circles of the human and social sciences there is now agreement that advancing human rights and social justice are praiseworthy goals. According to some theorists, these ought to be *among* the goals for research practices along with others such as seeking knowledge for its own sake, for example. For others, they are the *only* legitimate goals of social science inquiry. In the former camp, we find people like Martyn Hammersley (2008), who argues that the political activism and even radicalism inherent in some forms of qualitative inquiry today produces a polarization that indirectly encourages the neopositivism it otherwise aims to replace. He calls for "sound and realistic assessments" of qualitative research if its paradigms are to survive (p. 15). This, he finds, should involve downplaying its moral and political activism.

In the latter camp, we find pragmatists and social constructionists. Some pragmatists, who follow John Dewey and more recently the aforementioned Rorty, argue that we simply do not have sciences in order to copy the world in true representations but rather to cope with events in ways that are conducive to human growth. The results of social inquiry are valid, not when they magically "correspond to an independent reality," but when they allow us to collectively solve the problems that face us. Ultimately, social theories and ideas are evaluated in practice, when we see how practices and institutions change in response to them, and we further judge these practices and institutions "by the contribution which they make to the value of human life," as Dewey (1900) said in a classic presidential address to the American Psychological Association (p. 121). All sciences, in this pragmatist perspective, are therefore *moral* sciences insofar as they enable us to understand and improve the conditions and agencies through which human beings live (Brinkmann, 2004; Dewey, 1930 [1922]). Theories are validated when they enrich our lives by promoting human rights and democratic living.

Others of a social constructionist bent such as Kenneth Gergen find that social and psychological researchers ought to engage in what he calls "generative theory" by becoming "poetic activists" (Gergen, 2001b). Generative theories are theories about social life that not simply mirror the world, but change it. In fact, theories cannot do otherwise: "Theoretical accounts of the world are not mirror reflections of the world but discursive actions within a community" (Gergen, 2001a, p. 811). Poetic activists are those researchers who *know* that their theories work reflexively to constitute their phenomena and thereby to change aspects of the world. Knowing this will alert researchers, Gergen argues, to think about the moral and political values upon which their poetic redescriptions reside. On this account, all social science inquiry has a normative—moral and political—dimension. Or rather, we cannot really separate the normative from the descriptive for, in the constructionist framework, to theorize is to act.

Another recent example of a researcher who considers the advancement of human values as the intrinsic goal of social inquiry is Bent Flyvbjerg. Flyvbjerg (2001) has argued quite specifically that the social sciences are—or must become, if they want to matter—*phronetic*. Phronetic researchers, Flyvbjerg says, place themselves within the context being studied and focus on the values of the practices of communities by asking three value-rational questions: Where are we going? Is this desirable? What should be done? (p. 60). The *raison d'être* for the social sciences is thus developing the value-rationality of society (i.e., enabling the public to reason better about values and contribute to social justice). And the editors of the authoritative *Handbook of Qualitative Research* consider qualitative research as "a democratic project committed to social justice in an age of uncertainty" (Denzin & Lincoln, 2005, p. x). Today, it seems that epistemic criteria concerned with truth, reliability, validity, and simplicity in inquiry are increasingly replaced by ethical and political criteria that emphasize emancipation, empowerment, care, solidarity, and the advancement of human rights as generative aims of social research activities.

Many qualitative researchers are convinced by these arguments to the effect that human and social inquiry simply cannot neutrally mirror the world and that all such research has ethico-political presuppositions and implications. However, there is a great need, I believe, to continually reflect upon how to proceed from such insights. Along this line, Osbeck (1993) has applauded the pragmatic and generative viewpoint of social constructionism but also criticized it on the ground that if constructionists offer no basis for evaluation of cultural possibilities, then its relativism "undermines any reasonable means by which generative aims may be accomplished" (p. 345). Schwandt (2000) has likewise criticized "strong constructionism" and asked: "Absent any criteria for deciding across various frameworks which is the better (the more just, more democratic, and so on) practice and if there is no epistemic gain or loss resulting from this comparison, why would we bother to engage in the conversation?" (p. 200). Schwandt finds it deeply problematic and even paradoxical that constructionists claim to help improve the human condition while simultaneously arguing that all statements of the good "are the products of various particular communities of interpreters and thus to be regarded with suspicion" (p. 200). This is where the concept of human rights seems to be useful, because it may introduce a sense of direction in which to look if one as a researcher is interested in "poetic activism." Today, human rights are often used as the ultimate normative reference point in ethical and political discussions (Fields, 2003, p. 1). But it is certainly also a concept with its own pitfalls and lurking ethnocentrisms.

Some social researchers do in fact subscribe to specific predetermined moral standards and "statements of the good" that they want the social sciences to promote. One example is critical theory, the tradition that unites Marxian emancipation and Kantian ethics through critical analyses of social life. Jürgen Habermas has for decades worked on reformulating Kant's monological ethics into a dialogical procedure based on what Habermas (1990) calls "discourse ethics." Discourse ethics can be used when seeking social justice through critical research. It postulates an ideal speech situation of unconstrained communication where norms are evaluated according to a purely formal logic of argumentation, uncolored by any previously accepted moral views or power relations (Richardson & Woolfolk, 1994). The possibility of a pure procedural rationality is imagined here, which should be exercised by subjects who detach themselves from their prior commitments to substantive values: "Discourse ethics does not set up substantive orientations. Instead it establishes a *procedure* based on presuppositions and designed to guarantee the impartiality of the process of judging" (Habermas, 1990, p. 122).

In the language of rights, Habermas puts all the normative weight on what has been called "discursive inclusiveness" (Fields, 2003, p. 67): Everyone has a right to participate in the conversation, but no substantive rights as such are posited. The problem with this well-intentioned approach is what many would see as an illusion, namely that it is possible—or indeed desirable—to suspend entirely the concrete realities of substantive values, commitments, and power relations. Discourse ethics confines itself to the general (Western) principles of rational communication that are to prevail if humans are to be set free from oppressive ideologies, but were these phenomena suspended, there would be little left of human life as we know it, and social researchers would thus have no world to engage in, and participants would likely be unable to recognize their own worlds (see also the critique in Flyvbjerg, 2001, who favors particularistic Foucauldian power analytics over universalistic Habermasian discourse ethics).

Instead of Habermas's "thin" and "pure" ethics, I believe we need much "thicker" and more "impure" approaches to understand and act morally in the messy and contradictory world of multiculturalism. We should as researchers hesitate and think twice about whether we can really know a priori what human rights are, and what emancipation is. On the other hand, I also agree with some of the critics of social constructionism that we need to say more about how to conceive of human *progress* and *development* than simply calling for generative theorizing and poetic activism (some communities, for example, may not be interested in being "liberated" by well-intentioned researchers). For qualitative inquiry to engage responsibly in human rights and social justice issues, we need to be able to reflect on the directions of generativity and the values of poetic activism, so to speak. We need to find a middle ground between the abstract procedures of Habermas's universalism and the paralyzing relativism of some constructionists. To find this middle ground, we need a conception of rights that are at once more inclusive and "globalized" than any nation- or state-based account of human beings (e.g., in terms of citizenship), yet more flexible and situational than some of the ethnocentric articulations of human rights that are wholly individualistic. Bryan Turner (1993) has put the issue well in a discussion of the relationship between sociology and human rights:

> If sociology is the study of the transformation of *gemeinschaft* [sic] (organic and particularistic values and institutions) into *gesellschaft* [sic] (associations which are more universalistic in their definition of social membership) as a consequence of modernization, we can conceptualise human-rights solidarity as a historical stage beyond citizenship-solidarity. Whereas citizenship as a doctrine has been a progressive feature of western societies in terms of universalistic values behind the welfare state, human-right concepts can be seen as a progressive paradigm which is relevant to a world system. (p. 498)

In his book on human rights, Fields (2003) is searching for a similar middle ground by developing what he calls a "holistic approach" to human rights. This approach should be formulated

> without falling into idealist arguments such as the old natural law/natural rights formulation, without falling into a humanistic essentialism that sees human beings driven across time and culture

by invariable characteristics, and without falling into a relativism that would see humans as nothing more than constructs of their own cultures at any given moment, a view that would strip human rights of all cross-cultural relevance. (p. 74)

In what follows, I would like to chart and move on this middle ground between naturalism, essentialism, and relativism concerning human rights, trying to avoid all three pitfalls. I hope such an exercise will prove to be useful for morally and politically committed qualitative researchers. I will proceed in two stages. First, I will discuss in greater depth what rights are and argue that they are not just relevant for morally and politically committed researchers as something external to the practice of social research, but that they are, in fact, an intrinsic part of social life as such. Second, I will focus on the centrality of educating students in a way that enables them to deal with the qualitative human world and the injustices that people suffer and I shall point to literature as one important source of developing ethical and human rights sensitivity.

On Human Rights

What are human rights? Just posing a question like this will risk leading us astray, for it suggests that rights are timeless things or objects that "are" in a given way, perhaps with specific properties that can be investigated. But, in fact, there are no rights as Platonic entities that are magically attached to human beings. We should not ask what rights *are* in this way—as if they were naturally existing objects—but rather follow in the footsteps of Rom Harré, who asks: "What discursive tasks are they intended to accomplish or to facilitate?" (2005, p. 237). Rorty, who defended his own sentimentalist approach to rights as loyalty and solidarity, likewise advocated that "the question of whether human beings really *have* the rights enumerated in the Helsinki Declaration is not worth raising" (1998, p. 170). We should strive to avoid an essentialist reification of rights, for if we do not, we too easily come to the unhappy conclusion that they are "metaphysically queer," to borrow John Mackie's (1977) phrase concerning ethics more broadly. Or we may be led to conclude with the father of utilitarian moral philosophy Jeremy Bentham that they are "nonsense on stilts."

But although the word right does not refer to *things* that exist in the world independently of our discursive practices, it does not follow that the word is not extremely important. If we instead ask Harré's question about the *discourse* of rights—rather than the *entities* of rights—we should take an interest in those situations when we invoke the concept in our practices and conversations. And we obviously do this in talk "that expresses someone's belief that he or she has been denied something to which the speaker believes himself or herself to be entitled from someone else"(Harré, 2005, p. 224). Rights are what we invoke when something is denied or taken away from someone (often ourselves) in an illegitimate way. Fundamentally, rights arise from the fact that human beings are ontologically frail and that social institutions are precarious (Turner, 1993, p. 501). It is almost a matter of logic that if nothing could be taken away from us (e.g., life, liberty, integrity, health, self-respect, community, etc.); that is, if we were somehow invulnerable, we would have no rights. Rights are for frail human beings, not for invincible angels or gods.

I shall follow this lead below, but first it may be fruitful to briefly investigate the three most famous rejections of rights in the history of philosophy. A useful overview has been given by Fields (2003; see also this volume), whom I follow here. Ironically, one rejection comes from the very liberalist tradition that in other respects stands as the historical backdrop to the contemporary discourse on rights. The utilitarian tradition famously argues for a consequentialist theory of ethics according to which good actions are those that produce the greatest amount of happiness in a society. Legislators should thus not strive to protect any alleged human rights, but rather to maximize human happiness through a quantitative calculation of the likely consequences of our actions. On this account, slavery may be morally wrong, not because it violates human rights or the intrinsic value and dignity of human beings, but rather because it leads to reduced overall happiness. The standard critique of utilitarianism concerns exactly this point: This is simply not why slavery is wrong! Most of us would consider slavery to be wrong even under (the surely unlikely) conditions where this institution would produce greater benefit than harm—if it makes sense to imagine such calculations at all (e.g., if only a very small group of slaves were exploited by a large, sadistic majority to the great pleasure of this majority).

The other classical rejections of human rights come from the oppositional camps of conservatism (e.g., Burke) and Marxism. For Burke, a well-functioning society was an organic whole that ought to be preserved over and above any consideration of the rights of those humans that inhabit it. Thus, according to Burke, there are no *human* rights as such, for rights without a society are a pure social construction (Burke was a conservative communitarian). And for Marx, conversely, human rights talk was merely ideological. Rights are part of an ideology that has been installed to maintain the privileges of one class at the expense of others. Some contemporary Marxists, just as some utilitarians, will tolerate human rights talk on the assumption that it is the most effective language we have today to criticize the oppressive social structures that make us miserable. This is a quite common recourse to an instrumentalist view of human rights that ultimately deny their rational grounding.

Fields's own theory is what he calls a "holistic" approach, which, if I understand it correctly, does not conceive of rights as entities of any sort, but rather as a set of social practices that has an ongoing history (see Fields, 2003). Rather than being a priori determined by theorists or philosophers, the core values of human rights emerge out of the concrete struggles for human rights. It is a historical fact that theories about rights were "stimulated by concrete struggles that were going on at the time of their writing" (p. 21). Rights are thus not purely abstract philosophical reflections. If we philosophize without an eye to concrete struggles, Fields argues, there is a risk that we will look for one abstract and universal source of rights. There is all too often an impulse "to ground human rights on a single value, such as liberty, equality, or dignity" (p. 203). Instead of this, according to Fields, we should see human rights as "a struggle against domination by potentially co- and self-developing human beings" (p. 203).

There are a number of interesting philosophical questions that I have to leave untouched here. First and foremost whether the boundaries of human rights should necessarily be set around individuals or if groups can coherently be accorded rights. Another question concerns the ascription of rights to nonhuman animals and even plants. And a third one concerns the question of the differences and similarities between various kinds of rights— legal, civil, and human rights, for example. I shall not discuss these questions in detail here, but concentrate on human rights as such and try to develop an approach that cuts across many of the different issues here, while following Fields's approach to human rights as a set of practices that incorporate struggles against domination. I believe that Harré's theory is particularly useful in this regard (Harré, 2005; Harré & Robinson, 1995). Human rights, according to Harré (2005), should be conceived as social representations, as emergent properties of the joint performances of several people (p. 238)—or, in other words, as social practices. We should see our "rights practices" as performative instantiations or enactments of human rights.

Harré (2005) approaches the issue of rights within a larger discussion of the relationship between rights and duties. He argues that the bases for attributing rights and duties are vulnerabilities and powers, respectively. What he means by this is that rights are derived from vulnerabilities and duties are derived from powers. To begin with the latter: We can only meaningfully be said to have duties because we have the power to do certain things. As Kant famously said: "An 'ought' presupposes a 'can', i.e., a *power* to act and make a difference" (1996 [1788], p. 127). In principle, we are only responsible when we can act (this does not mean that those in less powerful positions are without personal responsibility, but it does mean that their responsibility is limited to what is within the range of their power). Harré notes that the issue of what constitute powers and vulnerabilities is context dependent. For example, the grandmother who looks after her grandchild has a duty to take care of the child, and the child has a corresponding right to be taken care of. But suppose the grandmother is going blind and they are about to cross a road together, then the child has a duty of guiding them safely across the road and the grandmother has a right to ask for help. This is context bound. As the philosopher Løgstrup (1956) argued, the ethical demand to take care of that of the other person's life that is in my power is given in virtue of human interdependency, but how to live up to this demand in concrete situations is based on a qualitative judgment that cannot be codified or summarized into universal rules or quantitative calculations (see also Brinkmann, 2007b). Living up to the ethical demand is a *practice* rather than something that can be stated in rules.

Conversely, we have rights because we have vulnerabilities. Invulnerable beings could not have rights, for rights are only conceivable for creatures that have something that can be taken away from them. We cling to what we value, but we cling (both logically and psychologically) only to what can be taken away from us (Jonas, 1992). The hungry have a right to be fed, because without food, they will die. Human beings, in this ontological account, are "members of a community of suffering from which they cannot escape" (Turner, 1993, p. 503). This is the basic source of human rights and possibly also human solidarity across cultures and tribes. This position is connected to the view that "while human happiness is notable for its cultural diversity, misery is characterised by its unity" (p. 504). Not every vulnerability, however, but only those that are tied to substantive *interests*, engender a right. Harré and Robinson (1995) define an interest as follows: "For an entity to have an interest is for it to be constituted in such a way that, where the interest is acknowledged and honoured, the entity more fully realizes whatever potentialities it possesses" (p. 520). Thus, it is senseless to claim that I have a right to become a millionaire, because there is nothing about being a millionaire that in itself helps me realize my potentialities. However, I do have a right to express myself through words and deeds, for denied of these possibilities I could not become the sort of creature that I otherwise could. That is why the full development of human beings—and in other words the realization of their interests—"is every bit as contingent on their exercise of [economic and social] rights as it is on the exercise of their political and civil rights" (Fields, 2003, p. 95), and this is clearly an argument in favor of including the latter among the human rights. On a holistic, practice-based account, political and economic rights are interrelated.

The issue of how powers and vulnerabilities are constituted is context dependent and historically relative. What is *not* relative, however, is the fact that there is a basis for the possibility of duties and rights in associated human living. It is a misconception to think that rights talk in this sense is particularly Western. A Huron Indian of Canada expressed the Huron notion of (what we call) rights to Baron de Lahontan, a Frenchman who lived with the Huron from 1683 to 1694, long before the American and French revolutions, by saying: "We are born free and united brothers, each as much a great lord as the other, while you are all the slaves of one sole man [the king]. I am the master of my body, I dispose of myself, I do what I wish, I am the first and last of my nation ... subject only to the great Spirit" (in Fields, 2003, p. 165).

Again, we should think about the question of rights and duties in terms of practices that protect vulnerable human beings and their interests against domination. Some of the core practices that uphold a moral order of a community and protect participants' rights are, for example, giving others their due as contributors to conversations and respect for those rituals that constitute and sustain the central practices of communities. Those vulnerabilities that arise from life within a community are the ground for "civil" rights, just as individual human rights are grounded in individual vulnerabilities (Harré & Robinson, 1995, p. 532).

Rights as the Basis for Social Life

Much of social life can be explained in terms of how we situationally negotiate rights and duties. This has been highlighted by Harré under the heading of positioning theory (what follows here builds on Brinkmann, 2007a). Positioning theory is quite unique as a social theory in foregrounding rights and duties as analytical social science concepts and it gives us a tool-box that is helpful in understanding the ways people do things and the meanings ascribed to what they do (Harré & Moghaddam, 2003, p. 3). For humans to understand each other and act meaningfully in the social world, they need first and foremost to understand rights and duties. They need to understand the positions that enable people to speak and act in specific situations. A position is defined as "a cluster of rights and duties to perform certain actions with a certain significance as acts, but which also may include prohibitions or denials of access to some of the local repertoire of meaningful acts" (Harré & Moghaddam, 2003, pp. 5–6).

In every social situation there exists a realm of positions in which people are located (e.g., student, teacher), and such positions are inescapably moral (Harré & van Langenhove, 1999, p. 6) because they involve "oughts" (e.g., being positioned as the teacher, I *ought* to try my best to develop the students' understanding of the world). Positions consist of rights to do certain things, to act in specific ways, and also of (moral) duties to be taken up and acted on in specific ways. Because positions are clusters of rights and duties, we identify them by identifying the powers and vulnerabilities that generate them. Furthermore, all positions exist within unfolding *storylines* that order social episodes. Social life—all of it—unfolds according to norms and already established patterns of development, which positioning theorists call storylines that can be expressed as narrative conventions (Harré & Moghaddam, 2003, p. 6). And finally, every socially significant action, including speech, must be interpreted as an *act*; that is, not just as an intended action (e.g., a handshake) but as an intelligible and meaningful performance (the handshake can be a greeting, a farewell, a seal, etc.). Actions are meaningful within social practices and as parts of some unfolding narrative. We understand people's acts when we understand the positions from where they act, which means that rights and duties should figure centrally in accounts of human action qua action.

Thus, when we, as qualitative researchers, want to understand how persons engage in social life—or when people as such are trying to understand each other—we presuppose certain normativities regarding rights and duties. It is impossible to understand the acts of a parent, a teacher, or a police officer without taking into account the positions and storylines that bring meaning to their activities. Social processes are therefore saturated with rights, negotiations of rights, and, alas, violations of rights. Consequently, my point is that an understanding of rights should not be a separate pastime activity, which the morally committed social analyst may engage in from time to time, for social life is epistemically inconceivable if stripped of the normativities generated by rights and duties. All social research thus needs an awareness of rights.

Educating Students for the Task

Probably the most direct way to change our human and social science disciplines into practices with more human rights awareness is by educating students. We should educate them in a way that enables them to deal with the qualitative human world of rights and duties and the injustices that people suffer. That we can change a discipline through the education of students—a kind of bottom-up approach—is often overlooked. We sometimes forget that we do have much power as university professors, and the ensuing responsibility, to change parts of the world by educating people who will act in this world. How to educate students in this way is a longer story, but if rights and vulnerabilities are situated and contextual, I think that it should involve a cultivation of their sensitivity to concrete issues and life problems that goes hand in hand with the ability to understand qualitative particulars, to engage in "thick description" without fleeing into abstraction. Philosopher Martha Nussbaum advocates the use of literature in cultivating students' sensitivity toward injustice and human suffering, and she talks about the perceiving, Aristotelian agent as an ideal. I think this is an ethical ideal *and* an ideal for qualitative researchers. Here are some of Nussbaum's words:

> Being responsibly committed to the world of value before her, the perceiving agent can be counted on to investigate and scrutinize the nature of each item and each situation, to respond to what is there before her with full sensitivity and imaginative vigor, not to fall short of what is there to be seen and felt because of evasiveness, scientific abstractness, or a love of simplification. The Aristotelian agent is a person whom we could trust to describe a complex situation with full concreteness of detail and emotional shading, missing nothing of practical relevance. (1990, p. 84)

If we follow Nussbaum here, there is a sense in which we need to blur the distinction between ethical goodness and epistemic goodness, that is, goodness in producing knowledge, when if comes to human lives (Brinkmann, 2007b). I think this is important to teach to students.

The use of literary examples in education can be used to train the capacity for understanding rights and duties in social life. To cite just one example, which has been discussed quite extensively by a number of different authors (Levine, 1998; McGinn, 1999; Rorty, 1989), reading Vladimir Nabokov's *Lolita* can be used as an exercise in the required form of ethical understanding (I elaborate on this in Brinkmann, 2007a). This complex and multi-layered story is told through the voice of Humbert Humbert, the educated European aesthete, who seduces the young girl, Dolores Haze, after her mother has died and whom he gives the name Lolita. The reader of the book is initially enchanted linguistically by the "sublime sensuality of the prose" (McGinn, 1999, p. 33), and Humbert as the confessing narrator positions himself as innocent and uses an array of rhetorical techniques to gain our sympathy.

Many readers and critics have, in fact, been seduced by the prose (Levine [1998] cites several critics that have taken Humbert's side against the 12-year-old girl; see p. 141), but, as I read it, the real point of the novel is to see through Humbert's "verbally induced hallucination" (McGinn, 1999, p. 35) and understand the real rights and duties that are in play, but hidden by the narrator: Lolita is, in fact, a 12-year-old girl, whose mother dies (actually, Humbert plans to murder the mother, but she dies in a car crash instead), and the girl ends up in the hands of an obsessive pedophile who disregards the girl's rights and his own duties and repeatedly rapes her until she escapes with another pedophile (named Clare Quilty—"Clearly Guilty"). Finally, the girl dies while giving birth to a still-born child. Humbert's prose is cultivated, aesthetic, and intoxicating, and stands in stark contrast to the life of Dolores Haze, which is, to quote the famous words by Hobbes, solitary, poor, nasty, brutish, and short. The reader's challenge is to see through the story line that Humbert's narration seeks to install and thereby understand the rights, duties, and the alternative story line that emerges through the cracks in the novel, which enables one to understand Humbert's acts in a way that is quite different from his own exposition. The reader needs to become detached from the immediate sensuality of the prose and see through Humbert's story line. In this way, reading the book is an ethical exercise in understanding the vulnerabilities and rights of the little girl:

[A]nd one that can help to train us in the art of behaving well: for ethical behavior is often a matter of understanding the interests and needs of our fellow human beings. On the other hand, *Lolita* will not yield obvious morals or maxims. But then, as Aristotle argued, doing the right thing is often not a question of knowing what is right in general, but of possessing techniques or skills, such as the interpretive skill that fiction teaches us. (Levine, 1998, p. 141)

I believe we have reasons to think that this "interpretive skill that fiction teaches us" is highly relevant for cultivating students' and researchers' sensitivity to situated human rights.

Not just fiction, of course, but also real instances of human rights violations could and should be used in educating students to navigate in the value-laden human world. The lesson will frequently be similar to that from *Lolita*: It is often necessary to read against dominant story lines to see the basic human rights that are threatened or violated. Learning to do so means acquiring a fundamental hermeneutic skill that capable qualitative researchers should be in a unique position to obtain and exercise if they want to make a difference in human rights discussions.

If we educate students in qualitative inquiry so that they see it as their duty to understand rights as a central part of social life in-the-making—both for ethical *and* epistemic reasons—then we could possibly educate people who will assist in generating a public where the sufferings and rights violations of each and every human being ultimately comes to matter. Working toward this goal, this utopia, should be a fundamental aim in qualitative research communities.

References

Brinkmann, S. (2004). Psychology as a moral science: Aspects of John Dewey's psychology. *History of the Human Sciences, 17*, 1, 1–28.

Brinkmann, S. (2007a). Practical reason and positioning. *Journal of Moral Education, 36*, 3, 415–432.

Brinkmann, S. (2007b). The good qualitative researcher. *Qualitative Research in Psychology, 4*, 1, 127–144.

Denzin, N. K., & Lincoln, Y. S. (2005). Preface. In N. K.Denzin and Y. S. Lincoln (Eds.), *The Sage handbook of qualitative research* (3rd ed., pp. i–xvi). Thousand Oaks, CA: Sage.

Dewey, J. (1900). Psychology and social practice. *The Psychological Review, 7,* 1, 105–124.

Dewey, J. (1930 [1922]). *Human nature and conduct: An introduction to social psychology.* New York: The Modern Library.

Fields, A. B. (2003). *Rethinking human rights for the new millennium.* New York: Palgrave Macmillan.

Flyvbjerg, B. (2001). *Making social science matter—Why social inquiry fails and how it can succeed again.* Cambridge: Cambridge University Press.

Gergen, K. J. (2001a). Psychological science in a postmodern context. *American Psychologist, 56,* 10, 803–813.

Gergen, K. J. (2001b). *Social construction in context.* London: Sage.

Habermas, J. (1990). *Moral consciousness and communicative action.* Cambridge, MA: The MIT Press.

Hammersley, M. (2008). *Questioning qualitative inquiry: Critical essays.* London: Sage.

Harré, R. (2005). An ontology for duties and rights. In N. J. Finkel and F. M. Moghaddam (Eds.), *The psychology of rights and duties: Empirical contributions and normative commentaries,* (pp. 223–242). Washington, DC: American Psychological Association.

Harré, R., & Moghaddam, F. M. (2003). Introduction: The self and others in traditional psychology and in positioning theory. In R. Harré and F. M. Moghaddam (Eds.), *The self and others: Positioning individuals and groups in personal, political, and cultural contexts,* (pp. 1–21). London: Praeger.

Harré, R., & Robinson, D. N. (1995). On the primacy of duties. *Philosophy, 70,* 274, 513–532.

Harré, R., & van Langenhove, L. (1999). The dynamics of social episodes. In R. Harré and L. van Langenhove (Eds.), *Positioning theory* (pp. 1–13). Oxford, UK: Blackwell.

Jonas, H. (1992). The burden and blessing of mortality. *Hastings Center Report, 22,* 1, 34–40.

Kant, I. (1996 [1788]). Kraus's review of Ulrich's *Eleutheriology. Practical philosophy* (pp. 119–132). (Cambridge edition of the *Works of Immanuel Kant*). Cambridge: Cambridge University Press.

Levine, P. (1998). *Living without philosophy: On narrative, rhetoric, and morality.* Albany: State University of New York Press.

Løgstrup, K. E. (1997 [1956]). *The ethical demand.* Introduction by H. Fink and A. C. MacIntyre. South Bend, IN: University of Notre Dame Press.

Mackie, J. (1977). *Ethics: Inventing right and wrong.* Hammondsworth, UK: Penguin Books.

McGinn, C. (1999). The meaning and morality of Lolita. *The Philosophical Forum, 30,* 1, 31–41.

Nussbaum, M. C. (1990). The discernment of perception: An Aristotelian conception of private and public rationality. In *Love's knowledge* (pp. 261–285). Oxford: Oxford University Press.

Osbeck, L. (1993). Social constructionism and the pragmatic standard. *Theory & Psychology, 3,* 2, 337–349.

Polkinghorne, D. (2004). *Practice and the human sciences.* Albany: State University of New York Press.

Richardson, F. C., & Woolfolk, R. L. (1994). Social theory and values: A hermeneutic perspective. *Theory & Psychology, 4,* 2, 199–226.

Rorty, R. (1989). *Contingency, irony, and solidarity.* Cambridge: Cambridge University Press.

Rorty, R. (1998). Human rights, rationality, and sentimentality. In *Truth and progress. Philosophical papers,* Volume 3 (pp. 167–185). Cambridge: Cambridge University Press.

Schwandt, T. (2000). Three epistemological stances for qualitative inquiry: Interpretivism, hermeneutics, and social constructionism. In N. K. Denzin and Y. S. Lincoln (Eds.), *Handbook of qualitative research,* (pp. 189–214). London: Sage.

Turner, B. S. (1993). Outline of a theory of human rights. *Sociology, 27,* 3, 489–512.

4. Human Rights, Social Justice, and Qualitative Research

Questions and Hesitations about What We Say about What We Do[1]

Julianne Cheek

Introduction: What Is This Chapter about and Why Write It?

Human rights and social justice have been, and continue to be, central considerations in qualitative inquiry. This is reflected, for example, in the emphasis that the writing and reporting of qualitative research gives to concepts such as transformation, emancipation, and giving voice to the underserved or marginalized. Denzin and Giardina (2009) capture this eloquently when they write,

> What is the role of critical qualitative research in a historical present when the need for social justice has never been greater? This is a historical present that cries out for emancipatory visions, for visions that inspire transformative inquiries, and for inquiries that can provide the moral authority to move people to struggle and resist oppression. (pp. 11–12)

Considerations of what such transformative qualitative inquiries might entail include, but are not limited to, the type of problems that form the basis of the research; the methods chosen for the research; the way that those methods are put into practice; the type and nature of the reporting of the research that is done; and the use to which it is hoped the research findings will be put.

The fact that qualitative research has as one of its central mantras a commitment to, and focus on, human rights and social justice is not surprising given the overt focus of qualitative inquiry on the social world and the way that world is thought about and understood. As Brinkmann (2009) points out, social processes are saturated with "rights, negotiations of rights, and, alas, violations of rights," leading him to conclude that awareness and understanding of rights is crucial to all social research. It is not an optional extra, a pastime activity or an activity that morally committed social analysts may engage in from time to time. However, as with most things, such centrality and familiarity can create a sense of comfort that may sometimes prevent us from pausing to think deeply and reexamine what we are assuming about qualitative research and advancing social justice and human rights—or, put another way, what we say about what we do.

For example, could it be that we sometimes have fallen into the easy assumption that because we are doing qualitative research we are "advancing" human rights? Muller (1997, p. 196) suggests that sociologists of education routinely use concepts like "social justice," "equality," and the "common good" as if they were self-evident. Could it be that qualitative researchers routinely position themselves in a type of comfort zone premised on the easy assumption that because they are doing qualitative research/using qualitative approaches it is self-evident that they are "doing" social justice? Muller's point applied to the qualitative research undertaking creates space for hesitation with respect to thoroughly scrutinizing the way the qualitative research approach is enacted at *every* point of the research process—especially the points where it is claimed that what is done is done in the name of social justice and/or human rights.

To develop this idea a little further, consider Mertens's notion of transformative research. Mertens (2009) draws on work by Maori and other researchers to emphasize the responsibility qualitative researchers have to challenge the "majoritized" spaces of the status quo. Such a challenge offers the potential for those in "minoritized spaces" to break out of a research process that can otherwise be fundamentally conservative in outcome and approach if it is premised on entry into, rather than the challenging of, majoritized spaces in the first place (Mertens, 2009).

In other words, building on Brinkmann's (2009) point that human rights should be viewed as social practices, the research process itself warrants scrutiny as the outcome of a series of social practices that are shaped by, and in turn shape, understandings of social justice and human rights. Could it be that some of the decisions and assumptions that we make at all levels of the research process actually emanate from, or place our research in, majoritized spaces? What assumptions do we make about the complicated, fraught, and dynamic nexus that exists between social justice, human rights, qualitative research, marginalized, and majoritized spaces? Where in the qualitative research process does, for example, social justice fit, why, and how do we know that it does? Posing such questions is a plea for us to hesitate before acting and to think deeply about both what we are doing and what we are saying about what we do. Such hesitation is imperative if research is to have the possibility to be located within a transformative paradigm. As Denzin and Giardina (2009) note, "The pursuit of social justice within a transformative paradigm challenges prevailing forms of human oppression and injustice. This paradigm is firmly rooted in a human rights agenda. It requires an ethical framework that is rights-and social justice based" (p. 12).

The discussion to follow shares and explores some hesitations I have been grappling with in relation to ways in which social justice and human rights have come to be thought about and positioned in the undertaking of the qualitative research process *itself*. In so doing, my level of focus is not on a particular instance of social justice or social injustice per se. Nor is it at a more philosophical level in terms of discussions of understandings of social justice and human rights. There are already many good examples of both these focuses in the extant literature (see, e.g., the recent volume *Qualitative Inquiry and Social Justice: Toward a Politics of Hope,* edited by Denzin and Giardina [2009]). Rather, I am interested in exploring aspects of the operationalization of the qualitative research undertaking *itself* and its relation to advancing—or not advancing—social justice and human rights. I structure the discussion using two points of hesitation that I have arising from reflecting on a research program that I was involved in for more than a decade. The first of these relates to what we say about what we do with respect to participant involvement and "sign on" to a qualitative research endeavor.

Hesitation One: Involvement and Participation Does Not Necessarily Equal Advancing Social Justice or Human Rights

This hesitation grew out of what at first glance may appear to be an unlikely place—namely, a review of literature about the nexus between research and practice in aspects of health care. Explorations of the research/practice nexus have ranged from a focus on "research translation" in the 1970s, shifting to "research utilization" in the 1980s, through to the more contemporary notion of "knowledge translation" (Garnham, Cheek, & Alde, 2009; Mitchell, 2004). Writings and discussions of research translation and research utilization tend to be premised, overtly or otherwise, on a model of research uptake that assumes a linear research process that involves a unidirectional and passive flow of information from research to practice. Research is done and then the challenge is how to get those findings taken up in practice, the so-called two communities issue (Canadian Institutes of Health Research, 2004). On the other hand, put simplistically, discussions about knowledge translation focus more on understanding how the practice setting(s) or context(s) in which the research is located affects the way that research and practice develop and interact. In other words, the focus is on understanding the dynamic that exists between research and practice with an emphasis on research as shaping, and being shaped, by the practice context rather than something that can be done and inserted into that context later. This applies to all parts of the research process including design, conduct, and findings (Graham & Tetroe, 2007).

As qualitative researchers, we can relate to issues emanating from a focus on, and questioning about, the dynamic relationship between research and practice. After all, isn't the breaking down of forms of the two communities idea at the basis of much of what we do and the very remit of qualitative research? Isn't our research a type of research where lines are blurred between research generators and research users? And for the purposes of our discussion here, isn't it this that, at least in part, gives our research its social justice inflection in terms of how it affects decisions about the areas we choose to study; the way we choose to study them; and the way we involve participants at all parts of the research process instead of, for example, viewing them as empty vessels into which we pour our research-derived wisdom? Well, here I find myself hesitating for the answers to these questions; it seems to me they are both yes and no. I turn now to unpack this hesitation and ambivalence a little more by posing a series of questions to you as the reader.

Pause to reflect on the last research project that you were developing or perhaps a new project that you are involved in developing. Think about it in terms of social justice and what it is hoped will be achieved. No doubt there are variations of the following elements/ideas involved: a desire to address something deemed as requiring change for reasons related to perceived injustices or inequalities and a desire to change something to make life better in some way for a group of people. This all sounds positive and even familiar in terms of the way that we read and speak about qualitative research. But perhaps there is a need for a bit more reflection on some of the implicit assumptions in such thinking.

Consider how the project was actually operationalized from the *outset*: that is, what is the genesis of the notion of the research project itself? Who decided that there was a need for research in the first place? Who made the choice of topic and how? Was a broad area identified and then a research team guided the decision making and the discussions based on the need to have a tight, researchable project acceptable to academics and/or governments and/or potential funders? Was it that the government or a funding body had decided on a priority area and that was the reason for the decision to work in this area? Was it a case of social justice but social justice after the need for the project was already decided and thus perhaps social justice according to the priorities of others?

Next, once the need and idea for the project was decided and it was going ahead, who decided who would be involved and how?

Who had the power to enable involvement at the outset about what exactly would be studied and how? Does reflection on these questions raise the issue of whether we most often describe participation as related to the development and unfolding of research once the players have been brought together or invited, perhaps not giving enough attention to how the players come together in the first place and/or who invites who? Could it be that this is in some ways a form of a linear or bounded research process *within* which there can be active participation and pursuit of social justice but within set parameters?

Still reflecting on this research project, now think about the idea of social justice itself. Was, and if so how and when, social justice explicitly talked about? Did the participants in the research have a shared understanding of, and vision for, social justice? Were social justice considerations something that a particular funding call highlighted and named as being important in the adjudication of grant proposals, so that the issue became how to address these criteria in a way that could lever funding? Was it ever discussed how the research team would know that social justice was being achieved or had been achieved in some way? Or was the assumption that the techniques employed and their associated rhetoric (for example, having participants and not subjects, giving voice to those in the research, sharing our findings with participants) in themselves reflected a commitment to social justice?

Such questions are challenging indeed and may well create a sense of discomfort for they force us to hesitate to examine some of the very core emphases in, and possibly sometimes assumptions about, qualitative inquiry. Qualitative researchers argue that they use iterative, reflexive, responsive, inductive, and emergent research designs—the antithesis in many ways of a linear research process and a linear way of thinking about knowledge transfer from research to practice. But could it be that surrounding this active and dynamic approach *within* individual qualitative research projects there is a more linear knowledge transfer process in operation, including that pertaining to social justice?

What I mean is that maybe the project, no matter how dynamic, is part of a more overarching linear conception of research designed to advance social justice that goes something like this: There is an issue about social justice, this is how to "fix" it and this is how we will know if it has been fixed. Without a doubt, we may have *within* the bounded research project strategies for a dynamic and complex translation of research results pertaining to social justice into practice related to the specific aims of the project and the specific substantive focus. But then is the assumption that this will percolate or permeate into changes in the situation of our participants or change our participants so they fit the situation deemed better and more just for them? Indeed, a lot of qualitative research is designed with and for "users," especially that drawing on action principles. But that does not necessarily ensure that uptake or translation of knowledge about findings and/or social justice occurs. Further, what uptake or actions are we actually talking about? Actions emanating from marginalized spaces or somewhere else? And how do we know?

This is an important discussion to have. Perhaps there needs to be a little more hesitation in our thinking and writing about this to assist in advancing social justice and human rights through qualitative research in a way that connects and resonates at all levels of a dynamic and active process—at the level of project design, conception, and execution to the levels of practice at policy and organizational levels. It is not enough to write, for example, "underpinned by a social justice agenda this project will..." We need to be explicit about what and whose understandings of social justice are in play and how they are being picked up and enacted within specific projects themselves as well as within wider communities—be they of researchers, citizens, policymakers, or politicians (and, of course, these are not mutually exclusive categories).

Hesitation Two: An Alternate Reading of a Research Program Raising Questions about What the Doing Actually Does

The second point of hesitation I will use to develop the discussion about pausing to think about what we say about what we do draws on reflections about a research program I was involved in for over a decade. The provision of care and services to and for older people is a matter of citizenship and social sustainability. I have had the privilege of being part of a research program in Australia (see Cheek [2010] for an overview of the program and an outline of the studies) designed to contribute to such citizenship and social sustainability. In many ways, the program is about how ordinary people cope with extraordinary circumstances and what they think about this and how they think things could be better. It was designed to make a difference. Findings from these studies have influenced practice in this area (Cheek, 2010; Cheek, Corlis, & Radoslovich, 2009) and attempted to address issues pertaining to social justice and human rights for this group of citizens.

At the end of this decade of research, it would be easy to sit back and consider this program as time and energy well expended. But that is too neat! For although I am sure that we have made a contribution to developing understandings that can advance the human rights of this group of Australians, I have been reflecting on whether or not we have in any way been complicit in impeding those rights. Or, if not actually impeded them, at the very least created possibilities where those rights might be impeded. The hesitation I will now explore is about how I believe receiving funding for a program of research has assisted in advancing human rights while at the same time possibly worked against the rights of some of those involved.

So what is the problem? We received considerable funding for our projects. Pursuit of this funding (as opposed to conducting smaller scale unfunded projects) was encouraged by the institutions in which we worked as researchers. That is because the institutions are rewarded financially by the government for research performance, one measure of which is the amount of funding received by researchers working at that institution (Cheek, 2005). Although the funding enabled us to conduct the research as well as build infrastructure, employ staff, support students, and pursue other small unfunded projects, this has come at a cost. We have had to tailor the focus of the research we do to the requirements set by funding bodies in terms of either the specific substantive research focus pertaining to older people and/or the methods used. Because the funder is paying for the research to be done, this in itself does not seem to be unreasonable.

However, reflecting on this further has posed a dilemma for me in terms of social justice and human rights considerations. On one level it seems reasonable to participate in the pursuit of funding in that the funding enables the research to be done and without the funds the research cannot be done. On another level, however, this may actually have worked to exclude other important focuses in this field because it is the priority areas of the funding body that determine what is, and even to a large extent what might be, researched and how. One effect of this is that the needs of some older people are served, namely those needs that are in line with government and policy agendas, whereas the needs of other groups of older people are ignored or not able to be pursued as they fall outside the priority areas set up by governments and/or funders. In this way, the politics of funding intrudes into the area of human rights. It is commendable that government funding schemes and projects might be premised on a human rights agenda. However, an effect of this, unintended or otherwise, may be that it is an agenda that constructs boundaries around what rights it is possible to pursue, explore, and promote, and how this can be done.

Considering this causes me to hesitate and reflect on my role as researcher in this program of research. I grapple with questions such as whether the research program of which I am part is a construction of certain understandings of human rights driven by funding and performance imperatives. If so, then in attempting to advance human rights, am I in fact only focusing on a delimited version of rights as an effect of the funding agenda where the boundaries are set by policymakers and funders? And is an effect of the fact that the funding received is also used as a measure of research performance to allocate research infrastructure money to the institutions to which the researchers belong, that the understandings of human rights in this area promoted by funders are sustained and confirmed? Could it be that in this way what I hoped might contribute to a more radical agenda of human rights advancement for older Australians might be viewed as a fundamentally conservative device? Social justice and human rights were advanced, but as constructed by financial incentives and parameters!

All of this is to demonstrate that it is important that we do not become comfortable with assumptions about the use of qualitative inquiry somehow being necessarily in and of itself as synonymous with advances in social justice. We need to make clear our decision making and thinking at all points of our research process including the concepts of social justice and advancing human rights in play. There cannot be assumed or implicit understandings of what such concepts are, nor can there be unstated and assumed understandings of a way of doing research as being the same as doing social justice or advancing human rights. In this way, boundaries between what we know and what we do are crossed at all points within and without (and these are not unambiguous categories) of the research and social justice endeavor.

Emphasizing the need to expose and explore how we think about advancing social justice and human rights through qualitative research resonates with contemporary challenges for qualitative research at a number of points. These include the interconnectedness of theory and method, implications for students of qualitative inquiry and their training/development, the relationship between research context and research method/design and uptake of that research, and the relationship between the researcher and the researched. Exploring and reflecting about these matters is as much about doing and incorporating social justice and human rights into our research as is any specific substantive focus. In so doing, perhaps we can move a little closer to an existential, interpretive social science able to offer a blueprint for cultural criticism such as that alluded to by Denzin (2000), where "we finally understand that the ethnographic, the artistic, the epistemological, the aesthetic, and the political can never be neatly separated. The boundaries that have traditionally separated ethics, the aesthetic, and epistemology are erased" (p. 261).

Coda: Where Does This Leave Us?

None of this should stop us from pursuing research and doing our very best to advance social justice and human rights through our research. However, what I hope this might do is to cause us to pause for a moment to think about what we are doing and why. This is not to limit what we can do; indeed, such hesitation and reflection can open up many new and different possibilities. However, it might limit, or at least make us think about and hesitate a little with respect to, what we say about what we do. This is part of exposing what Morse (2008) has referred to as the deceptive simplicity of qualitative inquiry: the panic, sweat and tears, the analytic struggles, the plain hard thinking that sits behind the elegance of the end product.

Thus, although this chapter can offer no definitive answers to the questions raised or arrive at a neatly bounded conclusion, it can open, and add to, a conversation that must be ongoing about qualitative research, social justice and human rights. As such, it should be viewed as "more a comment within an ongoing discussion" (Maxey, 1999, p. 206).

Note

1. This chapter is based, in part, on a presentation given at the Fifth International Congress of Qualitative Inquiry, May 20–23, 2009, University of Illinois at Urbana-Champaign as part of a plenary session entitled "Advancing Human Rights: How Can Qualitative Inquiry Play a Role in Influencing Health and Social Policy?" Svend Brinkmann, Donna Mertens, and Karen Staller were fellow presenters and thanks must go to them for very useful and constructive feedback and comments at various points in the process of preparing the material from which this chapter evolved. Truls Juritzen, Tony Bugge, and Camilla Hardeland also assisted in its preparation.

References

Brinkmann, S. (2009). Educating students and advancing human rights within psychology as a discipline of governmentality. Paper presented at the Fifth International Congress of Qualitative Inquiry, May 20–23, 2009, University of Illinois at Urbana-Champaign.

Canadian Institutes of Health Research. (2004). *Knowledge Translation Strategy 2004–2009 Innovation in Action*. http://www.cihr-irsc. gc.ca/e/26574.html (accessed August 19, 2009).

Cheek, J. (2005). The practice and politics of funded qualitative research. In N. K. Denzin and Y. S. Lincoln (Eds.), *Handbook of qualitative research* (3rd ed., pp. 387–409). Thousand Oaks, CA: Sage.

Cheek, J. (2010). A potent mix: Older people, transitions, practice development and research. *Journal of Research in Nursing, 15,* 2.

Cheek, J., Corlis, M., & Radoslovich, H. (2009). Connecting what we do with what we know: Building a community of research and practice. *International Journal of Older People Nursing, 4,* 3, 233–238.

Denzin, N. K. (2000). Aesthetics and the practices of qualitative inquiry. *Qualitative Inquiry, 6,* 2, 256–265.

Denzin, N. K., & Giardina, M. D. (2009). Introduction: Qualitative inquiry and social justice: Toward a politics of hope. In N. K. Denzin and M. D. Giardina (Eds.), *Qualitative inquiry and social justice: Toward a politics of hope* (pp. 11–53). Walnut Creek, CA: Left Coast Press.

Garnham, B., Cheek, J., & Alde, P. (2009). The research/practice nexus: Underlying assumptions about the nature of research uptake into practice in literature pertaining to care of the older person. *International Journal of Older People Nursing, 4,* 3, 219–226.

Graham, I. D., & Tetroe, J. (2007). Whither knowledge translation. *Nursing Research, 56,* 4S, 86–88.

Maxey, I. (1999). Beyond boundaries? Activism, academia, reflexivity and research. *Area, 31,* 3, 199–208.

Mertens, D. M. (2009). Integrating pathways: Research and policy making in pursuit of social justice. Paper presented at the Fifth International Congress of Qualitative Inquiry, May 20–23, 2009, University of Illinois at Urbana-Champaign.

Mitchell, P. H. (2004). Lost in translation? *Journal of Professional Nursing, 20,* 4, 214–215.

Morse, J. M. (2008). Deceptive simplicity. *Qualitative Health Research, 18,* 10, 1311.

Muller, J. (1997). Social justice and its renewals: A sociological comment. *International Studies in Sociology of Education, 7,* 2, 195–211.

5. Affirming Human Dignity in Qualitative Inquiry

Walking the Walk[1]

Frederick Erickson

Let me begin with a reminiscence. This spring will be the fiftieth anniversary of my first visit to the University of Illinois. I came here in the fall of 1959 for the annual Illinois-Northwestern football game. I was playing the clarinet in the Northwestern University Marching Band. Illinois won the game.

In the stadium I saw for the first time the Illini mascot, Chief Illiniwek. For those of you who are not familiar with the chief mascot, it is a Native American character that is nonhistorical, representing no actual tribe, wearing a hodgepodge of items of Native American dress, dancing in ways that imitate genuine Native American dance—a compendium image of "The Indian" that was created by white football fans. Over the years, objections to the chief were voiced by Native Americans, who considered him a false representation and thus demeaning—an offense against human dignity. After a sustained controversy, Chief Illiniwek no longer appears at football games here. His absence is still resented by some influential alumni, who claim that the image of the chief was not intended to disparage actual Native Americans and so should not be considered by them as an offense. Those alumni want to bring back the chief. At the football game in 1959 I recall not noticing Chief Illiniwek in particular—certainly his status as a made-up indigenous character was not salient for me. He was just the Illini mascot. Our Northwestern mascot was Willie the Wildcat; theirs was Chief Illiniwek, end of story.

My second visit was the next fall, again in the band, and that year Northwestern won. Six years later, I returned as a member of an interracial team of consultants and facilitators who were assisting local citizens and school personnel in their efforts to eliminate deliberate racial segregation in the Champaign public schools. That organizing process is described in Norman Denzin's recent book on performance ethnography (2003, pp. 95–101). (He had just arrived at the University of Illinois as a new junior faculty member—I was still in graduate school. We did not meet then, but it's a small world coincidence nonetheless.) I'm proud to say that in my third visit to the university I came as an outside agitator, part of an effort to foster social justice. However, although I was then aware of how racial segregation was being seen as an affront to human dignity by African Americans and by many white Americans as well, on my third trip to Champaign I still did not realize how Chief Illiniwek might offend Native Americans. Even as I was working to denaturalize the segregation of African Americans I was still caught up in the naturalization of Chief Illiniwek.

All that was preamble.

Now I want to say that at its best, qualitative social research advances human rights and affirms human dignity by seeking and telling the truth about what particular people do in their everyday lives and about what their actions mean to them. (In what may have been a providential moment while preparing these remarks, I saw a bumper sticker on a car with a quote from George Orwell: "In a time of universal deceit, telling the truth is a revolutionary act." It seems to me that we are always in a time of universal deceit because of the ubiquity of injustice.)

By truth, of course, I don't mean a disembodied "objectivity"— a voice from nowhere and no time, outside human positionality. But the conclusions of qualitative research, communicated in ways that combine advocacy with accuracy, can counter the promotion of structured deceit—that is, the deliberate and nondeliberate covering up of the truth about how particular sets of people actually live their lives. Many of us today consider privacy to be a human right, yet we can consider as complementary to privacy the right to have one's daily life portrayed in ways that do not distort its conduct and intentions, nor silence its subjective experience.

It follows that negatively stereotyped portrayals of the routine practices of people—portrayals that deceitfully distort the truth or silence it—are violations of human rights. I think of the depictions of happy African American slaves in the antebellum South, pictured as sitting on the front steps of the plantation house, playing banjos, singing, and eating watermelon, with Ole Massa in a white suit sitting contentedly on the porch in a rocking chair. I think of the advertisements in the 1920s by hotels in Hawaii showing a Hawaiian native chambermaid with a broad smile on her face, under the headline "Come to Hawaii, where the natives have a natural desire to welcome and help you!" And I've already mentioned Chief Illiniwek.

Qualitative research also advances human rights and affirms human dignity through its proper conduct during the process of inquiry by treating research subjects honorably: with respect, as genuinely informed about the researcher's purposes, as able to participate in the research without being coerced to do so. Thus, it is fair to say that there is a potential for affirming human dignity and fostering social justice through qualitative social inquiry, both in its conduct during fieldwork and in its reporting.

I hasten to add that we should not be naive about how hard it is to do good through social inquiry—genuine good—in a world in which evils and deceit persist so stubbornly. In the past generation, we have undergone a period of deep self-criticism in qualitative social research. The motives of such study have been questioned—for the implicit purposes of colonialism, patriarchy, and state domination that have often lurked within the research. Truth telling may have been a purpose of that kind of research, but not truth telling with the aim of affirming human dignity—rather with the aim of conducting Foucauldian panoptical surveillance.

In 1969, long before we were reading Foucault in English, a social philosopher colleague of mine named Charles Tesconi published an article on educational research titled "The School as Little Brother" (Tesconi, 1969). As an only child, at that time the full significance of Tesconi's metaphor escaped me. But after I had children of my own and saw sibling rivalry up close, the power of Tesconi's conceit became apparent. The little brother "tells on" the older sibling to the parents. It is a truth telling about what the sibling did, but truth telling in that the power situation gets the older sibling in trouble. This is directly analogous to the relation that in some contract research a qualitative researcher has with those he or she studies. The contractor is a relatively powerful govern-ment agency or "establishment" foundation, the staff of which is plugged into conventional policy discourse and conceives research topics in terms of the conventional assumptions that inhere in such discourse. The persons studied are usually not very powerful people—inner-city residents, immigrants, schoolteachers. The job of the qualitative researcher is to discover the daily practices of the powerless and report on them to the funding agency. That's to be contractually stuck in the role of little brother. (Such contracts, as Faustian bargains with the devil, get entered into because of the general academic careerism that tempts scholars to frame their work with glitter, make claims beyond their evidence, and chase big grant money.)

The conduct of qualitative research as fieldwork has also been criticized. Feminist scholars such as the Canadian sociolo-gist Dorothy Smith (1974) and my UCLA philosopher colleague Sandra Harding (1991), among many others, have claimed that those with privilege are blind to the ways in which that pos-session limits what they can see and affects how they are seen by those they are studying. It follows that the possibilities that fieldwork relationships will not be fully respectful or fair are magnified in situations of power difference between researchers and research subjects. Leaving those differences unremarked and thus transparent to reflective scrutiny will limit the researcher's capacity to learn what needs to be learned in the inquiry the researcher has undertaken.

In sum, qualitative researchers can be just as greedy and self-deceived as anybody else, and academics are especially tempted by the sins of envy and pride. All too often the reactions of academ-ics to those temptations are similar to those of Oscar Wilde, who said that the best way to get rid of a temptation is to yield to it. Moreover, postmodernist critiques of Enlightenment hubris have questioned the very possibility of "truth" as an aim in the arts and humanities as well as in the social sciences.

Let me now review—as briefly as possible—past and cur-rent approaches in qualitative research, identifying what I think is laudable in the aims of each approach and what I think are the difficulties in achieving those aims.

First, plain old ethnography—the general description of everyday lives of a particular set of people, taking account of the meaning perspectives by which everyday life is conducted. This is Malinowski's vision of an interpretively valid ethnography—to tell the truth about people whose lives were invisible (to Western Europeans), just as earlier study of working-class neighborhoods in London by Charles Booth and his colleagues (Booth 1891) and of an African American neighborhood in Philadelphia by W. E. B. DuBois (1899) had the purpose of revealing the lives of those who had been made invisible and silenced by polite society and academia in the late nineteenth century.

I believe that Malinowski's espoused aim was a noble one in spite of what we now can hear as political incorrectness in his choice of words in stating that aim: to inquire and report in a way that communicates "the native's point of view, his relation to life, to realize the vision of his world" (1922, p. 25). Malinowski's aim proved much more difficult to achieve than he told us it would be when he stated it in his first ethnographic monograph. He got things wrong in that very monograph, or only partly right, about the Trobriand Islanders of Melanesia. Even in describing the skill of their canoe building and the heroism of their sea voyages, he made a Eurocentric comparison, calling them "Argonauts" in the title he chose for the book—"Argonauts of the Western Pacific." For the Trobriand Islanders who read the book a generation later after literacy had become commonplace among them, there must have been a whiff of bad breath in that title. (The metaphor of bad breath in ethnography is particularly apt, for although Malinowski did not intend his manner of description to offend [remember Chief Illiniwek?], yet as the Trobriand Islanders read what he wrote, they have been reported as having experienced at some points in his text an alien aroma of things that were said not quite right [see the discussion in Young, 1979, pp. 15–16].) Moreover, Malinowski's fieldwork diary, published posthumously in 1967, shows that he did not consistently treat the "natives" with respect in the daily conduct of his fieldwork. And even DuBois, whose purposes as an African American reformer were noble indeed, had considerable trouble, as a Harvard-educated northerner, in learning how to relate to the African American sharecroppers he met in the rural South, as he tells us in *The Souls of Black Folk* (DuBois, 1903).

Next, critical ethnography—which aims to uncover the workings of oppression, including self-defeating actions by the oppressed themselves, that plain old ethnography may have failed to deal with directly. At their best, such critical studies do speak truth to power. Yet they face a fundamental ethical dilemma in recruiting research subjects who will be characterized as oppressors in their research reports. How to tell the truth to them? Could I say to a schoolteacher or social worker or nurse or physician "I'd like to study your everyday practices so that I can report in detailed narrative the ways in which you act in false consciousness as a witless tool of late capitalist, patriarchal, institutionally racist oppression. May I have your signature on this consent form?"

Next autoethnography, done sometimes as practitioner research. If outsider researchers, however well intended they may be, are liable to distort the meaning perspectives and practices of those they study—getting it less than fully right—insider researchers who report on their own experience can identify nuances that may well go overlooked or be misunderstood by the outsider researcher. This may avoid, for insider audiences, some of the clumsiness and "bad breath" of portrayals by outsiders who just don't quite "get it," interpretively, who misconstrue indigenous epistemologies to a greater or lesser extent. Yet insiders who report with overall interpretive validity may take the habitual too much for granted, underreporting some of it. And they may be blind to aspects of their own privilege. They may have their own axes to grind, their own self-deceptions. Just as there is a need for biography as well as for autobiography there are limitations inherent in autoethnography.

Next, participatory action research, sometimes called collaborative action research. This might seem to be the best of all possible approaches. It explicitly works for change, and so has an intrinsically critical edge, with the potential for addressing directly issues of power and equity in working to make things better. It requires that the outsider researchers and the local community members (practitioners of their own lives) collaborate on a more equal footing than in the traditional relationship between the studier and the studied, which is inherently asymmetric. As my own career has developed, I have found myself most comfortable in action research roles (for discussion, see Erickson, 2006).

For some years I've been working with early grades teachers in developing a website that shows how they teach science for deep understanding by 5 and 6 year olds. This makes visible teaching practice that would otherwise be invisible and it's assisting the teachers in telling their own stories of their practice. Yet our relationship is still not absolutely equal—there is still a worm in the apple—as a visitor to their classrooms I can go to the lavatory any time I want and they can't. (As I grow older, this difference between us becomes more and more salient!) This is as direct a way as I can think of to say that my privileges as an academic are reduced in collaborative action research relationships, but those privileges are never absolutely eliminated. Moreover, if the teachers and I are both blind to regressive aspects of the teaching practice we are portraying, critical awareness of that will not surface in the website we have built together, no matter how well intended and respectful we have been in working together. We wanted to show their teaching practice "warts and all"—its backstage aspects as well as a frontstage view—but we probably will not succeed fully in that.

Next, arts-based qualitative research and performance ethnography. This can help researchers escape from some of the delusions of "objectivity" (and omniscience) that go with a white coat-professional scientist self-image as a researcher. In poetry and fiction, one is not limited to considering only "facts" within in a prose-bound horizon (we need to remember that the word "prosaic" is not used as a compliment). I am reminded of Chinua Achebe's novel *Things Fall Apart*, which I read as a graduate student. It shows the clash of African and European cultures in the 1950s in an Igbo village in Nigeria in a palpable, direct way that was avoided in the ethnographic monographs produced by anthropologists at that time. Lady Murasaki's *Tales of Genji* and Jane Austen's novels provide narrative accounts of gentry life in medieval Japan and Regency England respectively—each with an incisiveness and subtlety that escapes most social scientific narrative reporting. Some of my mentors and colleagues in qualitative research are poets. One of my mentors, Paul Bohannon, turned to writing science fiction toward the end of his life. His former wife, Laura Bohannon, wrote early in her career a powerful account of the existential trials and the incompetencies that are entailed in fieldwork. She cast the book as a fictionalized autobiography with the title *Return to Laughter: An Anthropological Novel*, and published it under the assumed name of Elenore Smith Bowen (1964). As a beginning scholar she felt compelled to use a pseudonym because the candor in discussing fieldwork that she showed in the book was not at that time considered good form.

By comparison with great novels and poetry, qualitative research reporting is not a good read overall (my wife, Joanne Straceski, in looking over a draft of this presentation wrote in the margin at this point, "Ain't that the truth!"). Such reporting usually does not engage our sustained interest let alone inspire us to action on behalf of human rights and dignity. Much conventional ethnography has an antiseptic quality, inheriting its style from natural science description and specimen preservation (think of Charles Darwin's reporting on the physical characteristics of differing breeds of pigeons in the first chapter of his magnum opus *The Origin of Species* and of the collection and preservation of organisms using formaldehyde and alcohol). Such description kills the life of the actual real-time cultural practices it reports in order to transport them from their local scene of enactment and then to display those practices to an anonymous audience of readers in a reporting genre akin to the inanimate dioramas that we view through glass windows in a natural history museum—frozen action, outside time, and struggle.

In contrast, as Denzin (2003) observes in the recent book-length discussion of performance ethnography I mentioned previously, performance heightened reporting has the potential to portray the conduct of everyday life more vividly than does conventional ethnographic narrative—to reanimate that life, whether through evocative "performance writing" (Denzin, 2003, pp. 94–95) and reader's theater or by going beyond written texts entirely through ethnodrama, ethnographic documentary film, and multimedia displays in which real-time reenactment of everyday life is done. Folklore provides another source of vividness in reporting. I recall the trenchant social commentary and analysis contained in a joke I heard as a young volunteer in the Freedom Movement: "Used to call 'the Man' 'Mr. Charlie.' Now he's 'Chuck'—but he's still 'the Man.'"

And if you want to see a consummate example of affirming human dignity through the use of story, employing the power of personal stories, I commend to you the autobiography written by President Barack Obama, titled *Dreams from My Father: A Story of Race and Inheritance* (1995). If any of us could choose narrative vignettes so astutely and tell them so incisively as Obama has done, we could well be proud of our work. (I am pleased to see that two of our presenters at this congress agree with me in this assessment—Shante' Holley and Maja Miskovic will present a paper tomorrow morning titled "Barack Obama and the Power of Critical Personal Narrative" [Holley & Miskovic, 2009]). And it should be said that the force and significance of the stories Obama told would be the same whether he had become president or not—because they were stories about actual people—true in the sense of truth that I've been using in this speech. The people in his stories were engaged in making history (and that happened—they did what they did then) whether or not Obama would go on to become famous and powerful. Even if he had never moved beyond being a part-time law school professor and a state senator, his stories of people making small pieces of history would have the same value and validity, and they would manifest the same human dignity in the daily conduct of those persons' lives.

Despite all its affordances performance, ethnography still comes with some limits—the author does not escape the responsibility of trying to get the portrayal more right than wrong, in terms of interpretive validity. And just because a portrayal might attempt a heightened kind of evocation this does not mean that every such attempt would necessarily succeed—some performances and styles of writing captivate; others fizzle.

To conclude, we need to maintain healthy suspicion of the good that qualitative research can do, even as we eschew so thoroughgoing a cynicism as to doubt that any good at all could ever come from it. Malinowski's espoused aim of interpretive validity in ethnography, I want to reiterate, is indeed a noble one: to inquire and report in a way that communicates "the native's point of view, his relation to life, to realize the vision of his world" (1922, p. 25). I believe that in spite of the difficulties entailed in that project we still need to attempt it. But we need to do so with greater humility than qualitative researchers had in the heyday of realist ethnography, to try for a more reflexive and self critical qualitative inquiry than naively realist ethnography was able to achieve. My colleague Patti Lather (2009), in a paper presented this year at the American Educational Research Association's annual meeting, called for a sense of "constitutive unknowingness" in our work. I hear that as asking for greater modesty in our attempts at inquiry—modesty in the conduct of our fieldwork and modesty in what we claim to have learned from it. If through that modesty we can say something that is true about everyday life, even when as outsider researchers or as insider researchers we will still get part of the telling less than completely correct, that telling can advance the human right not to be invisible—not to be silenced and not to be stereotyped. Such modesty in our narration can affirm the human dignity of those whose lives we describe.

I greatly admire what President Nelson Mandela and Archbishop Desmond Tutu did in establishing and operating the Truth Commission in the new South Africa. At our best, qualitative researchers can serve as truth commissioners in our own societies—for every society needs its own such commissioners, as at the outset I quoted Orwell in saying so cogently. Yet we need to practice humility and self-critical awareness in the ways in which we go about our inquiry and in the ways in which we report what we have learned. Let us remember: It is not easy to do good, even when that is what we want to do.

Note

An earlier version of this chapter was presented as a keynote address to the 5th International Congress of Qualitative Inquiry, University of Illinois, Urbana-Champain, May 21, 2009.

References

Booth, C. (1891). *Labour and life of the people of London.* London: Williams and Nargate.

Bowen, E. Smith. (1964). *Return to laughter: An anthropological novel.* New York: Anchor Books.

Denzin, N. (2003). *Performance ethnography: Critical pedagogy and the politics of culture.* Thousand Oaks, CA: Sage.

DuBois, W. E. B. (1899). *The Philadelphia Negro: A social study.* New York: Schocken.

DuBois, W. E. B. (1903). *The souls of black folk.* Chicago: A. C. McClurg.

Erickson, F. (2006). Studying side by side: Collaborative action ethnography in educational research. In G. Spindler and L. Hammond (Eds.), *New horizons for ethnography in education* (pp. 235–257). Mahwah, NJ: Lawrence Erlbaum and Associates.

Harding, S. (1991). *Whose science? Whose knowledge?: Thinking from women's lives.* Ithaca, NY: Cornell University Press.

Holley, S., & Miskovic, M. (2009). Barack Obama and the power of critical personal narrative. Paper presented at the 5th International Congress of Qualitative Inquiry in session 1031, "Narrating the Political," University of Illinois, Urbana-Champain, May 22, 2009.

Lather, P. (2009). "Getting lost" in policy work. Paper presented at the annual meeting of the American Educational Research Association in session 31.032, Disciplined inquiry: From qualitative research to policy, San Diego, CA, April 14, 2009 [and forthcoming in *Educational Studies* under the title "Getting lost: Social science and/as philosophy."]

Malinowski, B. (1922). *Argonauts of the Western Pacific.* New York: E.P. Dutton.

Malinowski, B. (1967). *A diary in the strict sense of the term.* New York: Harcourt, Brace & World.

Obama, B. (1995). *Dreams from my father: A story of race and inheritance.* New York: Three Rivers Press.

Smith, D. (1974). Women's perspective as a radical critique of sociology. *Sociological Inquiry, 44*, 1, 7–13.

Tesconi, C. (1969). The school as little brother. *Changing Education,* Winter, 21–24.

Young, M. (1979). *The ethnography of Malinowski: The Trobriand Islands 1915–18.* London: Routledge & Kegan Paul.

Section 2: Method

6. In the Name of Human Rights

I Say (How) You (Should) Speak (Before I Listen)[1]

Antjie Krog

Introduction

It is the year 1872. A Bushman shaman called //Kabbo narrates an incident to a German philologist, Wilhelm Bleek, in Cape Town. In the narration, which took Bleek from April 13 to September 19 to record and translate from /Xam into English, the following two paragraphs describe how a young woman tracks down her nomadic family:

> She (the young widow) arrives with her children at the water hole. There she sees her younger brother's footprints by the water. She sees her mother's footprint by the water. She sees her brother's wife's spoor by the water.
>
> She tells her children: "Grandfather's people's footprints are here; they had been carrying dead springbok to the water so that people can drink on their way back with the game. The house is near. We shall follow the footprints because the footprints are new. We must look for the house. We must follow the footprints. For the people's footprints were made today; the people fetched water shortly before we came." (Lewis-Williams, 2000, p. 61)

For more than a hundred years, these words seemed like just another interesting detail in an old Bushmen story, until researcher Louis Liebenberg went to live among modern Bushmen. In his book, *The Art of Tracking: The Origin of Science*, Liebenberg (1990) insists that what seems to be an instinctive capacity to track a spoor, the Bushmen were using intricate decoding, contextual sign analysis to create hypotheses.

Liebenberg distinguishes three levels of tracking among the Bushmen: First, simple tracking just follows footprints. Second, systematic tracking involved the gathering of information from signs until a detailed indication is built up of the action. Third, speculative tracking involves the creation of a working hypothesis on the basis of: (1) the initial interpretation of signs, (2) a knowledge of behavior, and (3) a knowledge of the terrain. According to Liebenberg these skills of tracking are akin to those of Western intellectual analysis and suggests that all science actually started with tracking (Brown, 2006, p. 25).

Returning to the opening two paragraphs, one sees that the young widow effortlessly does all three kinds of tracking identified by Liebenberg. She identifies the makers of the footprints, their coming and going, that they were carrying something heavy and/or bleeding, that they were thirsty, that they drank water on the way back from hunting; she identifies the game as a springbuck; she establishes when the tracks were made and then puts forward a hypothesis of what they were doing and where and how she will find her family that very day.

The question I want to pose here is: Is it justified to regard Wilhelm Bleek (as the recorder of the narration), Louis Liebenberg (as a scholar of tracking), and myself (for applying the tracking theory to the narration) as the scholars/academics while considering //Kabbo (Bushman narrator) and the woman in the story (reading the tracks) as "raw material"?

How does this division respect human right number 19 in the Universal Declaration of Human Rights of the United Nations: "Everyone has the right to freedom of opinion and expression; this right includes freedom to hold opinions without interference *and to seek, receive and impart information and ideas through any media and regardless of frontiers*" (see http://www.un.org/en/documents/udhr/).

Who May Enter the Discourse?

The rights of two groups will be discussed in this chapter: first, the rights of those living in marginalized areas but who produce virtually on a daily basis intricate knowledge systems of survival

and second, the rights of scholars coming from those marginalized places, but who can only enter the world of acknowledged
knowledge in languages not their own and within discourses
based on foreign and estrange-ing structures.

Although Gayatri Spivak describes the first group as subaltern, she deals with both these groups in her famous chapter "Can
the Subaltern Speak?" suggesting that the moment that the subaltern finds herself in conditions in which she can be heard "her
status as a subaltern would be changed utterly; she would cease to
be subaltern" (Landry & Maclean, 1995, pp. 5–6).

Mrs. Konile as Subaltern

During the two years of hearings conducted by the South African
Truth and Reconciliation Commission two thousand testimonies
were given in public. Instead of listening to the impressive stories
of well-known activists, the commission went out of its way to
provide a forum for the most marginalized narratives from rural
areas given in indigenous languages. In this way, these lives and
previously unacknowledged narratives were made audible and
could be listened to through translation to become the first entry
into the South African psyche of what Spivak (1987) so aptly calls
in her piece "Subaltern Studies: Deconstructing Historiography,"
"news of the consciousness of the subaltern" (p. 203).

Covering the hearings of the Truth Commission for
national radio, one testimony stayed with me as the most incoherent female testimony I had to report on (First TRC Testimony of
Mrs. Konile, 1998). I considered the possibility that one needed
other tools to make sense of it and wondered whether clarification
could be found in the original Xhosa, or was the woman actually mentally disturbed, or was there some vestiges of "cultural
supremacy" in myself that prevented me from hearing her?

Trying to find her testimony later on the Truth Commission's
website was fruitless. There was no trace of her name in the index.
Under the heading of the Gugulethu Seven incident, her surname
was given incorrectly as "Khonele," and she was the only mother
in this group to be presented without a first name. Her real name
was Notrose Nobomvu Konile, but I later found that even in her

official identity document her second name was given incorrectly as Nobovu.

One might well ask: Is it at all possible to hear this un-mentioned, incorrectly ID-ed, misspelled, incoherently testifying, translated, and carelessly transcribed woman from the deep rural areas of South Africa?

I asked two colleagues, Nosisi Mpolweni from the Xhosa Department and professor Kopano Ratele from the Psychology Department and Women & Gender Studies, to join me in a reading of the testimony. Ms Mpolweni and Professor Ratele immediately became interested. Using the original Xhosa recording, we started off by transcribing and retranslating. Then we applied different theoretical frameworks (Elaine Scarry, Cathy Garuth, Soshana Felman, Dori Laub, G. Bennington, etc.) to interpret the text and finally, we visited and reinterviewed Mrs. Konile. What started out as a one-off teatime discussion became a project of two and a half years and finally a book: *There Was This Goat: Investigating the Truth and Reconciliation Testimony of Notrose Nobomvu Konile* (Krog, Mpolweni, & Ratele, 2009).

But first, some concepts need to be introduced that play a role the moment the voice of the subaltern becomes audible.

The Fluke of "Raw Material"

I was proud to be appointed by a university that, during apartheid, deliberately ignored the demands of privileged white academia and focused unabashedly on the oppressed communities surrounding the campus. The university prided itself, and rightly so, on being the university of the left and threw all its resources behind the poor.

Since the first democratic election in 1994, South Africa is trying to become part of what is sometimes called "a normal dispensation." So some months after my appointment 5 years ago, I was asked to send a list of what I have published that year. Fortunately, or so I thought, I was quite active: a nonfiction book, poetry, controversial newspaper pieces etc.—so imagine my surprise to receive an email saying that none of the listed writings "counts."

I went to see the dean of research. The conversation went like this:

"Why do my publications not count?

"It's not peer reviewed."

"It was reviewed in all the newspapers!"

"But not by peers."

Wondering why the professors teaching literature would not be regarded as my peers I asked, "So who are my peers?"

"Of course you are peerless," this was said somewhat snottily, "but I mean the people in your field."

"So what is my field?"

"The people working ..." and his hands fluttered "in the areas about which you write."

"Well," I said, "when I look at their work I see that they all quote me."

His face suddenly beamed: "So you see! You are raw material!"

Initially I thought nothing of the remark, but gradually came to realize how contentious, judgmental, and excluding the term "raw material" was. Who decides who is raw material? Are Mrs. Konile and //Kabbo and the Bushman woman raw material? Looking back onto our project, I find myself asking: Why did we three colleagues so easily assume that Mrs. Konile was raw material and not a cowriter of our text? Why are her two testimonies and one interview in which she constructs and analyzes, deducts and concludes less of an academic endeavor than our contribution? Her survival skills after the devastating loss of her son were not by chance but a result of her careful calculations and tested experiences. During our interview, we even asked her to interpret her text. Why should she enter our book and the academic domain as raw material? Should she not be properly credited as a cotext producer on the cover like the three of us?

I began wondering: What would another Gugulethu mother ask Mrs. Konile? Or to move to another realm: How would one cattle herder interview another cattle herder? How would one cattle herder analyze and appraise the words of a fellow cattle herder? How would such an interview differ from me interviewing that cattle herder? And, finally, how can these experiences enter the academic discourse *without* the conduit of a well-meaning scholar? How shall we ever enter any new realm if we insist that all information must be processes by ourselves for ourselves?

The Fluke of Discipline

After being downgraded to raw material, I duly applied to attend a workshop on how to write unraw material so as to meet one's peers through unread but accredited journals. The workshop was organized by the university after it became clear that our new democratic government wants universities to come up with fundable research. We were obliged to compete with the established and excellently resourced former white universities and their impressive research records.

I walked into this organized workshop. There were about forty of us. I was the only white person. During smoke breaks the stories poured out.

A professor in math told me the following:

> One Sunday a member of the congregation told me that he was installing science laboratories in the schools of the new South Africa, that it was very interesting because every school was different. So this went on every Sunday until I said to him that he should write it down. So after I had completely forgotten about it, he pitched up with a manuscript this thick (about four inches) and joked: Is this not a MA thesis? I looked and indeed it was new, it was methodically researched and systematically set out and riveting to read. So where to now? I said it was not math so he should take it to the science department. Science said it was more history than science. History said no, … and so forth.

Those who attended the workshop were by no means subaltern, but first-generation educated men and women from formerly disadvantaged communities in apartheid South Africa. As we attended subsequent workshops in writing academic papers, we became aware of how the quality of "on the ground experience" was being crushed into a dispirited nothingness through weak English and the specific format of academic papers. We learned how easily an important story died within the corset of an academic paper; how a crucial observation was nothing without a theory; and how a valuable experience dissolved outside a discipline.

The Fluke of Theory

The last story is about a seminar on the black body that I attended. Opening the seminar, the professor said that when he was invited he thought that the paper he was preparing would already have been accepted by an accredited journal and the discussion could then have taken place together with the peer reviews. The journal had, however, rejected the piece, so ... maybe the discussion should start from scratch.

The paper he presented was indeed weak. As he was speaking, one had the distinct feeling of seeing a little boat rowing with all its might past waves and fish and flotillas and big ships and fluttering sails to a little island called Hegel. The oar was kept aloft until, until ... at last, the oar touched Hegel. Then the rowing continued desperately until the oar could just touch the island called Freud or Foucault. In the meantime, you want to say forget these islands, show us what's in your boat, point out the fish that you know, how did you sidestep that big ship, where did you get these remarkable sails?

The discussion afterward was extraordinary. Suddenly, the professor was released from his paper and the black students and lecturers found their tongues and it became a fantastic South African analysis. Afterward I asked the professor: "Why didn't you write what you have just said?" He answered:

> Because I can't find a link between what I know and existing literature. It's a Catch 22 situation: I cannot analyze my rural mother if it is assumed that there is no difference between her mind and the average North American or Swedish mind. On the other hand, my analysis of my rural mother will only be heard and understood if it is presented on the basis of the North American and Swedish mind.

Academics from Marginalized Communities

Both of my colleagues, Nosisi Mpolweni and Prof. Kopano Ratele, were the first in their families to be tertiary educated, whereas I was the fourth generation of university-educated women. Right through our collective interpretative analysis on the testimony of Mrs. Konile, the power relations among us changed. The project started with my initiative, but I quickly became the one who knew the least. Prof. Ratele was the best educated of us three and had already published academically. Nosisi made an invaluable input with her translations and knowledge about Xhosa culture. I could write well, but not academically well. English was our language, but only Prof. Ratele could speak it properly. During our field trip to interview Mrs. Konile, the power swung completely to Nosisi, and I, not understanding Xhosa, had no clout during our field-work excursions.

However, during our discussions, I became aware that while we were talking, my colleagues had these moments of perfect formulation, a sort of spinning toward that sentence that finally says it all. We would stop and realize: Yes, this was it! This was the grasp we were working toward. But when we returned with written texts, these core sentences were nowhere to be seen in their work.

For the next discussion, I brought a tape recorder. We were discussing why Mrs. Konile so obsessively uses the word "I" within her rural collective worldview. I transcribed the conversation and sent everybody these chunks; here is the text returned by Prof. Ratele:

> Mrs. Konile dreamt about the goat the night before she heard that her son was killed. The TRC however was not a forum for dreams, but for the truth about human rights abuses. I suggest that through telling about the dream, Mrs. Konile was signaling to the TRC her connection to the ancestral worlds.
>
> The dream revealed that she was still whole, that she was in contact with the living and the dead and she clearly experienced little existential loneliness. ... Her son's death is what introduced her to a loneliness, a being an "I." She had become an individual through the death of her son—selected, cut off, as it were, to become an individual. She was saying: "I am suffering, because I had been forced to become an individual." The word "I" was not talking about her real psychological individuality. Mrs. Konile was using "I" as a form of complaint. She was saying: "I don't want to be I. I want to be us, but the killing of my son, made me into an 'I.'" (Krog, Mpolweni, & Ratele, 2009, pp. 61–62)

As a white person steeped in individuality, I initially didn't even notice the frequency of the word "I," but when I did it merely confirmed to me that the notion of African collective-ness was overrated, despite the emphasis it receives from people like Nelson Mandela and Archbishop Desmond Tutu. The conclusion Prof. Ratele came to, however, was the opposite and it was a conclusion I could not have come to, and up until now neither has any other white TRC analyst.

For me this was the big breakthrough, not only in the book, not only in TRC analysis, but also in our method of working. The confidence of the spoken tone, a confidence originating from the fact that somebody was talking from within and out of a world she knows intimately, had been successfully carried over on to paper. Prof. Ratele was crossing "frontiers" to get past all the barriers lodged in education, race, background, structure, language, and academic discipline to interpret his own world from out of its postcolonial, postmodern past, and racial awarenesses with a valid confidence that speaks into and even beyond exclusive and prescriptive frameworks.

My guess is that my colleague would never have been able to write this particular formulation without first talking it, and talking it to us—a black woman who understood him and a white woman who didn't.

We wrote an essay about Mrs. Konile's dream in our three different voices but the piece was rejected by a South African journal for allowing contradictory viewpoints to "be" in the essay, for having a tone that seems oral, for not producing any theory that could prove that Mrs. Konile was somehow different from other human beings, etc. The piece was, however, I'm glad to say, accepted by Norman Denzin, Yvonna Lincoln, and Linda Tuhiwai Smith (2007) for their *Handbook of Critical and Indigenous Methodologies*.

Conclusion: Research as Reconciliatory Change

These examples, ranging from a Bushman shaman to a black professor in psychology, expose the complexities of doing research in a country emerging from divided histories and cultures. It also poses some ethical questions about the conditions we set for people to enter academic discourse. Spivak (1988) indeed stresses that ethics is not a problem of knowledge but a call of relationship. When she claims that the subaltern "cannot speak," she means that the subaltern as such cannot be heard by the privileged of either the First or Third Worlds. If the subaltern was able to make herself heard then her status as a subaltern would be changed utterly; she would cease to be subaltern. But isn't the goal of our research "that the subaltern, the most oppressed and invisible constituencies, as such might cease to exist" (Landry & Maclean, 1995, p. 6).

French philosopher Gilles Deleuze rightly remarks that the power of minorities "is not measured by their capacity to enter into and make themselves felt within the majority system." At the same time, Deleuze points out that it is precisely these different forms of minority-becoming that provide the impulse for change, but change can only occur to the extent that there is adaptation and incorporation on the side of the standard or the majority (Deleuze & Guattari 1987, p. 520).

We have to find ways in which the marginalized can enter our discourses in their own genres and their own terms so that we can learn to hear them. They have a universal right to impart information and ideas through any media and regardless of frontiers, and we have a duty to listen and understand them through engaging in new acts of becoming.

Note

1. This chapter extends and inserts itself in the discussion of *testimonio* as given in John Beverley, 2005, pp. 547–558.

References

Beverley, J. (2005). Testimonio, subalternity, and narrative authority. In N. K. Denzin and Y. S. Lincoln (Eds.), *Handbook of qualitative research* (3rd ed., pp. 547–558). Thousand Oaks, CA: Sage.

Brown, D. (2006). *To speak of this land—Identity and belonging in South Africa and beyond*, Scottsville, South Africa: University of KwaZulu Natal Press.

Denzin, N. K., Lincoln, Y.S., & Smith, L. T. (Eds.) (2007). *Handbook of critical and indigenous methodologies.* Thousand Oaks, CA: Sage.

Deleuze, G., & Guattari, F. (1987). *Thousand plateaus: Capitalism and schizophrenia* (B. Massumi, Trans.). Minneapolis: University of Minnesota Press.

First TRC Testimony of Mrs. Konile. 1998. http://www.doj.gov.za/trc/hrvtrans/heide/ct00100.htm (accessed March 12, 2009).

Krog, A, Mpolweni, N., & Ratele, K. (2009). *There was this goat— Investigating the Truth Commission testimony of Notrose Nobomvu Konile.* Scottsville, South Africa: University of KwaZulu-Natal Press.

Landry, D., & Maclean, G. (1995). Introduction: Reading Spivak. In D. Landry and G. Maclean (Eds.) *Selected works of Gyatri Chakravorty Spivak* (pp. 1-13). New York: Routledge.

Lewis-Williams, J. D. (Ed). (2000). *Stories that float from afar: Ancestral folklore of the San of Southern Africa,* Cape Town: David Philip.

Liebenberg, L. (1990). *The art of tracking: The origin of science.* Cape Town: David Philip.

Spivak, G. C. (1987). Subaltern studies: Deconstructing historiography. *In other worlds: Essays in cultural politics* (pp. 197–221). London: Routledge.

Spivak, G. C. (1988). "Can the subaltern speak?" In C. Nelson and L. Grossberg (Eds.), *Marxism and the interpretation of culture* (pp. 271–313). Basingstoke, UK: Macmillan Education.

7. Autoethnography and Queer Theory
Making Possibilities

Stacy Holman Jones
Tony E. Adams

Just Stories

I am invited to speak at the critical methods pro-seminar my department offers for Ph.D. students in communication. These invitations are a matter of routine, and I welcome the opportunity to participate, along with the students, in a seminar. This time, I am invited as the guest on the evening slated for a discusison of queer theory. I wonder about this invitation. My work happens at intersections: of performance and feminsim, ethnography and fiction, personal writing and critique. I imagine that, if you're reading this book, your work also happens at intersections. I consider myself an auto/ethnographer, a performer, a writer, and a critical scholar. My work includes queer theory, but queer theory is not the center of my work or my identity as a scholar. Experience is the center of my work. Maybe the invitation was more about me, personally. If *I* am queer, then I should know about queer theory, right? Rather than decide, I embrace both options: My experience is queer theory and queer theory is me. I choose to critically engage—in text and in world—margin *and* center, experience *and* theory.

Along with the invitation to particiate in the discussion of queer theory, I am asked to assign one of my essays for the students to read. I have always been shy about this, uncomfortable with the compulsory knowledge students are supposed to have of their faculty and with how knowing the work collapses into, rather than complicates, knowing the person. Still, I comply, assigning an essay I wrote about adoption (Holman Jones, 2005b), about the intersections of performativity and performance, about how lives and the connections among us manifest in their telling and in the ways we tell on canonical narratives of what is and should be. The essay doesn't comment on queer theory directly, though it works to "redeploy" and "twist" from "prior usage" (often derogatory, accusatory, violent) the normalizing view of adoption, and does so in the "direction of urgent and expanding political purposes" (Butler, 1993, p. 228). And so it is—as I am—most certainly queer.

The students in the seminar tell me the essay is moving, even haunting. They also tell me my work is elliptical, referential, theory-laden, and overtly and overly scholarly. It is as if I am at once present and unavailable in my work, my words an apparition, a vanishing act. *I* cannot be read, known, or understood. My ideas, too, are abstract, undetermined, and difficult to decide. As the students tell me—tell of me, tell on me and my work—I think *yes*, that's *it*. The essay, my work, I—in its and my most compelling moments—ask the "unanswerable," seek indeterminacy, consider my own "unforeseen" (Gingrich-Philbrook, 2005, pp. 311, 312). And when someone asks the question the essay (my work, I) inevitably inspire(s)—"Why not just tell the stories? Why weight it down with all of that theory?"—I am ready.

"Because theory is a story. Theory tells us a story—in nonordinary language (which jolts us out of our complacency and into attention)—of how things are and helps us discover the possibilities in how things might be. The intersections among theory and everyday language are crucial to our ability to tell and re-imagine not only what we can say, but also who we can be" (Butler, 1997, p. 144).

When we say, "No theory, no politics, just stories," we forget the differentiating, strange-making impulse of critical inquiry and scholarship. Instead of stories *or* theory, emotionalism *or* explanation, seeking *or* representation, aesthetics *or* knowledge, we need a language that unsettles the ordinary while spinning a good story. We need the shifting, refiguring, and excessive talk of *maybe*, about what *matters*, that says something *queer*. This is why autoethnography and queer theory are good for each other. Told together, autoethnography and queer theory make stories—just stories—into insurrectionary acts (Butler, 1997, p. 145).

Good for Each Other

At parent-teacher conferences, I am told that my child is bright and a good student, but that he lacks focus. Thinking that he doesn't understand the lesson or that he's having trouble finishing his work, I ask about these things, but that's not it. Lacking focus means talking to his classmates when he's supposed to be listening, moving around the room when he's supposed to be sitting, sharing too much when he is called on, and—this last item jolts me back into my own second grade classroom—asking too many questions. Of course, I ask questions about all of these things, morphing my knowledge of docile bodies (Foucault, 1995 [1977]) and institutional structures (Bourdieu, 1977 [1972]) into parent-teacher conversation. But when we get to the questions, I am stuck. My child's questions aren't off-topic or meant to deflect attention from the teacher or the lesson. Rather, there are simply too many. I pause, reflecting on the self-imposed ban on asking questions that persisted for much of my second-grade year, then ask, "Would you rather he didn't ask questions?" This question is answered by a generative, open, and affirming silence.

When I get home, I retrieve my home-made grade school scrapbook from the attic and give my second-grade progress report to Noah. "Distracted by others when doing seatwork." "Participation in discussion good, but leaves little room for others."

"What does 'leaves little room for others' mean?"

"I think it means I asked too many questions and no one else got a chance."

"How can you ask too many questions?"

"I don't think you can. I think that without questions we can't talk and we certainly can't live" (Butler, 1997).

"Do I ask too many questions?"

"What do you think?"

"I think no."

"I think no, too. Do you know what else I think?"

"What?"

"I think we're good for each other."

Noah reminded me that asking questions is essential to living a free, peaceful, and *good* life. He reminded me that we must, as Butler (1997) reminds, interrogate "the terms that we need to live" and that we must take "the risk of living the terms that we keep in question" (p. 163). Autoethnography and queer theory are good for each other because they interrogate the terms that we need to live and live the terms we keep in question—recently, swinging, penetration, catastrophe, heresy, and closets, to name just a few (Adams, forthcoming; Berry, 2007; Holman Jones, 2009; Minge & Zimmerman, 2009; Spry, forthcoming). And like Noah and me, and Tony and me, and you and me, we are not good for each other when we are the same, interchangeable, never questioning. Rather than a mirror providing a self-affirming reflection, autoethnography and queer theory work together through and around the fulcrum and tension of the hinge. The hinge is an instrument of transitivity, a moral movement that is inspired and linked, acting and acted upon. The hinge asks us to align divided perspectives and provides a metaphor for promoting purposeful movement—to bring together the purposes and practices of autoethnography with the purposes and practices of queer theory.

In particular, we illustrate the possibilities of what can happen when a method and theoretical perspective are put into conversation, when we hinge experience and analysis, ambiguity and clarity, dialogue and debate, accessibility and academic activism, "just stories" and high theory. We are not after a homogenizing blend *or* nihilistic prioritizing of concerns. Rather, we want to try to "remap the terrain" of autoethnography and queer theory without "removing the fences that make good neighbors" (Alexander, 2003, p. 352); we want to ask what autoethnography and queer theory do, should do, and do to, for, and in research methodology and scholarship. We want to ask what autoethnography and queer theory do, should do, and do to, for, and in our efforts to honor the sanctity of life and human dignity.

Throughout this chapter, we use "I" to tell our stories to combine us, as authors and readers, into a shared experience. My experience—our experience—could be and could reframe your experience. My experience—our experience—could politicize your experience and could motivate and mobilize you, and us, to action. Our "I" is fashioned after Pollock's (2007, p. 246) "performative 'I,'" and away from a first-person scholarly narrator who is self-referential but unavailable to criticism or revision. By contrast, our performative I is "made real through the performance of writing," particularly in performances that link autoethnography and queer theory (Pollock, 2007, p. 247). Our I hinges us—Stacy and Tony—to "we," a community of scholars ready to write ourselves into new ways of being and becoming. We begin by taking a kind of relational inventory, exploring what joins and holds apart autoethnography and queer theory and asking about why these practices and politics are good for each other.

Inventory

One way to assess the goodness—of fit, of purpose, of goals—of a relationship is to think about commitment. Commitment is both personal and political; it is an investment in the now that anticipates a future based on common goals and cooperation (Foster, 2008, pp. 84–85). Commitment can also be an unquestioned value that elides difference and denies nonnormative identities and lives (Foster, 2008).

Autoethnography—a method that uses personal experience with a culture and/or a cultural identity to make unfamiliar aspects of the culture and/or identity familiar for insiders and outsiders—and queer theory—a dynamic and shifting, theoretical paradigm that developed in response to a normalizing of heterosexuality and from a desire to disrupt insidious, social conventions—share cooperative ideological commitments:

- Autoethnography, as a research method, rubs against and tries to disrupt canonical ideas about research and methodological orthodox, particularly ideas of what research is and how research should be done (Colyar, 2008; Ellis, 2007; Ellis & Bochner, 2000; Rambo, 2007; Slattery, 2001). Although not necessarily a research method, queer theorists advocate a similar sensibility in their attempt to deconstruct, pollute, and diffuse what passes as "normal" (Belkin, 2008; Bennett, 2008; Cobb, 2007; Gamson, 2000; Plummer, 2003).

- Queer theorists (re)appropriate extant research, language, texts, practices and beliefs in novel, innovative ways (Alexander, 2008; Hilfrich, 2006; Koro-Ljungberg, 2004; McCreery, 2008; Yep & Elia, 2007). Similarly, autoethnographers try to tell, recast, personal experience in inventive, tradition-breaking and -remaking ways, simultaneously critiquing and filling the gaps in existing scholarship (Aoki, 2005; Boylorn, 2006; Davis, 2009; Defenbaugh, 2008; Jago, 2002).

- Autoethnographers consider representations of identity and experience uncertain, fluid, open to interpretation, and able to be revised (Ellis, 2009; Goodall, 2006; Tillmann, 2009; Wyatt, 2005, 2008). Queer theorists share such a sentiment, all the while working against fixity and firmness, certainty and closure, stability and rigid categorization (Butler, 1999, 2004; Henderson, 2001; Plummer, 2005; Sedgwick, 1993).

- Queer theorists advocate for equitable, political change and conceive of ways research, texts, and bodies can serve as sites of discursive "trouble" (Butler, 1999, 2004; Chavéz, 2009; Irving, 2008; Muñoz, 1999; Solis, 2007). Such a desire constitutes much of current autoethnographic work as many autoethnographers do their best to make ideological and discursive trouble while, simultaneously, work to create humane and equitable ways of living (Berry, 2007; Dykins Callahan, 2008; Foster, 2008; Minge, 2007; Myers, 2008).

Autoethnography and queer theory are also good for each other because they share interrelated criticisms and deploy complementary responses to address their limitations:

- Queer theory is criticized for being too theoretical and impractical (Butler, 1999; Halberstam, 2005) yet praised for being able to make movement and motivate political action (Gamson, 2003; Wilchins, 2004). Autoethnography is criticized for being atheoretical (Atkinson, 1997) and poorly written (Gingrich-Philbrook, 2005; Moro, 2006) yet praised for being applicable to lived realities (Goodall, 2004; Tillmann, 2009).

- Autoethnography is criticized for being self-indulgent, too personally messy, too easy, and too narcissistic (Anderson,

2006; Buzard, 2003; Delamont, 2009; Fine, 2003; Gans, 1999; Madison, 2006); queer theory is assumed to be not personal enough and especially dense and difficult (Butler, 1999; Halberstam, 2005). Autoethnographers (Adams, 2009; Boylorn, 2006; Denzin, 2003; Holman Jones, 2005a; Neumann, 1996; Spry, 2001) and queer theorists (Butler, 2004; Corey & Nakayama, 1997; Glave, 2005; Nakayama & Corey, 2003) have replied by emphasizing the reciprocity of the I and the we, the reciprocity of story and theory, the reciprocity of the personal and political.

Queer theory is considered elitist, Western, colonialist, and white (Alexander, 2008; Halberstam, 2005; Johnson, 2001; Lee, 2003; Yep & Elia, 2007); autoethnography is considered a method dominated by theoretical colonialists and solipsists, patriarchy, and the tenured (Anderson, 2006, Buzard, 2003, Gingrich-Philbrook, 2005). Queer theorists have responded by refiguring queer and queer theory to signal, signify, and sound the concerns of diverse subjects and subjectivities on questions of race, ethnicity, class, sex, desire, gender, and ability (Alexander, 2008; Johnson, 2001; Lee, 2003; Moreman, 2009; Sandahl, 2003; Solis, 2007). Autoethnographers respond by appreciating the use of different media to represent "findings" (Adams, 2008), valuing embodiment, performance, and other so-called alternative ways of knowing (Denzin, 2003; Holman Jones, 2005a), embracing the cultural standpoints a researcher embodies (Boylorn, 2006; Marvasti, 2006), and respecting the relationships a researcher has with those she or he studies—no longer can a researcher enter a setting, mine others for data, and leave without empathetically acknowledging these others (Ellis, 2007; Tillmann-Healy, 2003).

Autoethnography and queer theory: complementary and in tension, accessible and able to engage complicated concepts, disruptive and open-to-revision, political and practical, humane and ethical—good for each other. By hinging autoethnography and queer theory, we work to be out and queer in autoethnography and work to use autoethnography to be out and queer. Being out and queer in autoethnography means making ourselves vulnerable to critique, by risking living—in language and in life—the terms we keep in question by embodying their possibilities (Madison, 1998). A focus on possibilities asks everyone involved in our exchange (writers and readers, performers and spectators, theorists and novelists, queers all) to claim and remake the terms we need, from the inner spaces of texts to the outer domain of society, so that we might make a material, concrete, and cathartic difference (Madison, 1998; see also Alexander, 2005; Holman Jones, 2005a; Madison, 2005). More specifically, we work to create possibilities by theorizing story and storying theory, embracing vulnerability while taking a political stand, creating conversation and trouble, and taking chances to make movement.

Possibility: Revising and Becoming

Hinging autoethnography and queer theory means making work that *becomes,* like a perpetual horizon, rather than an artifact of experience—making work that acts *as if* rather than says *it is*, recognizing that a (published) text fixes and solidifies experience but that experience is not fixed or solidified; it is always "partial, partisan, and problematic" (Goodall, 2001, p. 55). Such recognition means understanding, and embracing, the importance of being tentative, playful, and incomplete, and conceiving of experience as "overdetermined" (Wolcott, 2010), always in motion, and in need of (perpetual) revision (Ellis, 2009).

For instance, in May 2003 I received a call from my dad:

"I heard a rumor about you," he says. I become nervous. "I heard that you're living with a guy. In fact, not just living with, but fucking this guy. Is this true?"

"Weeelllll," I stutter, "no, it's not true. Who would say something like that?"

"That doesn't matter," he abruptly suggests. "I'm just glad it ain't."

"Yeah, me too, Father. That's silly. I'll talk to you soon." The conversation ends.

I realize that I can't stay silent any longer. I'm tired and I lied to my father. Guilt devours me. I pick up the phone and call him back.

"Hello," he answers in an upbeat, much happier tone.

"Yeah, Dad, it's me. I just wanted to tell you that it's true—I am living with a guy, my boyfriend in fact. Sorry to burst your bubble."

I hear nothing so I decide to make the situation better by making up a lie, telling him that his recently deceased mother, my grandmother, knew about my same-sex desire.

"And Grandma knew about my sexuality and my boyfriend but she thought it would be best if I didn't tell you. She was always fine with it, but realized, as did I, that you would not accept it. Sorry if I'm a disappointment."

"Shheee knneww?" he stutters.

"Yeah, she did, Father."

"Well," he utters more fluently, "I guess I'll call you soon."

"Bye, Dad. Take care."

Silence between us for the next six months (Adams, 2006).

Prior to my dad's call, I never thought I would tell him that I fit—and did not fit—particular labels, that is, gay and straight respectively. I planned to live my life not informing my father of significant others such as Brett (the guy I lived with) or of my same-sex desire. I feared being disowned and hated and did not feel I could deal with my father's response.

However, what I don't (or forget to) mention: Brett was with me when my dad called.

"Call him back," he pleaded. "This is your chance."

I don't mention Brett, a person who came into my life, loving me, teaching me the value of openness, giving me the strength to do what I never imagined doing before. I called my dad back.

However, I couldn't mention two events that hadn't happened yet: a call and a visit.

March 2006: a call.

"Tony?" I hear when I answer the phone.

"Yes?"

"It's Lynn. I can't believe I'm the one to tell you ... I'm so sorry, but ... Brett's dead," she says. "His sister just called me. You should call her."

We hang up; I call Brett's sister.

"Hi, Sarah?" I ask, unsure of her name. "This is Tony Adams. I lived with Brett in Carbondale."

"I've heard about you" she says through tears. "Brett died last night of diabetes. I've been calling people listed in his cell phone. I'm sorry. I didn't want to have to tell you this."

Brett's family—people I never met—told me that Brett died of diabetes, a condition he had since his early teens. But later, two of Brett's friends told me that on the weekend prior to his death, Brett told his dad that he fit—and did not fit—particular labels, that is, gay and straight respectively. Brett not only had diabetes, but also a history of attempted suicide.

Brett was 29. Before our relationship, he lived with a man for four years. Since he lived near his parents, I *assumed* he had come out to his family, assumed he told them he was gay. But prior conversations with Brett replay in my head:

"Are you 'out' to your family?" I ask.

"They know," he responds.

and

"How do your parents feel about your sexuality?" I ask.

"We don't talk about it," he responds.

and

"I'd like to meet your family," I say.

"Maybe one day," he suggests.

Brett never told me he had *said* anything to his family about his sexuality. He only said "they know," nothing more. What did "they know" mean?

To think that Brett may have died after telling his father that he found men attractive, that he identified as gay, makes me ill. I could contact his family and ask if diabetes really was the cause, but this might make for unnecessary, painful controversy. Even if they confirmed the diabetes story, I know an alternative, story exists. Besides, why would they tell me? Besides, Brett is dead. I miss him; nothing will bring him back.

March 2007: a visit.

My father visits me in Tampa, Florida. During our time together, I approach our coming out interaction.

"Dad," I say. "Do you remember when I told you that I was gay?"

"Yeah," he responds. "You lived in Carbondale."

"You called and said you heard that I was living with—*fucking*—a man. Remember?"

"Yeah."

"And I denied the rumor at first but then said it was true?"

"Yeah, I remember," he says. "That was a difficult time."

"That was a difficult time for me too," I reply.

Even though we didn't speak for a few months, I wanted to thank you for your response. You never told me I was bad. You didn't physically harm me. You didn't kick me out of the family. Some fathers respond to gay children in terrible, more drastic ways. Some force their children into therapy to change their same-sex desire. Some kick their children out of the family. Some children kill themselves because of their parents' negative reactions. You didn't do any of this and I appreciate that.

He said:

I heard you were gay a few days before I called. I was upset that you hadn't called in more than a month. I thought I had made you mad. I mentioned this to a friend and she said that you probably didn't call because you were gay and were scared to tell me. I asked her why she thought you were gay. She said she heard a rumor you were.

"So you didn't call me immediately after hearing I was gay?" I ask. "I assumed you did."

He continued:

No. I first called Jack [one of his friends] whose son came out to him a few years prior. We met for dinner and I asked him, as a father, how he responded to a gay son. Jack said that at first he was upset and angry, but knew that he did and should still love and support his son. He told me that even though I may be angry, I should love and support you as best I could. The best that I could do was unfortunately to not speak to you for six months.

By thanking my father, I get a glimpse of his processing of my gay identity, a glimpse of the person who I perceived to have reacted negatively to my coming out. An act of silence that made me mark him as homophobic and irrational I now learn was an effort to understand my same-sex desire, an effort that I cannot disregard when thinking about our relationship. My father stifled his own anger and decided not to express it openly; he waited until he could better accept it. My story of the call and of us, a story that changes with every writing of the event and with every interaction with him, and a story that only focuses on one call in the relationship, thus disregarding the numerous times we speak every week and month and the numerous times we have spoken in all of our years together. My story of the call and of us: overdetermined and destined for revision, a series of becomings, time after time.

Possibility: Talking Politics

Hinging autoethnography and queer theory means using— conversing about—our experiences in practical ways for political purposes. For me, it means talking about an aunt who, after I said, "I am gay," no longer allowed me to visit her home; Brett, an ex-lover, who may have killed himself after coming out to his father; and a student who reported me to the president of the university for being out in the classroom—the student and the president didn't think "gay" had any part in a college curriculum. It means talking about the man who interviewed me for a job and who told me, during the interview, that he was gay but no one else at his university knew (out of his fear that his same-sex desire would tarnish his case for tenure); the female student who, the week after I came out to the class, wrote in a paper that she liked women but refused to talk about it with anyone (as of this writing, three years later, she has only told one other person); and the high school acquaintance, who, after inferring from my Myspace.com webpage that I date men, emailed me for advice on getting out of reparative therapy, therapy required and funded by his parents to "correct" his same-sex desire.

For me, it means punctuating casual conversations with political questions and listening to the answers. It means repeatedly interrupting students' casual conversations before or after class, in my office or in the hallway, when they say, "That's so gay" to ask that they consider and revise their language. When they object—because they didn't mean any harm, because the phrase doesn't mean anything, I keep the conversation going by asking more questions: "Would it be okay for me to say: 'That's so black,' 'That's so Jewish,' 'That's so Asian,' 'That's so deaf, dumb, and blind,' 'That's so white, middle-class, suburban kid who wants to study hard and get a good job after college' and listening for answers?" It means asking one of my best students why he swings his hips and punctuates "s" sounds when rehearsing a monologue about the difficulties of coming out as a gay man that he's written as part of a performance about freedom of speech on university campuses and it means listening to his reply. It means staying on the line when my father calls to tell me that my mother ran into Cary, my junior high boyfriend, at the nursery where he works; when he tells me that Cary's best friend George is dead; when I hear my mother in the background correcting him, saying, "George isn't dead, he's gay; when my father repeats this information to me; when I say, "Well, gay is a whole lot better than dead"; and when my father says, "Depends on who you ask," so that I am able to ask in return, "Are you asking me?" and it means listening to his silent reply before telling him I love him and hanging up.

Possibility: Bearing Witness

Hinging autoethnography and queer theory means conversing about ways that we—as teachers, writers, researchers, activists, humans—try to document, ease or eliminate, and bear witness to harmful social practices, occasions of relational violence, and the trials and tribulations of (desiring) normalcy. For instance, soon after I share my autoethnographies in the classes I teach (e.g., Adams, 2006, forthcoming), I often get students who come to my office to share their stories of lesbian, gay, bisexual, and queer experience. "I'm not out to anyone," one says; "My parents disowned me," says another. The sharing of my politicized, practical stories motivates some people to share their stories with me. Together, we bear witness to the possibilities wrought in that telling.

For instance, sharing my open-ended, question-filled stories motivates other students to write their own queer experiences. Some say, "Your work gave me permission to do my research and my writing my way." Others say, "I am afraid of making myself vulnerable in my research as a young scholar—before getting a job, before tenure—but your work helps me see how I can take risks without being afraid." My stories and their stories, our stories and yours, together, make conversations about harmful situations go, make possible the ability to improve the world one person, family, classroom, conference, and essay at a time.

Possibility: Making Change

Hinging autoethnography and queer theory means conversing about what it means to live as a realistic and idealistic activist, as able to recognize limits while trying to push limits further to make something new. Consider, for instance, a conversation I often have with others, typically students, who identify as Evangelical, born-again Christians—people who have adoration for a typically anti-queer religion.

"Do you believe in Jesus?" a student will ask, in my office, at least once a year.

"I believe in being a good person," I respond. "I try to respect everyone. I try not to lie, or cheat, or do harm to others."

"But don't you find homosexuality, your lifestyle, a sin?" the other probes.

"I find it impossible to separate a lifestyle, a sin, from the person, the sinner," I say. "I consider communication constitutive—one is what one says and does, one is what one experiences, one is what one believes. Consequently, calling homosexuality, my lifestyle, a sin is no different from calling me and my existence a sin [Adams, 2009]. Furthermore, I value love, any kind of love, stemming from mutual consent. Love doesn't see categories or mixings of race, class, age, sex, ability, or gender."

"Yes, but what if you don't go to heaven?"

"All I know is that I want, and try, to be the best person possible."

"You model this well, particularly in the classroom," the other says. "But I find it difficult to believe that you don't follow Christianity or embrace Jesus explicitly."

"I could tell you that I follow Christianity and embrace Jesus, and that I find homosexuality a sin if that's what you want to hear," I say, "but I also value our relationship, and, in this conversation, honesty. I don't want to lie to you."

I often hear friends—and, most recently, a noteworthy queer scholar—say that these religious others are not worth our (queer) time and should be disregarded. However, for me, being a realistic and idealistic activist means keeping difficult conversations going (Ellis, 2009) rather than pretend these people don't exist or are not worthy of acknowledgment. It also means trying to engage in productive conversation, rather than something like

"Don't you find homosexuality, your lifestyle, a sin?" the other asks.

"No. And you're wrong, and homophobic, for thinking it is," I respond.

"But it is a sin ..." the other says.

"It is not ..." I reply.

Hinging autoethnography and queer theory means working our politics, innocently, into mundane conversation and refusing to chastise others' beliefs or make them out as monsters. It means recognizing, realistically, that people against same-sex desire exist, while, idealistically, find ways to productively question their beliefs—to make dissonance and trouble—together. It means recognizing that change happens in mundane conversation (hooks, 2000), and, in the words of Art Bochner, a refusal to "alienate the people we want to persuade."

Possibility: Moving

Hinging autoethnography and queer theory means trading in the debates around legitimacy, value and worth and for conversations about practicality, necessity, and movement. It means twisting autoethnography and queer theory from prior usages, whether diminishing or valorizing, and put them to use for innovative, politicized purposes. It means never becoming comfortable, always already wanting and being ready to (re)create. It means asking questions about now and making conversation on the way to somewhere else. For me, it means talking and listening to my father.

We are watching college football. Well, he is watching college football and I am reading and keeping an eye on the television. Every now and again I ask a question, keeping myself in the game.

We are sitting in the living room of the house I purchased when I left my husband after I fell in love with a woman.

We are sitting in the living room of the house I am renovating from just this side of wrecked, just this side of despair.

We are sitting in the living room of the only house I could

afford in the neighborhood where my old house—the house I shared with my former husband—sits. I am renovating this house, *my* house, so that my son and I might start a new life that resembles, however modestly, the old one.

My father is here to help me with the renovation. On the few occasions that he has visited me without my mother along, he has come to work: on the kitchen, on the yard, on the windows, on the porch. And today, as we take a break from our work, our renovation of my life, I want to talk. I want to ask him something, but I am afraid.

"Dad," I begin, feeling clumsy, but determined, "We've not talked about the 'gay thing.' I feel like we should. What do you think about it?"

My heart is pounding. Why is it so hard to get the words out? I watch him. He studies the screen. "Well," he begins, his eyes fixed on the blur of grass and uniforms, "I don't understand it. I don't think it's right. But it's your decision and I want you to be happy."

"I *am* happy, Dad."

"That's all that matters."

I wait, but that's it. He doesn't speak. I try again. "Anything else you want to say?"

"No. As long as you're happy, your mother and I are happy."

Not wanting to push him, not wanting this stiff discomfort, I say, "Okay. I'm glad to know that. If there's ever anything else, or you want to talk some more. ..."

Halftime begins and my father changes the channel, looking for another game.

Exactly a year later, I am visiting my parents at their home in Iowa. I haven't seen my father since he had a stroke a few months before. A *stroke* a year after he'd been in Tampa, strong and sure, helping to renovate my house. He'd had heart attacks before. He'd had bypass surgery before. But this time was different. This time, he'd had a stroke, left side paralyzed for several months, emergency surgery to repair a perforated bowel, the fall in rehab, the colostomy bag, the emptiness in his eyes and speech. There's a clear and sure line that demarcates before and after the stroke. Before: active, opinionated, capable, kind, a caretaker, body in the grip of unrelenting heart disease. After: dependent, angry, affable, unable to use his left arm but able to walk with a cane, forgetful in the immediate but a keen memory of the past, mind unsure of the structure and strictures of language and talk. During the visit, I sit with my father in the living room of his house, watching the evening news. My father is talkative and uncensored; speaking whatever comes into his mind. Sometimes this is funny, as when he needles my mother about the promises that "dinner will be ready in 15 minutes" she makes three times in 2 hours. Sometimes, this is enraging, as when he informs me that most states in the United States—including Iowa—have declared Spanish their official language, his racism seeping through his matter-of-fact delivery. And sometimes, my father's talk surprises, as when he asks about Noah and how he likes living in the renovated house. I tell him "Good," and "Yes," and he says, "Does he know you're a queer?" using a word his grandmother—my great grandmother—and not he, at least not before the stroke—would have used.

"Noah?"

"Yes, Noah. Does he know you're a queer?"

"Yes, Dad. He knows I'm gay."

"You can't be *gay*. You were married for 15 years for Christ's sake."

"Twelve."

"Twelve what?"

"I was married for 12 ... never mind. Yes, he knows I'm a queer," I say, then revise. "He knows I'm *queer*."

"Your mother and I should have known," he says, eyes on the set. "You were always strange."

At this, I smile. When I return home I'll tell Noah that he—that we—must keep asking questions and remember that our words imagine who we are and want to become. I'll tell him that our stories and our questions can be insurrectionary acts if we can just make room for movement, for what matters, for something more. And maybe you will ask and tell yourself—and your parents and children and students and teachers and readers and spectators—these questions and stories, too.

References

Adams, T. E. (2006). Seeking father: Relationally reframing a troubled love story. *Qualitative Inquiry, 12*, 4, 704–723.

Adams, T. E. (2008). A review of narrative ethics. *Qualitative Inquiry, 14*, 2, 175–194.

Adams, T. E. (2009). Mothers, faggots, and witnessing (un)contestable experience. *Cultural Studies ↔ Critical Methodologies, 9*, 5, 619–626.

Adams, T. E. (forthcoming). Paradoxes of sexuality, gay identity, and the closet. *Symbolic Interaction.*

Alexander, B. K. (2003). Querying queer theory again (or queer theory as drag performance). *Journal of Homosexuality, 45*, 2/3/4, 349–352.

Alexander, B. K. (2005). Performance ethnography: The reenacting and inciting of culture. In N. K. Denzin and Y. S. Lincoln (Eds.), *Handbook of qualitative research* (pp. 411–442). Thousand Oaks, CA: Sage.

Alexander, B. K. (2008). Queer(y)ing the postcolonial through the western. In N. K. Denzin, Y. S. Lincoln, and L. T. Smith (Eds.), *Handbook of critical and indigenous methodologies* (pp. 101–133). Thousand Oaks, CA: Sage.

Anderson, L. (2006). Analytic autoethnography. *Journal of Contemporary Ethnography, 35*, 4, 373–395.

Aoki, E. (2005). Coming out as "we 3": Using personal ethnography and the case study to assess relational identity and parental support of gay male, three-partner relationships. *Journal of GLBT Family Studies, 1*, 2, 29–48.

Atkinson, P. (1997). Narrative turn or blind alley? *Qualitative Health Research, 7*, 3, 325–344.

Belkin, A. (2008). Spam filter: Gay rights and the normalization of male-male rape in the U.S. military. *Radical History Review, 100*, 1, 180–185.

Bennett, J. A. (2008). Passing, protesting, and the arts of resistance: Infiltrating the ritual space of blood donation. *Quarterly Journal of Speech, 94*, 1, 23–43.

Berry, K. (2007). Embracing the catastrophe: Gay body seeks acceptance. *Qualitative Inquiry, 13*, 2, 259–281.

Bourdieu, P. (1977 [1972]). *Outline of a theory of practice* (R. Nice, Trans.). Cambridge: Cambridge University Press.

Boylorn, R. M. (2006). E Pluribus Unum (out of many, one). *Qualitative Inquiry, 12*, 4, 651–680.

Butler, J. (1993). *Bodies that matter: On the discursive limits of "sex."* New York: Routledge.

Butler, J. (1997). *Excitable speech.* New York: Routledge.

Butler, J. (1999). *Gender trouble: Feminism and the subversion of identity* (2nd ed.). New York: Routledge.

Butler, J. (2004). *Undoing gender*. New York: Routledge.

Buzard, J. (2003). On auto-ethnographic authority. *The Yale Journal of Criticism, 16*, 1, 61–91.

Chavéz, K. R. (2009). Exploring the defeat of Arizona's marriage amendment and the specter of the immigrant as queer. *Southern Communication Journal, 74*, 3, 314–324.

Cobb, M. (2007). Lonely. *South Atlantic Quarterly, 106*, 3, 445–457.

Colyar, J. (2008). Becoming writing, becoming writers. *Qualitative Inquiry, 1*, 52, 421 436.

Corey, F. C., & Nakayama, T. K. (1997). Sextext. *Text and Performance Quarterly, 17*, 1, 58–68.

Davis, A. M. (2009). What we tell our daughters and ourselves about <ssshhh!!!!> hysterectomy. *Qualitative Inquiry, 15*, 8, 1303–1337.

Defenbaugh, N. (2008). "Under erasure": The absent ill body in doctor-patient dialogue *Qualitative Inquiry, 14*, 8, 1402–1424.

Delamont, S. (2009). The only honest thing: Autoethnography, reflexivity and small crises in fieldwork. *Ethnography and Education, 4*, 1, 51–63.

Denzin, N. K. (2003). *Performance ethnography: Critical pedagogy and the politics of culture*. Thousand Oaks, CA: Sage.

Dykins Callahan, S. B. (2008). Academic outings. *Symbolic Interaction, 31*, 4, 351–375.

Ellis, C. (2007). Telling secrets, revealing lives: Relational ethics in research with intimate others. *Qualitative Inquiry, 13*, 1, 3–29.

Ellis, C. (2009). *Revision: Autoethnographic reflections on life and work*. Walnut Creek, CA: Left Coast Press.

Ellis, C., & Bochner, A. P. (2000). Autoethnography, personal narrative, reflexivity. In N. K. Denzin and Y. S. Lincoln (Eds.), *Handbook of qualitative research* (2nd ed., pp. 733–768). Thousand Oaks, CA: Sage.

Fine, G. A. (2003). Towards a people ethnography: Developing a theory from group life. *Ethnography, 4*, 1, 41–60.

Foster, E. (2008). Commitment, communication, and contending with heteronormativity: An invitation to greater reflexivity in Interpersonal Research. *Southern Communication Journal, 73*, 1, 84–101.

Foucault, M. (1995 [1977]). *Discipline and punish: The birth of the prison* (2nd ed., A. Sheridan, Trans.). New York: Random House.

Gamson, J. (2000). Sexualities, queer theory, and qualitative research. In N. K. Denzin and Y. S. Lincoln (Eds.), *Handbook of qualitative research* (2nd ed., pp. 347–365). Thousand Oaks, CA: Sage.

Gamson, J. (2003). Reflections on queer theory and communication. *Journal of Homosexuality, 45*, 2/3/4, 385–390.

Gans, H. J. (1999). Participant observation: In the era of "ethnography." *Journal of Contemporary Ethnography, 28*, 5, 540–548.

Gingrich-Philbrook, C. (2005). Autoethnography's family values: Easy access to compulsory experiences. *Text and Performance Quarterly, 25*, 4, 297–314.

Goodall, H. L., Jr. (2001). *Writing the new ethnography*. Walnut Creek, CA: AltaMira.

Goodall, H. L., Jr. (2004). Narrative ethnography as applied communication research. *Journal of Applied Communication Research, 32*, 3, 185–194.

Goodall, H. L., Jr. (2006). *A need to know: The clandestine history of a CIA family*. Walnut Creek, CA: Left Coast Press.

Glave, T. (2005). *Words to our now: Imagination and dissent*. Minneapolis: University of Minnesota Press.

Halberstam, J. (2005). Shame and white gay masculinity. *Social Text, 23*, 3–4, 219–233.

Henderson, L. (2001). Queer communication studies. In W. B. Gudykundst (Ed.), *Communication yearbook 24* (pp. 465–484). Thousand Oaks, CA: Sage.

Hilfrich, C. (2006). "The self is a people": Autoethnographic poetics in Hélène Cixous's fictions. *New Literary History, 37*, 1, 217–235.

Holman Jones, S. (2005a). Autoethnography: Making the personal political. In N. K. Denzin and Y. S. Lincoln (Eds.), *Handbook of qualitative research* (pp. 763–791). Thousand Oaks, CA: Sage.

Holman Jones, S. (2005b). (M)othering loss: Telling adoption stories, telling performativity. *Text and Performance Quarterly, 25*, 2, 113–135.

Holman Jones, S. (2009). Crimes against experience. *Cultural Studies«Critical Methodologies, 1*, 1, 608–618.

hooks, b (2002). *Feminism is for everybody: Passionate politics*. Boston: South End Press.

Irving, D. (2008). Normalized transgressions: Legitimizing the transsexual body as productive. *Radical History Review, 100*, 1, 38–59.

Jago, B. J. (2002). Chronicling an academic depression. *Journal of Contemporary Ethnography, 31*, 6, 729–757.

Johnson, E. P. (2001). "Quare" studies, or (almost) everything I know about queer studies I learned from my grandmother. *Text and Performance Quarterly, 21*, 1, 1–25.

Koro-Ljungberg, M. (2004). Impossibilities of reconciliation: Validity in mixed theory projects. *Qualitative Inquiry, 10*, 4, 601–621.

Lee, W. (2003). Kuaering queer theory: My autocritography and a race-conscious, womanist, transnational turn. *Journal of Homosexuality, 45,* 2/3/4, 147–170.

Madison, D. S. (1998). Performance, personal narratives, and the politics of possibility: The future of performance studies. In S. J. Daily (Ed.), *Visions and revisions* (pp. 276–286). Washington, DC: National Communication Association.

Madison, D. S. (2005). Critical ethnography as street performance: Reflections of home, race, murder, and justice. In N. K. Denzin and Y. S. Lincoln (Eds.), *Handbook of qualitative research* (pp. 537–546). Thousand Oaks, CA: Sage.

Madison, D. S. (2006). The dialogic performative in critical ethnography. *Text and Performance Quarterly, 26,* 4, 320–324.

Marvasti, A. (2006). Being Middle Eastern American: Identity negotiation in the context of the war on terror. *Symbolic Interaction, 28,* 4, 525–547.

McCreery, P. (2008). Gay activists appropriate the rhetoric of child protectionism. *Radical History Review, 100,* 1, 186–207.

Minge, J. M. (2007). The stained body: A fusion of embodied art on rape and love. *Journal of Contemporary Ethnography, 36,* 3, 252–280.

Minge, J. M., & Zimmerman, A. L. (2009). Power, pleasure, and play: Screwing the dildo and rescripting sexual violence. *Qualitative Inquiry, 15,* 2, 329–349.

Moreman, S. T. (2009). Rethinking Conquergood: Toward an unstated cultural politics. *Liminalities: A Journal of Performance Studies, 5,* 5, 1–12.

Moro, P. (2006). It takes a darn good writer: A review of *The Ethnographic I*. *Symbolic Interaction, 29,* 2, 265–269.

Muñoz, J. E. (1999). *Disidentifications: Queers of color and the performance of politics*. Minneapolis: University of Minnesota Press.

Myers, W. B. (2008). Straight and white: Talking with my mouth full. *Qualitative Inquiry, 14,* 1, 160–171.

Nakayama, T. K., & Corey, F. C. (2003). Nextext. *Journal of Homosexuality, 45,* 2/3/4, 319–334.

Neumann, M. (1996). Collecting ourselves at the end of the century. In C. Ellis and A. P. Bochner (Eds.), *Composing ethnography: Alternative forms of qualitative writing* (pp. 172–198). Walnut Creek, CA: AltaMira.

Plummer, K. (2003). Queers, bodies and postmodern sexualities: A note on revisiting the "sexual" in symbolic interactionism. *Qualitative Sociology, 26,* 4, 515–530.

Plummer, K. (2005). Critical humanism and queer theory: Living with the tensions. In N. K. Denzin and Y. S. Lincoln (Eds.), *Handbook of qualitative research* (pp. 357–373). Thousand Oaks, CA: Sage.

Pollock, D. (2007). The performative "I." *Cultural Studies ↔ Critical Methodologies, 7*, 3, 239–255.

Rambo, C. (2007). Handing IRB an unloaded gun. *Qualitative Inquiry, 13*, 3, 353–367.

Sandahl, C. (2003). Queering the crip or cripping the queer? Intersections of queer and crip identities in solo autobiographical performance. *GLQ, 9*, 1/2, 25–56.

Sedgwick, E. K. (1993). *Tendencies.* Durham, NC: Duke University Press.

Slattery, P. (2001). The educational researcher as artist working within. *Qualitative Inquiry, 7*, 3, 370–398.

Solis, S. (2007). Snow White and the Seven "Dwarfs"—Queercripped. *Hypatia, 22*, 1, 114–131.

Spry, T. (2001). Performing autoethnography: An embodied methodological praxis. *Qualitative Inquiry, 7*, 6, 706–732.

Spry, T. (forthcoming). Call it swing: A jazz blues of autoethnography. *Cultural Studies ↔ Critical Methodologies.*

Tillmann, L. M. (2009). Body and bulimia revisited: Reflections on "A Secret Life" *Journal of Applied Communication Research, 37*, 1, 98–112.

Tillmann-Healy, L. M. (2003). Friendship as method. *Qualitative Inquiry, 9*, 5, 729–749.

Wilchins, R. (2004). *Queer theory, gender theory.* Los Angeles: Alyson.

Wolcott, H. F. (2010). Overdetermined behavior, unforeseen consequences. *Qualitative Inquiry, 16*, 1, 10–20.

Wyatt, J. (2005). A gentle going? An autoethnographic short story. *Qualitative Inquiry, 11*, 5, 724–732.

Wyatt, J. (2008). No longer loss: Autoethnographic stammering. *Qualitative Inquiry, 14*, 6, 955–967.

Yep, G. A., & Elia, J. P. (2007). Queering/Quaring blackness in *Noah's Arc.* In T. Peele (Ed.), *Queer popular culture: Literature, media, film, and television* (pp. 27–40). New York: Palgrave Macmillan.

8. Some Ethical Considerations in Preparing Students for Performative Autoethnography

Tami Spry

We need to be advocates for the embodiedness of knowledge in a way that acknowledges human particularity while it strives toward a more radical humanism that crosses borders of knowledge and identity.

—Jill Dolan, 2001, p. 62

The stories that emerge in each case rise up against the norms that deny their integrity, that prefer silence, conformity, and invisibility. In the corporealities of performance, they break through normative reiteration into the time-space of terrifying exhilarating possibility.

— Della Pollock, 1999, pp. 27–28

Proem

Amanda's critical reflection upon rape.
Anthony's autoethnography of driving while black.
Trenton's critical work on his gay body in a Catholic church.

Anthropologist Victor Turner writes that performance is the explanation and explication of life itself. So what is at stake for these students while explicating their lives in the performance classroom? What is at stake for students when engaging the vulnerable, transformative, and dangerous terrain of critical performative autoethnographic performance, particularly and especially when they are not prepared with a theory/methodology praxis grounded in the discipline of performance studies? What are the human rights of students in this pedagogical performance process, and how are these pedagogical rights violated by a lack of substantive preparation in a performance praxis? I argue that it is an ethical imperative of their human rights for students to be provided the theoretical and methodological foundation in the study of performance when asked to engage the vulnerable, transformational, and dangerous terrain of critical autoethnographic performance.

Further, a grounding in performance praxis in autoethnography includes the politics of representation. Within the classroom, students have the right and responsibility to understand themselves as agents of the representations they create in performance. "The critical imagination," writes Denzin, "is radically democratic, pedagogical, and interventionist" (2009, 255); living within an unequal system of power requires a critical imagination for the purposes of radicalizing hope and materializing peace. What is at stake for an African American student in a majority white classroom, for the female student reflecting upon assault, for the GLBT student who will be coming out in the critical reflections of his gay body in a church? Knowledge is not innocent or apolitical. Viewing the autoethnographic performance classroom as a socially closed system or as ideologically benign is, it seems to me, a violation of a student's human rights as human rights are constructed as a special sort of inalienable moral entitlement, the minimum conditions for human dignity and a tolerable life. The classroom, as thoroughly articulated by Freire, McLaren and others, is a deeply political space.

Specifically, I assert that it is in an ethic of aesthetic epistemology in performance that underpins a foundation in the performance of autoethnography. An ethic grounded in the dialogic engagement between craft and emotion, between form and production, between technique and experience, between life and art. Such an engagement between these dialectics resist hierarchy; rather, it is in their answerability to one another—of aesthetics and epistemology as responsible to one another—that an ethic of care for performer and performance exists.

Though this chapter will focus primarily on autoethnographic performance, the basis of my arguments is derived from the long history and contemporary work in performance studies scholarship (e.g., Madison & Hamera, 2006). In discussing the ethical imperative of aesthetical epistemology in performance as a pedagogical human right, I will address the idea of epistemology as embodiment, of vulnerability as agency and then briefly map out an ethic of accountability and care in aesthetic representation in performance.

Em/Bodied Research: Epistemology as Embodiment

In considering the lived experiences that Amanda, Anthony, Trenton, and so many students chose to engage in, surely, performative embodiment is not to be taken lightly. The body in performance is not to be taken lightly because "a piece of paper, whatever the reason, can't carry the weight of a body," as Elyse Pineau (2000, p. 4) deftly articulates. In the performance studies classroom, one learns just how much a body weighs when representing sexual assault, or racial violence, or homophobia. We live in our bodies and learn about self, others, and culture through analyzing the performances of our bodies in the world. The performing body is at once a pool of data, a collector of data, and then the interpreter of data in knowledge creation, in the process of epistemology. Performance is not about donning a hat or coat or costume or turning one's back to the audience to indicate that one is "not in the scene." These are performance conventions and, although relevant, mean nothing when the body itself is not engaged as an agent of embodied knowledge. Madison's (2006) thick description of performative embodiment helps:

> Like good theory, performance is a blur of meaning, language, and a bit of pain. Whirling past, faster than I can catch up. Testing me, often refuting me, pulling away and moving toward me. I'm almost there with it. I hold on. I keep my hands on the performance and my eyes on the theory. I am playful, but I am not playing. I do not appreciate carelessness. I pay attention. I do not let go or look away, because I have learned that all the meanings, languages, and bit of pain will come into clarity and utility like

a liberation song. I need this clarity for the ones I love. (p. 245)

Embodied performance can be a liberation song within the violence, loss, and confusion of our personal/political lives when engaged as a studied performance praxis of research, meaning, language, and pain. "When the students in the course," writes Joni L. Jones (2002) of her own performance pedagogy, "take on cultures they believe are other than their own, they expand themselves through the bodily incorporation that is performance" (p. 176). Being vulnerable to the process of performance, or privy to its transformative possibilities means full engagement of the body and/in theory. The body blurs the boundaries of culture.

Judith Hamera (2002) refers to "body building" as the process of recognizing how we live in and make meaning through our bodies (p. 122). For example, how is the body a part of, or held apart from, particular social practices based on race, gender, geography, religion? How, Hamera asks, does the social construction of the body impact the meaning-making process, and meaning made through performance in the classroom? I will never be pulled over for "driving while black," but Anthony has been and most likely will continue to be. So what is the body-building process he goes through to explicate that experience, to articulate those meanings in performance, particularly within the still largely traditional pedagogical separation between mind and body?

Performance surely intervenes in this faux separation as performance itself is the enactment of scholarly analysis of text and/or culture. And though performance foundationally includes the body in knowledge construction, Hamera cautions romanticizing this meeting of the mind and body lest we think of this joining as a "eureka" moment that may apolitically sanitize knowledge of the complex power structures and constraints on everyday embodied existence, undercutting the central aim of performative autoethnography and the performative-I liminal disposition of embodiment (Spry, 2006, forthcoming). Although being pulled over because of skin color may be a eureka moment for a white audience, this action is grossly mundane in Anthony's racially lived experience. Hamera's caution moves us further into an understanding of what is personally/politically at stake in engaging the interventionist critical imagination without proper methodological preparation in performance. She writes, "It is paramount to me to explore what knowledges we think we are restoring. ... I believe it can frame how we, as embodied educational subjects, survive and what we survive" (2002, pp. 129–130)—especially, I would argue, when engaging the focused, structured, theoretically grounded critical reflection of performative autoethnographic method. So how does the researcher approach embodiment and the vulnerability required to survive?

Vulnerability as Agency

Growing out of a critical imagining of performative autoethnography in my performance courses is a process of *practiced vulnerability* designed to assist the student/researcher to move into the liminal embodiment of the performative-I disposition. In autoethnographic performance, the student is made aware that this is *h/h* story, that no one gets to tell this story but her; however, she must also be made aware that the way she represents that story through language and performance is a politically contested and personally accountable praxis. Performative autoethnography requires that Amanda be the only one to tell the story of her assault, not the media, not the social worker, not the councilor, not her friends, her boyfriend, or her mother. Autoethnography gives her permission, gives her the space, the time, the *right* to critically reflect and carefully craft the story of her experience. Usually in the classroom, this constitutes the first time a student has engaged in a focused, structured, theoretically grounded critical reflection and construction of the transformative experience. Also, it is most likely the first time that the student has put his body on the line in performance. Autoethnography is critically performative when experiences are aesthetically crafted to reveal the personal as political, the private as public analysis, or the emotional as epistemologically evocative. Long before students decide what they want to compose and perform, they are made aware of the risks involved and thus the vulnerability required to compose and perform critical autoethnography.

A practiced vulnerability is a methodology of moving out of one's comfort zone of familiarity, a strategic surrendering into a space of risk, of uncomfortability, of uncertainty that one experiences when critically reflecting on *h/h* own experience. It is a purposeful movement into the liminality—the betwixt and betweeness—of the critical creative process. When speaking of the performative body, Pelias (2007) writes, "It offers a vulnerable self, exposed, presented bare for its personal and social curative value, for its articulation of a site for identification, and for its power as political intervention" (p. 185). To be in this space "presented bare" is to experience a letting go of fixed meanings of long held familial and societal beliefs and values, a loss, to various extents, of a controlled sense of experience. Practiced vulnerability is strategic surrender to an inbetweenness of self and other, to a relation, to a letting go of fixed meanings for the purpose of "keep[ing] my hands on the performance and my eyes on the theory." It is a space of active reflexion where one inhabits the intersections of *h/h* own personal experiences with the intimate politics of others. It is the practice of being vulnerable to meaning making, to the collisions and communions of our experiences with others. A practiced vulnerability is not a binary or linear process of replacing one fixed meaning for another; rather, it is a space of exploration, understanding, and continual critical reflection.

Through a series of exercises involving writing and the body, the student learns how to step into the undefined, unrefined space of liminality that exists between experience and text, between emotion and craft, between theory and practice, between body and knowledge. As the performer articulates experience through language, the language turns back on itself, changing, redefining, breaking, and remaking the performer's understanding of the negotiation between self, other, and context within the transformative experience. Body and word, experience and craft are simultaneously reformulating meaning, revealing possibilities for usually subaltern understanding of self in the world. The student learns that this is not a space or a process of endings or answers but of a continuation of meaning and transformation where one might experience calm in the inchoate, comfort within uncertainty.

With a practiced vulnerability, the performer decides to move deeper into reflecting on what happened, what sociocultural expectations and norms served to silence or inhibit his voice; or what ones did he perpetuate at the expense of others? In his performance of "Driving while Black," Anthony put us in the car with him as he jumps into the backseat of an Escalade driven by an African American friend in Little Jamaica in New York City. It is late in the evening, they are laughing, talking, listening to music. And then. And then Anthony narratively stops time as he and his friends see the lights of a police car in the rear view mirror. The driver had done nothing wrong, had not disobeyed any streetlights, traffic signs, or cross walks. Anthony allowed himself and performatively us, to move deep into that defining moment, into the complexities of racial construction, of fear, of power structures, and of masculinity as he narrated his body's reaction to the lights in the mirror and critique of the events that ensued, events that are, to be sure, made grotesquely mundane because of their frequency.

Thus, one does not invite a student to enter these spaces lightly or to stumble into this process without strategy, without method, without a practiced vulnerability so that Anthony, Amanda, and Trenton can decide through their own agency what and when and how they would do this telling, this negotiated meaning, this strategic surrendering, so that they decide the weight of their body on the page; they create and define the lines they would put their body on upon the stage. It is a practice in being vulnerable to living in one's body when that body may be viewed as abject, abnormal, unsociable, unruly.

Performance, which at its heart is the embodiment of language, has also taught me a skepticism of language's ability to represent me or others outside of the dominant master narratives that it is meant to serve. This skepticism of language's ability to represent the body is, I believe, a necessary preparation in a practiced vulnerability. A linguistic skepticism demystifies the imperializing of language and motivates the critical reflection upon the systems of power held in place through language. I have written elsewhere that I neither trust nor can live without language. But, whether I trust it or not, language will represent me, others, and culture, based on its collective will composed by those in various kinds of power at the moment of utterance. A critical skepticism can be a reliable counterpart in preparing students for the practiced vulnerability needed in interrupting and reinventing the collective will.

The unlikely dialectic of skepticism and vulnerability provides the possibility for a substantive embodiment where the student does not leave the classroom feeling exposed by inappropriate self-disclosure but rather strengthened by critical reflection about lived experience crafted from her own wisdom and use of theory. This is a human right of performance pedagogy. Words can construct but cannot hold the weight of the body. But classroom performance might assist the student in the kind of "body building" needed in lifting that weight and understanding how and what we survive.

Ethic of Aesthetic Epistemology

Surely, performative autoethnography provides the opportunity for personal empowerment; *however*, a practiced vulnerability enables the realization that the performer, the agent in representation, is responsible for and answerable to her representation of others in the autoethnographic context. Any methodology of critique that does not exercise as fundamental sociocultural systems and discourses of power sanitizes and imperializes critical reflexivity into a parlor game of identity construction where the Self stands in front of a mirror trying on different cultural hats to see the "world" from the eyes of the Other.

Thus, as the *ethical* agent of her experience, Amanda must also understand her*self* as answerable for the representations of self-others-context in the autoethnography. Judith Butler refers to this as giving an account of oneself. She writes:

> When the "I" seeks to give an account of itself, it can start with itself, but it will find that this self is already implicated in a social temporality that exceeds its own capacities for narration: indeed *when the "I" seeks to give an account of itself, an account that must include the conditions of its own emergence, it must, as a matter of necessity, become a social theorist.* (2001, pp. 8–9, emphasis in original)

Language is, of course, socially constructive of race, gender, religion, and other categories that reflect cultural values and hierarchies that perpetuate or deconstruct, that make or interrupt systems of power. It is in Amanda's and Anthony's and Trenton's knowledge of the power of aesthetic production as representation that they not only become empowered agents of self representation, but also understand themselves as responsible for the power in representations of otherness. In other words, representation has risks. Those risks can be negotiated by an ethic of care for aesthetic representation.

This ethic of aesthetic representation is realized through what Mindy Fenske (2004) calls an ethic of answerability where, in this case, the autoethnographer is responsible for and ethically liable for linguistic representations of the interpolations of self with others in contexts (p. 8). The strength and elegance of Fenske's position, in her article "The Aesthetics of the Unfinished: Ethics and Performance," is in her argument that no hierarchy exists between craft and emotion, form and production, theory and practice, art and life. "Instead," Fenske writes, "such relations are unified and dialogic" (p. 9). She continues, "Art and life are connected, one is not meant to transcend the other. Both content and experience, form and production ... exist inside the unified act in constant interaction" (p. 9). In this dialogical ethic of care, emotion is not touted as the scholarly cure for objectivity, nor is aesthetic craft viewed as a mechanized technique handcuffing the raw essence of experience; rather they are interdependent on one another, responsible to one another, liable to one another to represent the complex negotiations of meaning between selves and others in power laden social structures. Here, art is not a reflection of life; they are, rather, answerable to one another. "Form," writes Fenske "becomes a location inciting, rather than foreclosing, dialogue" (p. 11). Here, the student does not make an epistemological choice of craft over emotion, or practice over theory; rather, because they are mutually answerable to one another, the student seeks knowledge through the dialogic engagement of these entity.

Clearly, embodiment is crucial in this ethics of aesthetics. Just as emotion is not inherently epistemic, Fenske reminds us that "events are not ethical simply because they are embodied. ... In order to achieve answerability, the embodied action must be responsible for its meaning, as well as liable to meaning" (p. 12). The material body cannot be erased in performative auto-ethnography; rather, the corporeal body is made fully present in performance and represented through critical reflections upon the body's social constructions. In his autoethnographic performance "Driving while Black," the truths of Anthony's life are not com-promised by artistic craft; rather, it is in the dialogic process of articulating, of crafting life that Anthony embodies knowledge that is epistemic and generative. To operate as if there is a hier-archy in art or life, in craft or emotion, in theory or practice is to engage, Fenske argues, "a type of aesthetic that lets the artist off the ethical hook" (p. 13). Ethically, these dialectics are liable to and answerable to one another. Epistemologically, these dialectics engaged in collaboration expand the depth and breadth of critical conversations and implementations.

Building Body

It is final performance time in my performative writing class. Students are working on the development of one piece through-out the 15-week semester. This student, who I will call Amanda, has been working on an autoethnography about the sexual assault she survived in high school. Her first two texts were incredible, beautifully crafted, and fully and elegantly embodied in perfor-mance. In this last development, she had the class get up on stage and stand at the back of the stage facing the wall. She then stood on the floor in front of us where she was three feet below us as we stood on the raised stage looking down. Looking up at us, she began her performance critically reflecting on where she stands in relation to the assault; looked down on. She then took autoeth-nography to task commenting on what is at stake in excavating pain for critical pedagogies of hope and transformation.

All this while, Amanda had on a backpack. She then told us the last name of her attacker: Lemon. As she took the backpack off, she began to tell us about something that happened a few days after the attack. She came out to her driveway one morning and in the driveway was a brown paper bag. As she opened the bag she found that it was full ... of lemons. Students at her school had found out about the attack and this was their response. As she told us this story, she reached into her backpack and handed each of us a lemon. On the lemons were written words. As we read the words, Amanda went into a treatise on the symbology of language, ethics, group think, and The Lucifer Effect (how violent or unethical behavior becomes normalized within groups). As we peeked around at each other's lemons, some said "courage," "insecurity," "power." I was given the last one. On it was written "self-reflection." In her last line, Amanda confessed to still feeling looked down on and expressed her desire to someday stand eye-to-eye with others as she thinks about her assault.

Silence.

One of those classroom performances where there is just ... silence.

And surely, one of those classroom performances where we allow ourselves to weep.

I swear to you, she was radiant.

Radiant during and after the performance.

She made this experience HER story.

Her pain.

Her hope.

Her meaning.

No longer Lemon's.

Hers.

Afterword

Anthony is fully aware, it seems to me, that his African American body is constructed in dominant culture as always and already potentially dangerous. Trenton is aware of the narrative of immorality imposed on his body in and out of the church. Amanda is aware of the sedimented cultural responses to the assaulted body who dares to speak. This awareness comes from a pedagogical performance praxis and space where they are encouraged to "keep [their] hands on the performance and [their] eyes on the theory." They do not look away from the complexity and difficulty of bodies feeling and knowing through the embodied practice of rigorous performance praxis. A practiced vulnerability provides the opportunity to live into and craft one's own corporeal narrative exploring the values, motives, and constraints of social construction. It is a conscious preparation for possibilities, vulnerable to the fluidity, partiality, multiplicity, and contextuality of meaning making. When dealing in the personally political weight of performance, it is her pedagogical human right, her inalienable moral entitlement to be provided a firm foundation in the theory praxis of performance studies. These are, it seems to me, minimum conditions for human dignity and a life made tolerable through a libratory performance pedagogy, through the enactment of a critical imagination.

References

Butler, J. (2001). *Giving an account of oneself.* New York: Fordham University Press.

Denzin, N. K. (2009). A critical performance pedagogy that matters. *Ethnography and Education, 4,* 3, 255-270.

Dolan, J. (2001). *Geographies of learning: Theory, practice, and activism.* Middletown, CT: Wesleyan University Press.

Fenske, M. (2004). The aesthetic of the unfinished: Ethics and performance. *Text and Performance Quarterly, 24,* 1, 1-19.

Hamera, J. (2002). Performance studies, pedagogy, and bodies in/as the classroom. In N. Stucky and C. Wimmer (Eds.), *Teaching performance studies* (pp. 121-130). Carbondale: Southern Illinois University Press,

Jones, J. L. (2002). Teaching in the borderlands. In N. Stucky and C. Wimmer (Eds.), *Teaching performance studies* (pp. 175-190). Carbondale: Southern Illinois University Press.

Madison, D. S. (2006). Performing theory/embodied writing. In. J. Hamera (Ed.), *Opening acts: Performance in/as communication and cultural studies* (pp. 243-266). Thousand Oaks, CA: Sage.

Madison, D. S., & Hamera, J. (Eds.). (2006). *The Sage handbook of performance studies.* Thousand Oaks, CA: Sage.

Pineau, E. L. (2000). Nursing mother and articulating absence. *Text and Performance Quarterly, 20,* 1, 1-19.

Pollock, D. (1999). *Telling bodies performing birth.* New York: Columbia University Press.

Spry, T. (2006). A performative-I copresence: Embodying the ethnographic turn in performance and the performative turn in ethnography. *Text and Performance Quarterly, 26,* 4, 339–346.

Spry, T. (forthcoming). Performative autoethnography: Critical embodiments and possibilities. *The Sage handbook of qualitative research* (4th ed.). Thousand Oaks, CA: Sage.

Section 3: Politics

9. This Is Our Moment (So) Yes We Can

Shifting Margins, Centers, and Politics of Difference in the Time of President Barack Obama

Cynthia B. Dillard,

(Nana Mansa II of Mpeasem, Ghana, West Africa)

How we enact and construct our politics depends profoundly on who and what we see as the center—and the margins—of our work, including our qualitative research. This chapter explores the ways that the recent election of Barack Obama as the 44th president of the United States fundamentally shifted the margins and centers of our collective discourses, practices, and imaginations around the globe in ways that have implications for qualitative inquiry.

I want to start by telling a story. It is not a linear one, but one that is circuitous, recursive, and very personal. It starts when I was an undergraduate at one of the most racist small-town universities in my home state of Washington. I studied and worked harder than many undergraduates, as I wanted desperately to leave Ellensburg, to get out of the sticks and move back to the diverse and urban center of Seattle where I'd grown up. On several occasions, I had face-to-face encounters with the Ku Klux Klan (sheets and all). I'll share one encounter in detail. I was walking home from the library, on my way to the grocery store near my house. I had just crossed the street and was nearly in front of my apartment when a blue sedan slowed down next to me. Sensing something was wrong (and remembering my dad's advice to stay in a public place if I ever felt threatened), instead of running into my house, I faced forward and walked just a little faster, attempting to use my peripheral vision to catch a glimpse of who was in the car that had now pulled up right next to me. All I could see were the white sheets and I knew this was not good. Looking for an exit, a way to escape, I felt my heart beating faster. "Nigger!" they yelled. "We're gonna' get you nigger! We know where you live!" They sped off. After a few minutes, I began to breathe again. And for a black girl in Ellensburg on a block that was truly not her own, I felt fortunate to be alive. However, being called out of my name has been a common experience, including in Columbus, Ohio, where I now live. And it is the experience of countless other Blacks as well, both historically and contemporarily.

Fast forward to November 4, 2008. Election Day in the United States. I don't need to tell you the contested, racialized, and contentious nature of the presidential campaign: From Reverend Wright to Bill Ayers, much had threatened to derail the candidacy of Barack Obama. And much was centered around one of our most volatile subjects as a nation (which is also the center of the ever-present harassment often felt by black people and other people of color): RACE. Like many, I worked tirelessly on behalf of the Obama campaign: This was the first time in my life I did so. On that November day, I was canvassing in my community of Clintonville, one of the more progressive in Columbus and certainly in the traditionally red state of Ohio. Wearing my "Yes We Can" t-shirt and jeans and carrying my clipboard, I was hyper-aware of the characterization that was commonly assumed and that I had heard countless times from friends, acquaintances, strangers, and the media: That I would automatically vote for Barack Obama, given our shared blackness, our shared ethnic heritage. I also admit to feeling slightly anxious in Ohio, as I walked home after my final shift of the campaign. Like in Ellensburg, I was about a block from my house when an off-white Suburu slowed down, clearly trying to get my attention. Flashback. Three young white guys in the car. I look for an exit. I steel myself for the name calling that I assume will follow. Instead, the guy driving the car smiles, waves his hand, and shouts "THANK YOU!" at the top of his lungs and speeds off.

I tell these stories to both illustrate and argue a point: That regardless of our political affinities, the campaign and election of Barack Obama fundamentally shifted and disrupted our individual and collective taken-for-granted interactions across differences, witnessed in the many months of the election and beyond. This questioning of margins and centers has also shifted our former discussions of paradigms to potentially transformative moments and discussions of larger cultural notions such as race, democracy, freedom, community, and the place and importance of history. This new collective consciousness—contested, messy, and emergent—is what I would like to explore a bit here.

From a Black-Eyed Female Squint: Endarkened Feminist Perspectives on Margin and Center in Brief

According to many black feminist scholars (Bethel, 1982; Collins, 1990, 2000; hooks, 1984; Lubiano, 1991; Moraga & Anzaldua, 1981), the relationship between margins and centers has always been contested space, particularly for those outside the mainstream and hegemonic frameworks guiding public life. Black women's experiences and bodies are certainly one of these sites of contestation. Critics have suggested that much published feminist theory arises from those who live in the center, whose realities rarely include knowledge, awareness, or understanding of the lives of women who live in the margin (Collins, 1990, 2000; Dillard, 2006a, 2008; Royster, 2000). Many further suggest, as hooks (1984) does, that the body of feminist theory "lacks wholeness, lacks the broad analysis that could encompass a variety of experiences" (p. iv). To be in the margin is to be part of the whole but outside the main, entering worlds that we can serve or work in, but where we cannot *live*. hooks (1984) goes on to say that our survival as black women in the United States has always "depended on an on-going public awareness of the separation between margin and center and an on-going private acknowledgement that we were a necessary, vital part of that whole" (p. iv).

It is this particular sense of wholeness, based in the structure of daily lives as black people in the United States that provides us an oppositional world view, a black-eyed (female) squint (Bethel, 1982; Canon, 1995; Collins, 2000; Dillard, 2006a; Freire, 1970; hooks, 2000; Royster, 2000). This way of seeing, despite often brutal lived realities is "a mode of seeing unknown to most of our oppressors, that sustained us, aided us in our struggle to transcend poverty and despair, strengthened our sense of self and our solidarity" (hooks, 1984, pp. 4–5).

Given this ability to "squint" in more than one world, a visionary feminist politics, from my view (and those of many indigenous and women of color researchers, highlighted in Denzin, Lincoln, and Smith's edited *Handbook of Critical and Indigenous Methodologies* [2008]), is an emboldened, endarkened, transformative one, emerging from those who have strong knowledge and wisdom about *both* the margin and center. Further, Moraga and Anzaldua (1981) caution us to recognize that "the passage is *through*, not over, not by, not around, but through ... as long as I see it for myself as a passage through, I hope [it] will function for others, colored or white, in the same way" (p. xiv, emphasis in the original).

What we witnessed in the Obama campaign and in these early stages of the Obama presidency embodies such passage, a theory in the flesh that Hurtado (2003) and Madison (2007) speak of, where, in this moment, the theory (the center) is born out of and being created *through* a black man. For the first time in U.S. political history, the most prominent figure in the U.S. cultural milieu was black. Further, he was not a black religious figure but a political one. According to Willis (2009), the social and spiritual shift for all Americans has been just as dramatic:

> Obama's presidency will mark the first time in American political history that the voices ... of those driven more by the greater social good than by personal moralizing will be privileged inside of the White House. ... He will have to liberate the very notion of faith, which has been hijacked during the Bush administration for very narrow political interests ... all geared toward a racially inclusive, religiously pluralistic, non-hierarchical conception of faith that celebrates human dignity, values economic equality and has a global sensibility.

What we witnessed was theory in the flesh, where the physical realities of the man of Barack Obama and all of our "bodies"—raced, ethnicized, nationalized (gained by whatever means), sexualized, partnered "all fuse to create a politic born out of necessity" (Moraga & Anzaldua, 1981), a bridge *through* the contradictions of our experiences in all of their diversity and the conditions of the national and world stage.

Lessons from Margins to Center: Paradigms, Legacies, and the Obama Presidency

There are four lessons that I am positing (with the help of Cherrie Moraga and Gloria Anzaldua [1981]) that characterize the nature of both the conversations that have opened up/become possible and the character of the paradigm (Dillard, 2006b) within which they are being shaped and are shaping this moment. I also want to suggest that these lessons might serve as touchstones and considerations for the character and conduct of our qualitative inquiry in this moment as well.

> *Lesson #1*: In the shifting margin and center of the Obama campaign (and in the way the politics of margins and centers played out on the Obama body), *new connections* (not always painless) were made across/within/among differences, particularly around race.

I was standing at the deli counter at Whole Foods, proudly wearing one of my favorite Obama buttons. Black and white, it is a profile of Barack Obama with John F. Kennedy in the background, his famous quote in white letters: "Change is the law of life. And those who look only to the past or present are certain to miss the future." As I stood, I noticed a white woman aside me at the deli counter continuous looking at me, as if she wanted to say something. Mustering enough courage, she finally leaned over her cart and said: "I like your button." As with many a white woman at this time in particular, I read this comment as recognition of a sort of common ground we (maybe? suddenly? for the first time?) shared in our support of Barack Obama. But I also read it as a desire of hers to have conversation with a woman of African ascent about the meanings of the elections for me, for both of us. One of many such "at random" conversations I had during the campaign, we stood there for nearly 20 minutes, talking about our differences and similarities as women. About our deeply divided nation, particularly along race and class lines. About the wars in Afghanistan and Iraq and the wrong-headedness of both. About the bullying and imperialism of our government's current actions in the world. About how fear had been the prevailing common ground between us. About the hypocrisy and hopelessness that seemed to have pervaded the very fabric of the United States and the ways work on the campaign was a powerful and positive antidote to them. Most often, as was the case on this day, we ended by talking about the moral and *über* cool nature that typified Obama's spirit. In his natural grace, eloquence, intelligence, and fearlessness about the important stuff, he embodies a sense of diverse collective and individual *hope*.

Freire (1996) speaks of hope as an ontological need: "My hope is necessary, but it is not enough. Alone it does not win. But without it, my struggle will be weak and wobbly … [because hope] demands an anchoring in practice. As an ontological need, hope needs practice in order to become historical concreteness" (p. 8–9).

Barack Obama's (2006) *The Audacity of Hope: Thoughts on Reclaiming the American Dream* grounds this ontological need in chapters that address the U.S. constitution, faith, race, family, politics, values, and the like, all fundamental to the common ground that inspired us to trust in what President Lincoln described (and President Obama reminds us regularly) as "the nature of our better angels." So to the astute question Handel Wright (2003) has often asked as to "what difference difference makes (p. 206)," I suggest that Obama's marshaling of hope and change was the practice that Freire called for, that opened space for an *ontological common ground* for many in this country. This ground is not "post" race or without the desire and willingness to flatly ignore the ways that race has structured inequities across along all sorts of lines of difference. Instead, it was both about marshaling hope *and* change AND race *and* difference. A black feminist move at its finest!

> *Lesson #2*: The space of the campaign provided us a *new set of recognitions*, particularly around race. We could see one another more clearly.

I had just watched the inauguration of President Obama on television, an emotional and transformative day for me. My Christmas-turned-Obama tree displayed a newfound sense of patriotism that, as an African American, I am still learning to embrace. Little U.S. flags and small lights covered the tree. There was even an Ohio state flag there, signifying the fact that even my state of Ohio made a change, did the "right thing," foot soldiers of all races and stripes organizing and working to garner this victory. I was talking with a white researcher friend of mine after the inauguration, who asked me a very telling question. Again, it was a question or comment that was heard often through the voices of the media, as the news commentators described the huge and very diverse crowd who had gathered for the inaugural ceremony in Washington, DC. The question? "Where did all those black people come from?" *We've always been here*, was my response to her. But for many, it was the first time that *we'd* been seen (I might add as "Americans," but Michelle Obama has already taken the heat for that one).

A substantive shift was very visibly enacted in *who* became visible during the campaign and post-campaign. Whether in the rather bold move to take up of the topic of race through theorizing his life within the systemic and profoundly racialized, privileged, and too often inequitable contexts of the nation and world, President Obama invited us into an intimate conversation about "the tar baby in our midst" (Golden, 1995, p. 3). His "A More Perfect Union" speech (delivered during the course of his 2008 campaign) recognized and articulated both the margin *and* the center: That race, although structurally powerful and oppressive must be verbalized, talked about, and examined in a way that moves us toward the *inspiration* to change, toward something that breathes new life into our very way of being. We saw spiritual concepts like hope, humility, and freedom marshaled in a way that inspired people to recognize that, often despite our misunderstandings, tragedies, and feelings about what race has meant in our lives, we, as a whole nation and world are the only ones who can deconstruct it, can build a new way to be together. That recognition of our common humanity inspired us to mobilize for change.

Lesson #3: There was a *new site of accountability*, particularly for everyday people. "We the people in order to form a more perfect union" took on new meaning.

Barack Obama was an improbable choice as the Democratic flag bearer. But what he seemed to understand deeply was that what was needed (in addition to the spiritual imperatives of "hope" and change we could "believe in") was a combination of grassroots mobilization and activism through which we the people would become involved and invested in both his ideas and the creation of a movement. He used on-line technology and a very disciplined team of advisors who he listened to and trusted. He tapped into the desire, power, and the passion of everyday people across our differences in a way never seen in history. For many, the power of his message had us doing things we'd never imagined: Canvassing, holding house parties, attending mega-rallies, standing on street corners with big signs, donating on-line even when we couldn't afford to, donning Obama wear as everyday fashion, making thousands of phone calls, talking to strangers and finding whatever common ground we held together. We, the people, became the eyes, ears, arms and legs, stomping for Obama. But what we really knew, given the confluence of the message, the candidate, the state of the union and its place in the world was that we were stompin' for *ourselves*. The campaign, as President Obama reminded us time and time again, belonged to *us*: It was *e pluribus unum* for real. As *Rolling Stone* writer Tim Dickinson (2009) reported: "The team Obama built had little experience electing a president—and that was exactly the point: We were all in this together" (p. 101).

> *Lesson #4*: We gained a *new source of power*, both here and abroad. And given our always multiple and different versions of being human, we are being called to re-vision our individual and collective place(s) in the world.

In January 2009, *The Atlantic* published a special "State of the Union Issue." In black, white, and shades of Barack Obama, the headline questioned boldly from the cover: "THE END OF WHITE AMERICA?" The subsequent article by Hua Hsu (2009), spoke to the ways that the election of Barack Obama as the first African American president is the manifestation of a growing trend toward "the gradual erosion of whiteness" as the touchstone of what it means to be American. He goes on:

If the end of white America is a cultural and demographic inevitability, what will the new mainstream look like—and how will white Americans fit into it? What will it mean to be white when whiteness is no longer the norm? And will a post-white America be less racially divided—or more so? (p. 46)

Contrast the *Atlantic* piece with anther black and white cover, this time from *Ebony* magazine. The bold words on the cover? "REAL LOVE: The Obama's Story of Commitment Inspires America." The article begins:

When you take a moment and think about it, we got far more than we voted for last November. Barack Obama's electoral victory has reshaped the landscape of American politics forever. His and wife Michelle's popular appeal has redefined success in the minds of even the most critical skeptics. But more, the commitment, passion and devotion Barack and Michelle Obama have for each other have fundamentally changed the look of Black love. (Cole, 2009, p. 64)

Although the focus and nature of these two magazines are quite different, they literally point in black and white to the ways that power is being contested and redefined at this moment in our histories (plural on purpose), toward the way that the margins and centers of power are felt to be shifting, where the ground— of race, sexualities, class positions, nationality, and so on—have taken on a different history, given the election of Barack Obama. Filmmaker Spike Lee suggested that historians will mark two distinct phases in American life: "B.B. and A.B.—Before Barack and After Barack." That is a bold pronouncement, but one that seems to be true. The world as we had always known it was different in a fundamental way, especially related to race. But I am also struck by what is also being *whispered*, what is the *not* said in these two articles and our conversations—but said anyway. It's what I alluded to in a paper about paradigms that I wrote a number of years ago (Dillard, 2006b). What is whispered is what Richard Wright (1957) calls *perspective*:

Perspective is that part of a poem, novel or play which a writer never puts directly upon paper. It is that fixed point in intellectual [and spiritual] space where a writer stands to view the struggles, hopes and suffering of his people. There are times when he many stand too close and the result is blurred vision. Or he may stand too far away and the result is a neglect of the important things. (p. 62)

Like many, I received emails, text messages, and phone calls on or around the days of the election and the inauguration of Barack Obama. Most came from African-ascendent people in the United States, Ghana, and the Caribbean. The central message was one of congratulations "for *your* election of Barack Obama." Like many Blacks in the United States, we felt we'd taken a leap forward that day, that we'd become new in some way, finally acknowledged as 5/5ths or full human beings. We were *vital*, central to our U.S. democracy, despite our strained and often tenuous relationship historically and contemporarily with the still unmet principles of justice and equity. What these congratulatory messages taught me (and the articles above echo) is that, as black folks, too many of us are still in Ellensburg, Washington, still "facing the Klan." But what these messages also suggest is how important this moment is to our collective possibilities as African-ascendent people *within* a nation of diversity, *within* the grand experiment that is the United States of America.

It is very difficult to describe the profundity of this moment in the depth of the souls of many Blacks. It's as if, just for a moment, we were in the center, not the margins of the view. But what we also knew was that the view, if for just a moment, had space for all, for *we the people*. The emails I received suggested that this moment was a humanizing space for African-ascendent people around the world, given legacies of hatred, oppressions, apartheid, slavery, colonization, and continued inequities and injustices for Blacks everywhere. I'd like to think that it was also a humanizing and transformative moment for qualitative researchers, a moment to examine our perspectives, the not-said that Richard Wright suggested. To consider more carefully our methods and approaches and their relevance today, post-Obama, but pre-"justice for all." To see where and whether our ethics of research are ones that bear witness to hope, to the racialized memories and possibilities that are always present within the research that we do, whether acknowledged or not. To study our purposes and reasons for engaging in inquiry, our selections of communities to "study" and on behalf of whom we do our work. We, too, must find a means to marshal hope and change in our research in ways that asks new questions, that opens spaces for ontological common ground like hope and change and difference and equity (see Dillard & Okpalaoka, in press).

I'll end with an excerpt from an open letter, written by Alice Walker (2008) to Barack Obama. I believe her words are both a praisesong and a challenge to examine our histories, biographies, and motivations in order to create, through our research, the spirit we experienced and saw possible in the campaign:

Dear Brother Obama,

You have no idea, really, of how profound this moment is for us. … But seeing you deliver the torch so many others before you carried, year after year, decade after decade, century after century, only to be struck down before igniting the flame of justice and of law, is almost more than the heart can bear. And yet, this observation is not intended to burden you, for you are of a different time, and, indeed, because of all the relay runners before you, North America is a different place. It is really only to say: Well done. We knew, through all the generations, that you were with us, in us, the best of the spirit of Africa and of the Americas. Knowing this, that you would actually appear, someday, was part of our strength. Seeing you take your rightful place, based solely on your wisdom, stamina and character, is a balm for the weary warriors of hope, previously only sung about. … And your smile, with which we watch you do gracious battle with unjust characterizations, distortions and lies, is that expression of healthy self-worth, spirit and soul, that, kept happy and free and relaxed, can find an answering smile in all of us, lighting our way, and brightening the world. We are the ones we have been waiting for.

Yes, we can. And so it is.

References

Bethel, L. (1982). "This infinity of conscious pain": Zora Neale Hurston and the black female literary tradition. In G. T. Hull, P. B. Scott, and B. Smith (Eds.), *All the women are white, all the Blacks are men, but some of us are brave* (pp. 176–188). New York: The Feminist Press.

Cannon, K. G. (1995). *Katie's canon: Womanism and the soul of the black community*. New York: Continuum.

Cole, H. (2009). Real love: What we crave, what Barack and Michelle Obama have. *Ebony, 54,* 4, 64–49.

Collins, P. H. (1990). *Black feminist thought: Knowledge, consciousness, and the politics of empowerment*. New York: Routledge

Collins, P. H. (2000). *Black feminist thought: Knowledge, consciousness, and the politics of empowerment* (2nd ed.). New York: Routledge.

Denzin, N. K., Lincoln, Y. S., & Smith, L.T. (Eds.). (2008). *The handbook of critical and indigenous methodologies*. Thousand Oaks, CA: Sage.

Dickinson, T. (2009). Obama's brain trust: How the candidate and his team created the most formidable political machine in modern history. *Rolling Stone Commenmorative Edition*, pp. 96–101.

Dillard, C. B. (2006a). *On spiritual strivings: Transforming an African American woman's academic life*. Albany: State University of New York Press.

Dillard, C. B. (2006b). When the music changes, so should the dance: Cultural and spiritual considerations in paradigm "proliferation." *International Journal of Qualitative Studies in Education, 19,* 1, 59–76.

Dillard, C. B. (2008). Endarkened feminist epistemology and healing methodologies of the spirit. In N. K. Denzin, Y. S. Lincoln, and L.T. Smith (Eds.), *The handbook of critical and indigenous methodologies* (pp. 277–292). Thousand Oaks, CA: Sage.

Dillard, C. B., & Okpalaoka, C. L. (in press). The sacred and spiritual nature of both/and: Towards a transnational black feminist praxis in qualitative research. In N. K. Denzin and Y. S. Lincoln (Eds.), *The handbook of qualitative research* (4th ed.). Thousand Oaks, CA: Sage.

Golden, M. (1995). Introduction. *Skin deep: Black women and white women write about race*. New York: Doubleday.

Freire, P. (1970). *Pedagogy of the oppressed*. New York: Continuum.

Freire, P. (1996). *Pedagogy of hope: Reliving pedagogy of the oppressed*. New York: Continuum.

hooks, bell (1984). *Feminist theory: From margin to center*. Boston: South End Press.

hooks, bell (2000). *All about love: New visions*. New York: William Morrow and Company.

Hsu, H. (2009). The end of white America? *The Atlantic, 303*, 1, 46–55.

Hurtado, A. (2003). Theory in the flesh: Toward an endarkened epistemology. *International Journal of Qualitative Studies in Education, 16*, 2, 215–225.

Lubiano, W. (1991). Shuckin' off the African-American native other: What's "po-mo" got to do with it? *Cultural Critique, 18*, Spring, 149–186.

Madison, D. S. (2007). Dangerous ethnography and utopian performatives. Keynote address presented at the Third International Congress of Qualitative Inquiry, University of Illinois at Urbana-Champaign, May 2.

Moraga, C. & Anzaldua, G. (1981). *This bridge called my back: Writings by radical women of color.* New York: Kitchen Table Press.

Obama, B. (2006). *The audacity of hope: Thoughts on reclaiming the American dream.* New York: Crown.

Royster, J. J. (2000). *Traces of a stream: Literacy and social change among African American women.* Pittsburgh: University of Pittsburgh Press.

Walker, A. (2008). An open letter to Barack Obama. http://www.theroot.com/views/open-letter-barack-obama (accessed November, 5, 2008).

Willis, A. (2008). Faith-based politics, the Obama way. http://www.theroot.com/views/faith-based-politics-obama-way (accessed November 15, 2008).

Wright , H. K. (2003). And endarkened feminist epistemology? Identity, difference and the politics of representation in educational research. *International Journal of Qualitative Studies in Education, 16*, 2, 197–225.

Wright, R. (1957). *White man, listen!* New York: Harper.

10. Triangulation of Micro-Perspectives on Juvenile Homelessness, Health, and Human Rights

Uwe Flick

Introduction: Human Rights, Homelessness, and Health Care

The Universal Declaration of Human Rights (United Nations, 1948, Article 25) proclaims that "everyone has the right to a standard of living adequate for the health and well-being of oneself and one's family, including food, clothing, housing, and medical care." Similar claims are made by the FEANTSA[1] Report (2006). The World Health Organization (1999) has formulated four strategies against poverty and social exclusion, which can be taken as a starting point for qualitative inquiry addressing human rights issues in the context of health: (1) Act on the determinants of health by influencing development policy; (2) Reduce risks through a broader approach to public health; (3) Focus on the health problems of the poor; and (4) Ensure that health systems serve the poor more effectively (Hepworth, 2006, p. 337).

This agenda gives a helpful orientation for acting against inequality, poverty, and problems linked to it from a global perspective and can be used for addressing several specific problems in the context of relatively rich countries. Homelessness is a phenomenon that can be encountered in different contexts and it includes various forms of living. Rough sleeping is perhaps the most obvious one and it can be witnessed in most of the bigger cities in the Western world. But there are other forms of homelessness—people losing their homes, living a sporadic, nonpermanent way in shelters, or staying at other people's houses (e.g., with partners or relatives). Homelessness brings a risk of social isolation and exclusion or is a manifestation of both. Homelessness can have a negative impact on human rights—the homeless are often not treated as though they were human beings or they are deprived of social and health support. Homelessness is also connected to health risks, either specific ones or higher rates of general risks. Qualitative inquirers can look at homelessness and its link to health issues on several levels:

- analysis of the risks of becoming homeless;
- the living conditions of being homeless and their impact on health risks and problems;
- homeless youth as a specific phenomenon;
- health problems in the context of being homeless; and
- service utilization and barriers and effects of interventions in the context of being homeless.

Risk of Becoming Homeless

In most countries in Western Europe and the United States or Canada, homelessness can become relevant for a wider part of the population than has been true previously. It has been shown that some of the currently homeless people have been leading conventional lives before the present, and some have had higher education and led professional lives for some time. Homeless youth have backgrounds in all levels of society, although those from a lower socioeconomic status are more likely to become homeless. In many cases, a specific life event turned the person into being homeless—ejection from an apartment, insolvency of an enterprise, losing a job, breaking up of a relationship, certain forms of illness. Yet all these events do not necessarily lead to homelessness. Therefore, we need more research that addresses how people become or became homeless, which psychological and social factors prevent this state or development, and which contribute to making it more likely.

Being Homeless: What Characterizes the Life Situation of Homeless People and Implications for Health?

The second question addresses the life world of people being homeless—How do they live? How do aspects of inequality and deprivation become relevant and concrete for them? How are they experienced and what are their implications for health? There are some more or less obvious features of the homeless—they have no regular place to stay or live; they have no money or not enough of it for living on usual standards in areas like clothing, eating, consumption, etc. This can lead to hygienic problems as well as to mental stress (because of a lack of privacy, for example). Panhandling as an attempt to raise at least some income can lead to experiences of rejection by the public and to being subject to verbal and physical aggression and violence. Drugs and alcohol become functional for those coping with these conditions. All these features have more or less direct implications on health in general and on specific areas of health problems.

Homeless Youth as a Specific Phenomenon

Juvenile homelessness is of particular interest for three reasons: First, a general trend can be seen in Germany, for example, but also elsewhere: The trend is now for younger people to become homeless. In Germany, statistics show that from 1992 to 2002, fewer people aged 50 and over have become homeless. In particular, street kids have become a media topic—mostly in countries like Romania, the GUS countries,[2] and Latin America. But in Germany, too, there is growing number of homeless adolescents. It can be expected that this trend will continue. Second, the earlier someone is confronted with street life or being homeless, the longer he or she will have to live with this problem. And third, preventive efforts can have a stronger impact on a life history, if they address the people while they are younger.

Service Utilization and Barriers

This leads to a fourth question, and it is one that qualitative inquiry can respond to. Is the range of services that is available for homeless people adequate to their needs? Are there services they can turn to in case of health problems? Do homeless people use these services or, asked the other way around, do these services reach their addressees? And on what does it depend? For Germany again, we find estimations that 80–90% of the homeless people urgently need some form of medical treatment, whereas 60% said in interviews that they do not have a doctor they go to if they have health problems (Armut und Gesundheit in Deutschland 2000; Trabert 1995). Both the homeless and health-care providers have viewpoints and attitudes that make it more unlikely that homeless people with health problems utilize professional help in time and sufficiently. Distrust toward and negative experiences with the medical system, living conditions that are dominated by other more pressing needs, and so on build up barriers for possible clients. And lack of knowledge about homelessness, aversions, and prejudices on the part of health professionals may contribute to keeping the barriers high (at least around regular health services). Providing more doctors and institutions that specialize in supporting homeless patients may be one solution.

Homelessness and Health in Adolescence

Homelessness and adolescents living on the street can be observed in many countries, including rich ones like Germany. Adolescents who live in the streets face numerous risks. They are subjected to these risks, but sometimes they take them on purposely. They are not only subjected to social exclusion because of their instable housing situation but also because of their chronic lack of money. They have to spend their money for what is absolutely necessary for their daily survival. Standards of healthy eating and appropriate clothing are often reduced or given up. Those who live under such conditions of social exclusion have precarious health situations. Releatively minor health problems like respiratory, gastrointestinal, or skin diseases can often occur, as can more serious illnesses like AIDS or hepatitis (Barry, Ensign, & Lippek, 2002, p. 146). Consuming drugs and alcohol may help the homeless withstand life in the street but those contribute to severe somatic and mental health problems. Only limited medical support is available for the adolescents because they cannot afford to pay their share for actual treatment. Poor living conditions and the risk behaviors connected with them directly influence the adolescents' health status. They also influence the representations of health held by the individuals—what they understand as health and on what health seems to depend for them. Individuals' representations of health again influence how they react to symptoms and what they do (or do not) to maintain or promote their health (Flick, 2000, p. 316).

Features of Juvenile Homelessness

In the literature, studies addressing juvenile homelessness in Germany and other relatively rich countries had the following features. Adolescents in the studies are mostly between 14 and 24 years old. They have spent at least one night on the street, in the public sphere, in parks, at train stations, or at specific shelters without the option of going home to their parents' or their own place. These adolescents live in precarious housing conditions or institutionalized shelters. They are dependent on ones giving shelter (e.g., friends, relatives, youth authorities, etc.). They partake of controlled substances, which often prevents them from reaching a long-term solution to their housing situation.

Approaches to Juvenile Homelessness and Health

To study adolescent homeless with the particular focus on health, we can take the following approaches. First, describe the world of being homeless: What does it mean to be in this situation, and what experiences do people have in it? Second, describe health-related practices of homeless adolescents: How much are they different from what other adolescents do about their health? An aim should be to give voice to homeless adolescents in and through the research. With a focus on human rights in this context, it will be fruitful to analyze the institutional and professional perception and reaction to homelessness and health problems of adolescents in institutions providing (potential) social and health-related support. This can lead to the identification of needs and options for change and development from both perspectives.

As this brief outline may have demonstrated, to study homeless adolescents and their health and illness from a human rights perspective we need a combination of several approaches. In what follows, I outline my recent study into the issue, while also offering it as an example of our methodological point of view.

Using Triangulation for Studying Homeless Adolescents' Health and Chronic Illness

To address the issue of health and homelessness from a human rights standpoint, a fruitful perspective would be to look at health services and their accessibility and experiences for homeless people. To address this on an empirical level, we need different approaches for understanding this issue in its complexity. For this, we turn to the application of triangulation as a methodological principle. Norman Denzin (1970) has distinguished several forms of triangulation: Besides triangulation of several investigators and of various theories, we find triangulation of data and methodological triangulation, which again is differentiated in "within-method" (e.g., the use of different subscales within a questionnaire) and "between-method" triangulation. The latter were applied in the study on which this chapter is based. The background of this application was the following definition of triangulation I developed after working for quite some time on the concept of triangulation both on practical and methodological levels:

> Triangulation includes that researchers take different perspectives on an issue under study or more general in answering research questions. These perspectives can be substantiated in using several methods and/or in several theoretical approaches. Both are or should be linked. Furthermore it refers to combining

different sorts of data on the background of the theoretical perspectives, which are applied to the data. As far as possible, these perspectives should be treated and applied on an equal footing and in an equally consequent way. At the same time, triangulation (of different methods or data sorts) should allow a principal surplus of knowledge. For example, triangulation should produce knowledge on different levels, which means they go beyond the knowledge made possible by one approach and thus contribute to promoting quality in research. (Flick, 2008, p. 41)

In the study underlying this chapter, I used several methodological approaches. I applied between-methods triangulation by combining three methods: With participant observation, I studied health-related practices and interactions in the field under study; in "episodic interviews" (see Flick, 2008), I addressed the adolescents' health concepts and experiences with health services; in expert interviews, I focused on the perception of homeless adolescents by health professionals and on what they think how health care for this group works and which obstacles exist. Finally, the episodic interview is an example for "within-methods" triangulation, as it combines question-and-answer approaches with narratives of situations that result from invitations to recount situations in which specific experiences (e.g., with health services) have been made by the interviewee (for more details, see Chapter 5 in Flick, 2008).

For applying triangulation as a methodological strategy, a number of practical issues become relevant, which I shall briefly address.

Design and Sampling

First, design and sampling should be considered in the application of different methods, whether they call for different samples each. For interviews, sampling will address people. In the example discussed here, I used theoretical sampling for selecting the adolescents and purposive sampling for finding and choosing the experts. In observations, it is the situation that is in the focus of sampling. In general, it will not necessarily be the same persons who have to be included in the observation as were selected for the interviews. It also should be considered whether to use the same cases for each method or not. The danger here is that an overchallenge of the participants may produce loss—they might be ready for one of the method (e.g., being interviewed) but not for the other one (being observed, or vice versa). The consequence of this is that you might lose possible participants for your study who are not willing to accept both methodological approaches you want to apply.

Levels of Triangulation in Qualitative Research

In triangulating different methods in qualitative research, the question is which level the triangulation concretely addresses. Here we have two alternatives: Triangulation of different qualitative methods can be applied to the single case. The same persons who are interviewed are also members observed. Their answers to questions in the interviews and their observed practices are compared, brought together, and related to each other on the level of the single case as well. The link can be established in addition—or only—on the level of data sets. The answers to the interviews are analyzed over the whole sample, and a typology is developed. The observations, too, are analyzed and compared for regularities or common themes. Then these commonalities are linked to the typology and compared with it.

Possible Results of Triangulation

Applying triangulation in a study like the one presented here can have three kinds of outcomes: The results coming from different methods converge, mutually confirm, and support the same conclusions. This was the aim in the beginning of using several methods. However, it is more interesting when both results focus on different aspects of an issue (e.g., subjective meanings of a specific illness and disease-related practices) but are complementary to each other and lead to a fuller picture. And, of course, results may diverge or contradict, which means we should look for (theoretical and/or) empirical) explanations for the contradictions.

Juvenile Homelessness, Health, and Chronic Illness in a Big German City

Approaching Homeless Adolescents

To access homeless adolescents and interviewing them, I participated in social street work and in a low barrier drop-in center. I informed the adolescents I met in this context about the study and asked them to make this project known to their peers. The drop-in center allowed me to make appointments with the adolescents in a room without external disturbances.

I worked with two samples subsequently. The first one included adolescents from 14 to 20 years old; the second one focused on chronically ill homeless adolescents from 14 to 25 (see Table 1).

Table 1: Samples

Age (in years)	Homeless adolescents		
	Male $n = 12$	Female $n = 12$	Total $N = 24$
14–17	5	9	14
18–20	7	3	10
	Chronically ill homeless adolescents		
	Male $n = 6$	Female $n = 6$	Total $N = 12$
14–17	1	3	4
18–25	5	3	8

With few exceptions, the adolescents were ready to participate in the interview and to answer "unpleasant" questions. The episodic interviews (Flick, 2008) combined concrete, focused questions (e.g., about what health means for the interviewee) and narrative stimuli focusing on specific situations and experiences. The adolescents were asked for their concepts of health and their experiences of health, health problems, and how they dealt with them. They were invited to recount situations referring to such experiences. The interview guide included several topics: how interviewees turned to street life, their subjective definitions of health, their current situation (housing, financial problems, nutrition) and its consequences for health, and how they handle health problems and risks (drugs, alcohol, sexuality). The interviews were carried out in 2005 and 2006 and lasted between 30 and 120 minutes (60 minutes on average). Participant observation complemented the interviews for better understanding the health practices of the interviewees and their peers. Data analysis uses thematic coding (Flick, 2009), beginning with all statements referring to an area (e.g., the meaning of health) for every interviewee. Comparative dimensions were defined across cases for finding similarities and differences. Cases were grouped along these dimensions and analyzed for specific combinations of features. Contrasting cases allowed comparing the cases in one group for similarities and comparing cases across the groups for differences among them. Interpretive and practice patterns were found and analyzed.

From Family to Street Life

I first asked the interviewees to tell me about their way into homelessness or life in the street. Compared to the other parts of the interview, narratives about this issue are relatively limited. The adolescents mainly refer to conflicts in the family as to why they were homeless. In some cases, a permanent stress in the family or in school is mentioned as the cause for one's own decision to leave. In other cases, interviewees see themselves as victims of family dynamics or mention a general emptiness of the family relations. Mostly, the interviewees seem not to be aware of what made them leave their families and turn to living in the street (or do not want to talk about this). I find more or less strong idealizations of the families they left. It was astonishing that the adolescents did not express a clear idea of how they ended up in their current situation (see Table 2).

When I interviewed them, the interviewees had been living in the street or in some part of the homeless adolescents' subculture from 1 month to 6 years. The majority had left school without finishing it; two held a very basic degree; and one still attended school more or less regularly. Different from Eastern Europe or

Table 2: From Family to Street Life

Interpretive Pattern	Adolescents								
	All			"Health"and homeless			Chronically ill		
	All	Male	Female	All	Male	Female	All	Male	Female
Being a victim	17	8	9	11	6	5	6	2	4
Idealization	7	4	3	7	4	3	—	—	—
Taking responsibility	5	4	1	2	1	1	3	3	—
Emptiness in family	4	1	3	4	1	3	—	—	—
Illness	3	1	2	—	—	—	3	1	2
N	36	18	18	24	12	12	12	6	6

developing countries, fewer homeless adolescents in Germany have been sleeping rough for a longer period. They spend their days at busy inner-city places for panhandling money from pedestrians or to meet friends living a life similar to theirs. At night, they turn sooner or later to mostly provisional accommodations of (otherwise also homeless) peers or to assisted housing or they have short-term apartments. However, homeless adolescents rarely find access to appropriate housing or can maintain it financially (Avramov, 1998, p. 15), which is also true of these interviewees (see Table 3). When

Table 3: Housing Situation at the Time of the Interview

Form of housing	Adolescents		
	Male *n* = 18	Female *n* = 18	Total *N* = 36
Staying with friends and acquaintances	11	8	19
Assisted living	3	6	9
At relatives' or partners' places	1	2	3
Quarters for staying overnight (Only chronically ill adolescents)	4	1	5

I interviewed them, they said that they were provisionally staying overnight at friends' or relatives' places or in assisted living. When the adolescents stay overnight at their peers' places, the houses are often very poorly equipped and unhygienic, often full of rats and mildew. Some of the chronically ill adolescents had an apartment for short-term use when I interviewed them.

Utilization of Medical Services

The following is a discussion of the group of the chronically ill adolescents I studied. I was interested in what the participants do when they need (medical) help and what their experiences in this situation are like. In the interviews and observations, I identified a number of interpretive patterns.

Seeing a Doctor as Self-evident

One example for the first pattern is Daniel,[3] suffering from Hepatitis C, amputation of the right leg, and facing the threat of amputation of the left lower leg:

> (...) as long as the virus degree is not in an area, that you have to treat it, I don't have it treated (...) it is controlled by the doctor and that is actually thes most important thing you should do if you have this disease. (Daniel, 24 years old)

Other participants in this pattern have neurodermatitis or allergies to dyestuff and band-aids and strong skin irritations. These adolescents have no doubts about the relevance of the doctors' prescriptions. They see them as mandatory, so they keep appointments with doctors. They are ready to invest time and money for handing in prescriptions. Professionals' suggestions about how to deal with their disease are taken up for changing their illness behavior. However, more extensive changes in daily routines are rarely considered.

Seeing a Doctor as a Distant Option

Denise is an example of the second pattern. Although other adolescents suffer from asthma, hay fever, obesity, and alcoholism, Denise suffers from allergies to animal hair and milk and, most evident in her daily life, extreme obesity. She refers to her allergic reactions on her skin when she says:

> If it is impossible to stand it, if my whole body is really full from head to feet and there is no part free of it at all, then I would go (see the doctor ...). But it was not so serious so far. Lucky me. (Denise, 16 years)

Again, these adolescents have no doubts about their need of medical treatment. However, currently they do not seek or receive treatment. They delay seeing a doctor as long as possible and don't do so as long their symptoms are not urgent enough to make professional help necessary. Their lack of insurance is seen as an obstacle for using medical services; they also see living on the street as an obstacle for medical treatment.

The Doctor as a Risk

This pattern applies to a number of adolescents suffering from lactose intolerance, hay fever, Hepatitis C, anorexia, neurodermatitis, cardiovascular problems, chronic bronchitis and asthma, and so on. Romy is 14 and suffers from a chronic bronchitis. She describes her experiences:

> (...) I took many drugs in addition, drank alcohol and afterwards some aspirin or so because of my headache and all that did not really fit together and then I passed out. (Romy, 14 years)

She and the other interviewees to whom this third pattern applies express a strong distrust of any doctors. This has to do with experiences of feeling abandoned when the diagnosis they were given produced a shock. In general, they see doctors as incompetent. Another reason for their skepticism is that they felt they were treated like laypeople by doctors. Finally, they see treatments as experiments at their expense. And as Romy's statement shows, these adolescents experience treatment as risk rather than as help.

Table 4 summarized the patterns I found. It shows that the last pattern applies to half of the interviewees, although the patterns were found across the different diseases in or group.

I found another pattern I labeled as "fatalism":

Jan has fully developed AIDS. Asked about how he feels, he answers, it has to be ok, he still could get along with it, and now it was too late anyway to expect a substantial improvement, there is nothing that could be done for him anymore. He would attend the Homeless Doctor, she would provide him with painkillers and there is nothing else he still wants anymore. (Field notes, February 22, 2005)

Table 4: Utilization Patterns of Medical Services

Interpretive Patterns	Adolescents		
	Male $n = 6$	Female $n = 6$	Total $N = 12$
Interpretive Patterns	2	1	3
Assisted living	1	2	3
At relatives' or partners' places	3	3	6

Jan expresses a rather fatalistic attitude toward his disease and his future life. He does not expect treatment or improvement anymore but only pain relief. He disappeared from the field soon after.

For those who are affected, chronic illness may subjectively be experienced in different ways from how they appear when "objective" or professional criteria are applied. In the next step, the subjective views of the adolescents will be complemented by the external perspective of people working in social and health services who are working with chronically ill homeless adolescents. These people can be seen as experts for estimating the adolescents' situation, needs, and problems. I analyzed the experts' views on the adolescents' need for support and which health-care deficits might exist in supporting this target group. I included physicians and social workers specialized in working with homeless people (not necessarily adolescents) or working in institutions for specific target groups (like Hepatitis C) and thus might be relevant for our adolescents because of their diseases (see Table 5).

Table 5: Sample for the Experts Interviews

Fields of Work	Experts		
	Physicians	Social workers	Total
	n = 5	*n* = 7	*N* = 12
Basic service (social street work and minor surgical procedures for homeless people; general practitioners)	3	3	6
Medical and social assistance for specific groups (e.g., prostitutes, hustlers, hepatitis-C patients; drug users)	2	4	6

When looking at what the experts say about deficits in the health care for homeless adolescents with a chronic illness, four areas are mentioned. Five experts mention particular subgroups who do not receive support among chronically ill adolescents on the street. Here, migrants from Eastern Europe living illegally in Germany are mentioned. These adolescents can neither make claims for appropriate housing or for medical treatment. Seven experts talk about a lack of specific institutions or professional knowledge necessary for appropriate support for the adolescents. In particular, social workers complain about a lack of physicians visiting the adolescents at their meeting points who could offer medical basic support. Doctors who treat the homeless, especially those who work with people without insurance, do not really meet the adolescents' needs, the social workers say. Four social workers say that the existing health projects miss the adolescents' needs because of the way the projects are structured or how they operate. Further, the institutions are too specialized and networking among them is weak. Competition rather than cooperation are dominant, and knowledge about what other institutions could contribute is limited:

> [They] should be better coordinated and linked. ... Support for homeless people, institutions for people with addictions, for youth

in general is available, but among these three areas there is hardly any coordination in the help that is offered. (Social worker)

Beyond that, there are not enough services and people are not trained for working with homeless adolescents. These problems are complemented by the limited accessibility of health care for people without insurance or who have their papers not with them. Only one doctor sees no deficits in the health care for homeless adolescents (see Table 6).

Table 6: Health Care Deficits Seen by the Experts

Health care deficit	Experts		
	Physicians	Social workers	Total
	$n = 5$	$n = 7$	$N = 12$
Lack of health care for certain target groups	3	2	5
Inappropriate way of working or structure of existing services	—	4	4
Lack of institutions or competence	3	4	7
Limited accessibility of health care	1	1	2
No deficit	1	—	1

What to Do? Implications of This Study

As the experts in these interviews stress, it is important to see the adolescents and their health issues in the context of the street life they lead. Treatment and prevention will fail as long as the adolescents live in the street. Barriers in services have to be very low if the adolescents are to utilize the services.

As the adolescents in these interviews point out, it is important to be taken seriously by those providing the services and to develop trust to the doctor. Health is a secondary problem in street life. Finally, interventions should go beyond health to become relevant for them. This means that services should be organized in an interdisciplinary way and should include health and other social support to become relevant. Those who work in institutions in this field have to try to find their clients on the street and offer their services rather than waiting until the clients come in and ask for help. Although different from the situation in the United States—in Germany, almost everybody is in the health insurance system—our study shows the difficulties existing in this particular field, if health service access as a human right is to be guaranteed if homelessness is the context in which a health problem arises.

Conclusion: The Use of Triangulation in Studying Human Rights

Taking the three methodological approaches used in this study, different perspectives on the issue of access to and utilization of medical and social support become apparent: The observations show in which situation and circumstances participants refrain from expecting help from services. In interviews with the adolescents, I heard detailed accounts of experiences and evaluations of utilization of medical and social services and explanations and interpretations and why these are utilized or not. Here, perceptions of treatments as a risk dominated the interviews. In interviews with experts, I learned about how social workers and physicians perceive these adolescents, why they think the latter do not make use of existing services, and why these services are not adequate or are not used by their potential addressees. Altogether, these three perspectives outline a fuller picture of practical conditions under which a human right—and medical care—becomes difficult to be claimed or supported, once another one—housing—is not given for one or the other reason. The three micro-perspectives on homelessness, health, and human rights make accessible:

- professional images of clients and service problems;
- experiences of a vulnerable group with health problems and services; and
- health-related practices in everyday life beyond institutional realities.

These add up to a comprehensive picture of the problem. The combination of the three methodological perspectives gives a fuller picture from complementary angles—the view of the adolescents is also complemented by observing their practices by the experts' views "from the outside."

Acknowledgments

This research was funded by the German Research Council (DFG – FL245-10/1-2). The author thanks Dr. Gundula Röhnsch for collaborating in collecting and analyzing the data.

Notes

1. Fédération Européenne d'Associations Nationales Travaillant avec les Sans-Abri (English: European Federation of National Organisations working with the Homeless).
2. Gemeinschaft Unabhängiger Staaten (GUS). In English, Commonwealth of Independent States (CIS); the former Soviet Republics.
3. All names have been changed.

References

Armut und Gesundheit in Deutschland e.V. (2000). Die Gesundheitssituation wohnungsloser Menschen. In R. Geene and C. Gold (Eds.), *Gesundheit für Alle! Wie können arme Menschen von präventiver und kurativer Gesundheitsversorgung erreicht werden?* (pp. 49–50). Berlin: b_books.

Avramov, D. (1998). Homelessness in the European Union: Changes and continuities. In D. Avramov (Ed.), *Youth homelessness in the European Union. FEANTSA transnational report 1997* (pp. 13–34). Brussels: FEANTSA.

Barry, P. J., Ensign, J., & Lippek, S. H. (2002). Embracing street culture: Fitting health care into the lives of street youth. *Journal of Transcultural Nursing, 13*, 2, 145–152.

Denzin, N. K. (1970). *The research act*. Chicago: Aldine.

FEANTSA. (2006). Annual European report. The right to health is a human right: Ensuring access to health for people who are homeless. www.feantsa.org/files/Health_Annual_Theme/Annual_theme_documents/European_report/EN_Annual_theme_report_2006_Health.pdf (accessed January 10, 2010).

Flick, U. (2000). Qualitative inquiries into social representations of health. *Journal of Health Psychology, 5*, 3, 315–324.

Flick, U. (2008). *Managing the quality of qualitative research*. Thousand Oaks, CA: Sage.

Flick, U. (2009). *An introduction to qualitative research* (4th ed.). Thousand Oaks, CA: Sage.

Hepworth, J. (2006). The emergence of critical health psychology: Can it contribute to promoting public health? *Journal of Health Psychology, 11*, 3, 331–342.

Trabert, G. (1995). *Gesundheitssituation (Gesundheitszustand) und Gesundheitsverhalten von alleinstehenden, wohnungslosen Menschen im sozialen Kontext ihrer Lebenssituation*. Bielefeld, Germany: VSH Verlag.

United Nations. (1948). The Universal Declaration of Human Rights. http://www.un.org/en/documents/udhr/index.shtml (accessed January 10, 2010).

World Health Organization. (1999). Poverty and health. Report by the Director-General. Executive Board, RB105/5. Geneva, Switzerland: World Health Organization.

11. Poverty and Social Exclusion

The Everyday Life of the Poor as the Research Field of a Critical Ethnography

Elisabeth Niederer
Rainer Winter

If you are poor, you're badly off! In fact no one cares about what you've got to say. Neither how it is—my life as a single mother of four kids and no money at all. …. You have to go to work, when the kids are sleeping in bed and you just hope that none of them will wake up or become ill. It doesn't matter to other people if I can buy food, pay the heating or if we get ill from our musty apartment. Neither of the kids can go the birthday party, because I'm even not able to get a little something as a birthday present. No one cares about those things, also no politician. Because we are just the ones who are poor.

—Annemarie, age 39, single mother, housewife,
waitress and cleaning woman

What are you nowadays without having a job? Nothing, nothing at all—even less than nothing! My bad, isn't it? If you are in work everything is great. You have friends and everything. In that case you are somebody. But people look down on you as soon as they notice that you are unemployed and poor. It has always been like that. Long ago when I was working in the factory it was different. You want to know about poverty? Everybody who does not have a job is poor.

But not only because there's no money for food, going out or a car.
Without work there is no respect. Nobody is treating you nice.
Worthless—that exactly describes how I feel and what I am.

—Peter, age 42, molding cutter, unemployed

Introduction

The voices of the poor are mostly unheard. Actually, they get lost
in the noisy din of our everyday life, so most of the time we do
not notice them at all. Hence, we have to look and listen closer to
realize that the reason why we cannot hear the poor is because they
are too weak, too fragile, and/or too ashamed to raise their voices.

Annemarie is one among thousands of people affected by
poverty in Carinthia, a small state in Austria, one of the richest
countries in the world. She is also one of eighty-five poor human
beings who participated in our ethnographic research project about poverty. This explorative study on poverty and social
exclusion in a wealthy country is the result of an attempt to hear
the voices of the poor. More than that, the study is about giving
voice to the unemployed, the less qualified, people without any
professional education, welfare recipients, single-parent families,
immigrants, and retirees. We did applied qualitative empirical
research so as to disclose the social and cultural realities of poor
people from their very specific perspectives.

To unveil the neoliberal strategies and institutions that
actively contribute to the circumstances of poverty, a critical
ethnographical analysis requires a macro-contextualization of
structural circumstances. Through this methodological approach
to the politicization of structural inequality, we can see beyond
the bizarre blame-the-victim and sensationalist debates ongoing in the media. Thus do we problematize and deconstruct the
awry and diffuse representations of postmodern poverty, its views
among the public, and its social backgrounds.

Overall, we hope that our qualitative empirical research
project makes a committed contribution in the name of civil
society, which strongly urges social justice and equal opportunities for poverty-stricken people. In addition, we go beyond most

one-sided discussions of poverty—which generally ignore the voices of the poor—and present an inside perspective in a sensitive and respectful way.

The Qualitative Inquiry of New Poverty

Poverty and social exclusion are parts of our daily lives. They are found not only on the fringes of society but are also commonly in our so-called social middle. The terms "poverty" and "social exclusion" mean different things to different people. There are many different explanations of what causes poverty, different measurements of poverty, and different descriptions of poverty, but only a few approaches consider the perspectives of the people concerned. Likewise, few scientific approaches consider poverty within the context of scandalous structural inequality and systemic distributive injustice.

The scientific findings of this study are found in the contextualization of theories, methods, and qualitative empiricism, which contributes to the articulation of social and cultural realities of poor people, the actual experts on the subject of poverty. To the extent that new poverty and social exclusion are considered as postmodern risks, which always have to be analyzed in relation to the contexts of development of their social structure, general validities and standardized definitions are becoming obsolete. Unequal power relations producing new poverty are consequently the result of a broken and corrupt social order in the twenty-first century.

Methodologically, qualitative methods of postmodern social inquiry are gaining relevance, especially when working with marginalized groups, as circumstances of poverty are considered a research field described and analyzed through a new interpretative and performative ethnography (Denzin, 2003). Correspondingly, the concept of "sensitive research" (Liamputtong, 2007, pp. 5–9) is applied in this study to consider research participants as social, vulnerable, and exposed human beings who must be treated with empathy and respect. In particular, our consideration and theorization of women in poverty draws from basic elements of postmodern feminism such as standpoint theory (Code, 1991; Collins,

2000 [1990]; Haraway, 1988, 1989; Harding, 1991; Hartsock, 1983a, 1983b; Smith, 1990). Besides gendered disparities, this conjunction of perspectives reveals that poor people are pauperized and Othered through specific social structures that hold the individual accountable for being poor.

In research practice, the methodological triangulation (Denzin, 1989) of focus groups, reflexive interviews, and autoethnography has an important function. It is believed that by this strategy comprehensive knowledge and detailed insights in the everyday lives of poor people can be achieved. The basis of social change is therefore grounded in a critical and interpretative social science, which unveils social injustices and growing tendencies of inequality and discusses them via case studies. Accepting and appreciating the poor as experts and research partners empowers them to aim for agency, to receive it back, or to sustain it with a focus on turning away from social restraints and individual feelings of guilt and to turn toward a critical, emancipating, and political perspective.

Fields of New Poverty: Research Findings of the Qualitative Ethnographic Study

It is vital to understand the heterogeneous dimensions of poverty circumstances of poor people[1] because the dimensions reveal individual insights about the people's everyday lives. Poor people's statements about their sociocultural experiences and activities illuminate their marginalized standing and uncover differences, similarities, types, and coping strategies, which will help us understand their poverty and social exclusion.

According to Bourdieu et al. (2005 [1993]), a critical analysis and reflection of the interview texts is only possible through crossing the frontiers of objectivity. So, the purpose of this study is not to adopt the objective position of a neutral and detached observer; rather, it is based on a postmodern understanding of social science (see Denzin, 1997; Harding, 2004), in which it is generally accepted and actually even required to contribute with subjective perspectives. Only then, at the intersection of combining inner perspectives of poverty, lived experiences, and knowledge production can we be led to new and original findings.

The outstanding problem areas of poor people result from lack of income—they are working poor or workless poor—and are the basic categories in which the research participants are affected in their everyday lives. Labor, family, health, habitation, education, and sociocultural participation are intrinsically tied together because they reciprocally determine and influence each other. New poverty is a matter of multidimensional circumstances that cannot be analytically separated from each other. Furthermore, a context-specific analysis has to include individual aspects of personality development and the political situation of the area the affected people are living in. Specific patterns of action and interpretation pertaining to gender, immigration, coping strategies, and dreams of the future are major categories of the study.

By this exploration of a culture of poverty, we present insights in social and cultural realities of the everyday lives of the poor, who are considered precarious, marginalized, subordinated, excluded, or decoupled. Within a detailed and thick description of the poverty circumstances, where the experiences, needs, wishes, and ideas of poor as "findings of social committed perspective" (Weiss, 2005, p. 195) are central, social, cultural and political structures, and discourse formations become visible by reference to the earlier mentioned basis categories. It may be true that the mini-narratives of the poor are characterized by individual estimates and interpretations, but nevertheless they articulate massive structural and systemic imbalance and discrimination. In sum, the analysis of the social conditions of the poor people in this explorative project points at established power relations and neoliberal economic ideologies, which substantiate Bourdieu's (2001) assumption of "an illusion of a equality of opportunities" (p. 27).

It can therefore be said that through multidimensional microanalysis of several fields of new poverty social justice does not exist for all human beings. Fair participation in many aspects of life is denied to people affected by poverty.[2] By determining minimum standards of a material and monetary supply regarding the basic coverage of necessities, health and habitation deficits can be seen that have negative effects on physical and psychological health and on the individual sense of well-being. Likewise, sociocultural and political mechanisms of exclusion, which, according to Bourdieu, are a lack of social and cultural capital, are firmly connected to available or unavailable resources and prevent poor people from leading an unrestricted and self-determined life. In fact, this lack of equal opportunities and fair participation are the most compromising and harmful parts of poor people's lives, as Sen (2001) also points out. In many cases, poor people do not have opportunities to make decisions and choices, which leads to their successive retraction and exclusion from all social, cultural, and political spheres.

Poverty and social exclusion cause difficulties and burdens, which render impossible the active and steady ambition to qualify for jobs, earn degrees, retrain, or obtain key competences. Educational aspirations are smothered and cannot be realized for lack of money. Related to occupational skills, cultural competences of reflexivity and empathic role taking and sharing of aspects is the emergence of a specific political and critical education to question and challenge established power relations. Preventing educational inequality and poverty are the keys to increasing professional and social opportunities, personal abilities, and individual chances in the present and future.

Women, especially single mothers, are affected more often and more strongly by structural poverty and social exclusion.

> You know, I don't have any choice at all. If I didn't work in my lousy job, we would starve. How that sounds! Very dramatically. But it's true. I'm really good in operating economically. Nevertheless it is never enough. As a single mother, all alone as a woman it just can not work. Despite you are a doctor or something like that. ... I want everything to be right for my son. But sometimes I have to pick him up at 8 or 9 pm at day care. That is so hard for both of us and it costs a fortune. The apartment plus heating are also very, very expensive. After I have paid all my bills there are just 70 euros left over. But at least I am able to handle my payments. This is no mean feat given that I'm alone with everything. I'm sure that not everybody is getting through that way. But it's never easy or funny. But may be life isn't like that for some people. (Vanessa, age 27, nurse)

In general, educational injustice, which is also a major indicator of the inheritance of poverty from one generation to the other, is clearly revealed as the key factor of particular poverty circumstances. Women, young children, and young people with immigrant backgrounds tend to have multiple disadvantages.

Lena has a similar story:

> I grew up with my mother and my brothers. I haven't met my father. For my mum raising us up all alone was very hard. School and education did not play any role in our childhood. We had to deal with things more important—like where from to get food. Not one of us kids was too stupid or lazy for high school, but we all had to earn money for the family. That was clear from the beginning on. Nobody was sad or offended. That's just the way it is. Nobody was ever interested in how it worked at school, what I had to study or about exams or grades. That was absolutely irrelevant. Although I was a good learner. (Lena, age 41, shop assistant)

We also found that bad health and a lack of health awareness increase with long duration of poverty and social exclusion. During the period of the research, there were some diagnoses of serious diseases such as heart attacks, cancer, depression, and anxiety attacks. Single mothers with migrant backgrounds have increased risks of poverty and social exclusion. This is the most precarious life situation at present. In Carinthia, sexist and racist discourse productions are everyday occurrences and take place in outspoken and shameless ways. The right-wing populist government in Carinthia, begun by Jörg Haider, is producing institutional xenophobic discourses. So the social and cultural practices of the Carinthian people are based on forms of discursive knowledge, as can be shown through our interviews and discussions.

Practices Dealing with New Poverty

For cultural studies, it is of particular interest to determine the discursive practices and alliances poor people use to cope with their social and cultural reality. The broad range of poverty-coping strategies, which have to be interpreted within the context of immediate experiences, exposes different cultural practices (e.g., denying poverty, accepting poverty, compensating poverty, or fighting against poverty). Moreover, we also notice the special tactics of stigma management to hide one's social identity of being poor in order to assimilate to social norms and standards. In this process, strength-sapping attempts were made to conceal poverty circumstances from other people.

Despite hopeless poverty, poor people do wish for an alternative and better future. They clearly dream of "an ordinary life," where basic material and immaterial resources are available (even if those aspirations are not more than a low standard to the average of the Carinthian population).

> Hope dies last. Right? Why are you asking me about my dreams? Seriously, I don't have any dreams anymore. At least nothing special. Not as I used to dream about my future when I was a child. I dreamed about being an astronaut or an actress, things like that. And now? There is not much left anymore. ... If anything I would like to have standard things. Like a larger TV set and a new winter coat. And that I'm able to settle my accounts, my rent, electricity, cell phone. And of course finally to celebrate a festive Christmas. Those are my dreams! Maybe they come true some day. (Michaela, age 44, welfare recipient)

Traditional poverty stereotypes can be determined through the focus groups and the reflexive interviews. They reflect social, cultural, and individual knowledge about supposed distinctive characteristics of poor people and their everyday lives. At this point, generally shared assumptions and forms of collective knowledge are reflected in our interview texts. Even some of the poverty-affected participants label other poor people as "lazy," "rotten," "boozy," "no-good," "good for nothing," "characterless," and "work-shy." It is commonly accepted as fact that the other poor are "fully responsible" and "to be blamed" for their conditions of life. In other words, and invoking Beck's (1992) concept of individualization within a risk-oriented society, poverty can be seen to be a socially individualized force to the extent that the poor often see themselves as having no other choice but to hide their circumstances to avoid criticism from those who are in the middle- or upper class. This behavior increases the daily stress of poverty-affected people.

As our findings show, all research partners are stigmatized through the "social vulnerabilities" (Beck, 2008a, p. 317; 2008b, p. 26) caused by poverty and social exclusion. This social vulnerability is grounded in the particular discourse that misinterprets poverty as shame, discredit, and personal failure. In fact, structural inequality is an effect of social conditions being intentionally suppressed in public and political discussions. That implies that, by this standard line of thinking, poverty and social exclusion cannot be fought or avoided. Measures against poverty are continually propagated, but they cannot possibly be implemented by currently existing policies. Job-creating measures, educational programs, and tax reforms are lacking—notwithstanding the importance of these measures—new perspectives of distributive justice and the redistribution of wealth, which increases to the same extent as poverty.

Despite all the difficulties in everyday life, the research findings reveal remarkably creative personal resources and capabilities of the poor. Christian, for example, carves rocking horses out of wood and restores antique cupboards; Daria cooks and boils Serbian delicacies or tells people their futures via tarot cards; Moni makes dolls, planters, bags, or fancy paper out of old newspapers.

By giving the poor a participating voice, those details of everyday life can be perceived that are rarely noted in the traditional field of poverty research. By representing the voices of the poor, starting points dealing with the empowerment of personal skills and capabilities emerge, in addition to the negative details of concrete structural causes and effects of poverty and social exclusion. Thus, and through such a critical ethnography, we can gain a more nuanced understanding of the poor, their particular circumstances, and their agency.

Political Perspectives in the Fight against Poverty and Social Exclusion

The fight against poverty and social exclusion and the fight for poverty prevention are undoubtedly among the most pressing issues of our time. However, it would probably be naive to believe that there is any political consent regarding poverty and social exclusion, especially considering the various, often conflicting, viewpoints concerning their causes. On the one hand, neither collective resentment, with generalized claims about alleged social delinquency, the work-related and meritocratic impetus of our society, nor historical anchored alms will disappear overnight; on the other—economic—side, billions of euros are made. In contemplation of these neoliberal policy strategies, an outrageous cynicism makes doubtful that there is political will for social change. Nevertheless, it is important to offer possible strategies, solution options, measures, and corrections that are supposed to at least reduce the risk of poverty and social exclusion within the realm of political possibilities. Contentious debates about poverty have to take place, along with simultaneous consideration of the socioeconomic conditions that consider the devastating social developments as the outcome of a lack of distributive justice (Butterwegge, 2009). Thus, sweeping tax reform to excuse the poor and call on the rich and super-rich to their democratic account is essential in the fight against poverty. Endorsing the suggestions of several NGOs, a national finance sales tax and the global introduction of the Tobin tax, which taxes stock market transactions and foreign currency exchanges, would be a real opportunity to transfer wealth and reduce poverty. In fact, these financial considerations are rendering a national and international redistribution of means to responsible political resorts.

Conclusion

The qualitative inquiry presented here is pursuing a number of political active and caring goals, which follow Denzin's idea of a "utopian project" (2008, p. 139) and contain "ideological and utopian moments" (Kellner, 2005, p. 13): (1) The first concern was to illustrate new poverty caused by social injustices and tendencies of inequality within the framework of a political and critical social inquiry by using case examples. (2) Poverty-affected people are interviewed about their ways of life and the associated lived experiences by which means, in some cases, for the first time they got the chance to talk about their everyday lives in new poverty and the issues that are relevant to them. (3) By use of sensitive research practices in communication, where research partners and researchers are on the same level, the participants are taken seriously and reflect their own situation. (4) This, in turn, leads to possibly the most important point of our project. That is, the research partners shall be empowered by the talks in the focus groups and reflexive interviews to cultivate, strengthen, or get back their personal agency that involves first and foremost avoiding social constraints and individual feelings of guilt moving toward a critical, emancipating, and political perspective. (5) Sociocultural and political participation possibilities ought to enhance what is leading to new prospects and opportunities for the research partners. (6) The potential to contribute to the transformation of our society and to foster the development of democracy and social justice is arising from taking these small steps.

In sum, it can be said that our main concern is not only to hear the voices of the poor but also to enable themselves to join the social, cultural, and political dialog and to participate with equal rights in our society. As Tijana, a 34-year-old shop assistant reminds us:

> Barely enough to keep body and soul together, but just about too much to die, like they say, right? Exactly that's life for me and my son. In fact I don't even wish for much. Just a life without sorrows. Bathing in the lake and eating ice cream in the summer and celebrating little parties at Christmas or for birthday. Maybe with some presents. And Italian food. This sort of things. And going to the bank without being afraid of that the other people in the queue hearing about ... (pause) ...Well, without them hearing me begging for 20 euros. Like this I can't look in the mirror anymore. Because I have slumped everything totally!

Notes

1. A full elaboration of the research findings are to be found in Niederer (2009, pp. 185–382). Relexive interviews were carried out with five focus groups with six to eight participants from August 2007 to September 2009.

Thirty-four women and twenty-one men aged between 19 and 61 were interviewed. In some cases, the research partners participated in both focus groups and reflexive interviews. In total, eighty-five poor people took an active part in our study.

2. The concept of relative poverty refers to poor people's relation of resources in comparison with the average of the society they are in living in.

References

Beck, U. (1992). *Risk society: Towards a new modernity.* New Delhi: Sage.

Beck, U. (2008a). *Weltrisikogesellschaft. Auf der Suche nach der verlorenen Sicherheit.* Frankfurt: Suhrkamp.

Beck, U. (2008b). *Die Neuvermessung der Ungleichheit unter den Menschen.* Frankfurt: Suhrkamp.

Bourdieu, P. (2001). *Wie die Kultur zum Bauern kommt. Über Bildung, Schule und Politik.* Hamburg: VSA Verlag.

Bourdieu, P. et al. (Eds.) (2005 [1993]). *Das Elend der Welt.* Konstanz, Germany: UVK.

Butterwegge, C. (2009). *Armut in einem reichen Land. Wie das Problem verharmlost und verdrängt wird.* Frankfurt: Campus Verlag.

Code, L. (1991). *What can she know? Feminist theory and the construction of knowledge.* Ithaca, NY: Cornell University Press.

Collins, P. H. (2000 [1990]). *Black feminist thought: Knowledge, consciousness, and the politics of empowerment.* New York: Routledge.

Denzin, N. K. (1989). *The research act. A theoretical introduction to sociological methods.* New York: McGraw-Hill.

Denzin, N. K. (1997). *Interpretive ethnography: Ethnographic practices for the 21st century.* Thousand Oaks, CA: Sage.

Denzin, N. K. (2003): *The cinematic society and the reflexive interview.* In J. F. Gubrium and J. A. Holstein (Eds.), *Postmodern interviewing* (pp. 141–155). Thousand Oaks, CA: Sage.

Denzin, N. K. (2009). *Qualitative inquiry under fire. Toward a new paradigm dialogue.* Walnut Creek, CA: Left Coast Press.

Haraway, D. J. (1988). Situated knowledges: The science question in feminism and the privilege of partial perspective. *Feminist Studies, 14,* **5**, 575–599.

Haraway, D. J. (1989). *Primate visions: Gender, race, and nature in the world of modern science.* New York: Routledge.

Harding, S. (1991). *Whose science? Whose knowledge? Thinking from women's lives.* Ithaca, NY: Cornell University Press.

Harding, S. (Ed.) (2004). *The feminist standpoint theory reader. intellectual and political controversies.* New York: Routledge.

Hartsock N. (1983a). Difference and domination in the women's movement: The dialectic of theory and praxis. In A. Swerdlow and H. Lessinger (Eds.), *Class, race and sex* (pp. 157–172). Boston: Hall.

Hartsock, N. (1983b). The feminist standpoint. Developing the ground for a specifically feminist historical materialsim. In S. Harding and M. Hintikka (Eds.), *Discovering reality: Deminist perspectives on epistemology, metaphysics, methodology, and philosophy of science* (pp. 283–310). Dordrecht, the Netherlands: Reidel.

Kellner, D. (2005). Für eine kritische, multikulturelle und multiperspektivische Dimension in den Cultural Studies. In R. Winter (Ed.), *Medienkultur, Kritik und Demokratie. Der Douglas Kellner Reader* (pp. 12–58). Cologne, Germany: Herbert von Halem Verlag.

Liamputtong, P. (2007). *Researching the vulnerable.* Thousand Oaks, CA: Sage.

Niederer, E. (2009). Die Kultur der Armut und ihre sozialen Kontete. Eine ethnographische Studie über Armutslagen in Kärnten. Ph.D. dissertation, University of Klagenfurt.

Sen, A. (2001). *Development as freedom.* Oxford, UK: Oxford University Press.

Smith, D. (1990). *The conceptual practices of power: A feminist sociology of knowledge.* Boston: Northeastern University Press.

Weiss, H. (2005). "Frühe Hilfen" für entwicklungsgefährdete Kinder in Armutslagen. In M. Zander (Ed.), *Kinderarmut. Einführendes Handbuch für Forschung und soziale Praxis* (pp. 182–197). Wiesbaden, Germany: VS Verlag.

12. Human Rights and Qualitative Health Inquiry

On Biofascism and the Importance of *Parrhesia*

Geneviève Rail

Stuart J. Murray

Dave Holmes

There is a time when the operation of the machine becomes so odious, makes you sick at heart, that you can't take part: you can't passively take part, and you've got to put your bodies upon the gears and upon the wheels, upon the levers, upon all the apparatus, and you've got to make it stop. And you've got to indicate to the people who run it, to the people who own it, that unless you are free, the machine will be prevented from working at all.

—Mario Savio, 1964

Our title invokes issues of (qualitative) method. Method is the means by which knowledge claims obtain their validation. It exposes the basis on which we come to understand claims about subjects, bodies, health, illness, and prescriptions to constitute a truth that deserves our observance in collective action. We agree with Koch (2007) that this specific methodological issue brings about questions of context as knowledge claims are always generated out of a context where the perspectives and values of a culture preexist matters of judgment and action. The discussion of political power, therefore, cannot be removed from the discourse on method. We, along with other qualitative inquirers, particularly those of the poststructuralist type, have written about a framework highlighting the inherent problems with the modern epistemology underlying the evidence-based movement and mainstream health research (Cohen, Stavri, & Hersh, 2004; French, 2002; Freshwater & Rolfe, 2004; Goldenberg, 2006; Holmes, Perron, & O'Byrne, 2006; Holmes et al. 2006; Murray, 2009; Murray et al., 2007; Rail, 2009a, 2009b; Rail & Lafrance, 2009; Staller, 2006; Traynor, 2002; Walker, 2003; Winch, Creedy, & Chaboyer, 2002). The result of our deconstructive effort has been to reveal the power dimension of knowledge construction in health inquiry.

Speaking out against a powerful aggregate of coordinated forces from a position of relative powerlessness was bound to be met with extreme resistance. Unsurprisingly, then, proponents of "normal" health sciences have shot back at us, from blogs to journal articles, accusing us of relying on jargon-filled postmodern theories that stand in the way of the number-one priority, to "better man's lot," as one author put it (Jefferson, 2006, p. 393). This chapter briefly addresses this rhetorical strategy but mostly extends some of our previous discussions to comment on the contemporary discursive terrain characteristic of health inquiry in neoliberal societies. In doing so, we note the biomedical, bioeconomic, and biocultural discourses that we associate with biofascism. We then present two problematic and interconnected examples of the effects of such discourses on health inquiry: evidence-based health sciences and medical ghostwriting.

Discussing the epistemological conditions that invite such phenomena, we then argue that qualitative inquirers are better positioned to address the matters of "speech" they pose, to exercise and defend this most fundamental human right in academia, and to perturb the current politics of health knowledge production. We conclude the chapter with a call to qualitative health inquirers to inscribe themselves in the role of the "specific intellectual" (Foucault, 1980) and to engage in *parrhesia* or "fearless speech" as a way to disrupt the epistemological status quo and to unpack the play of power in health research. Our antifoundational stance thus contains a political commitment of its own. In our endeavor to undermine the foundational claims of dominant health sciences discourses and order, we aim to promote plurality, difference, conversation, and freedom of dissent as the ethical elements of de/re/ constructed health sciences and research. Furthermore, we aim to disrupt demands for conformity to singular and universal bodies, subjectivities, care, prescriptions, and ways of being healthy or not as we argue that they increasingly take on the character of biopolitics and biofascism, phenomena to which we next attend.

From Biopolitics to Biofascism

Foucault's (1997) concept of "biopolitics" is useful for the understanding of current phenomena within contemporary health care and inquiry. Foucault defines biopolitics as "the endeavor, begun in the eighteenth century, to rationalize the problems presented to governmental practice by the phenomena characteristic of a group of living human beings constituted as a population: health, sanitation, birthrate, longevity, race" (p. 73). Foucault thus argues that, in modernity, *bios* or the "life" of the population increasingly comes to inform the ways in which individuals are subject to governmental control, surveillance and regulation. Gradually, he claims, individuals are replaced by "biological processes" and individual lives are displaced by "species-life." This conception of life gets adopted as an ideology, soon becoming a pervasive public morality that is internalized and perpetuated at the micro-level.

As a form of "biopower," this ideology is invisibly deployed in the ways that individuals come to understand, govern, and care for themselves. Through the concept of healthism, Crawford (1980) discusses how this political ideology shifts the responsibility for health from the state to the individual. In his 1994 book entitled *The Death of Humane Medicine and the Rise of Coercive Healthism*, Skrabanek picks up the discussion and links healthism to fascism as he discusses how governments begin to use propaganda and coercion to establish norms of health and "healthy lifestyle." Skrabanek claims that healthism either leads to or is a symptom of totalitarianism in that it justifies racism, segregation, and eugenic control. According to him, what is "healthy" is moral, patriotic, and pure, whereas what is "unhealthy" is foreign and impure. Skrabanek adds that state actions to prescribe what is healthy or forbid what is unhealthy are limitless in scope and jeopardize many civil and human rights. Although Skrabanek's version of healthism may seem useful to our arguments, we actually find Rose's (1999) version of healthism more useful in that, according to him, capitalist society finds coercion unnecessary. Because people desire health, the apparatus of advertising and other means of capitalist persuasion lead to people appropriating the dominant discourse of healthism without much need for coercion. For Rose (2006), the burden of remaining healthy shifts from the government to individuals, who then are blamed if they get sick.

Rose's conceptualization of healthism aligns with our view of biopolitics in the context of health inquiry. Indeed, in recent years, health research has been marked by biopolitics. Furthermore, we agree with Murray that such research has entered an era of "biofascism," which is understood as the nexus of three interrelated phenomena: biomedicalization, bioeconomics, and biocultural discourses (Murray, 2009). In brief, the first link to fascism rests with the biomedicalization of health care management and delivery and what they mean for health research. In a previous piece (Murray et al., 2007), we argued that the health care and research "industries" are a mind-boggling nexus, a tangled web that includes Big Pharma, innumerable government lobbies, government agencies and public policymakers, academic health sciences and its research sponsors, the convergence of research and business with its multiple public and private "stakeholders," and the insurance industry, to name just a few. For the average person, this complex system can be incomprehensible, if not barely navigable, and it is not farfetched to imagine the individual disappearing into this apparatus, subject to its "disciplining" (Foucault, 1977 [1975]). These multiple nodes of influence and control are not simply the expansion and reticulation of medical authority and practices into new realms; together, they represent a new way of understanding the relation between medicine, health, and life itself. We take our term from Clarke and her colleagues who have dubbed this phenomenon "biomedicalization" (Clarke et al., 2003). Biomedicalization is characterized by the new political economic valences of biomedicine, the rise of risk surveillance, the medicalization of risk factors, technologization, and the emergence of biomedical and technoscientific identities, to name a few elements.

The impulse of biomedicalization maps seamlessly onto the political economy of neoliberalism, the reigning hermeneutic and narrative of contemporary Western democracies. Here, mainstream health care and research are aligned with a second discussion of "fascism" where neoliberal political economic discourses feed on and supplement biomedicalizing discourses. Both types of discourse demand greater efficiency and greater economy in the face of dwindling public resources and soaring health care costs. Biomedicalization is enabled by the neoliberal ideology that expresses an almost evangelical faith in free market capitalism, where nonmarket forces are either monetized or ignored (see Barry, Osborne, & Rose, 1996; Bunton & Petersen, 1997; Miller & Rose, 2008). From academe and its research-granting bodies to hospital ethics review boards and the medical insurance industry, dominant discourses are purchased wholesale from the corporate sphere, an Orwellian catalog that includes: the client-based mantra, key performance indicators, outcomes, best-practice guidelines (BPGs), knowledge mobilization and transfer (also known as scientific transfer), capacity building, operationalization, commercialization, and so on. "Client" patients are encouraged to conceive of themselves in entrepreneurial terms: They begin to relate to their own bodies and genetic material in instrumentalist and economic vocabularies. Here, we can think about "biocapital" (see Sunder Rajan, 2006) or the phenomenon of "biobanking," where the storage of umbilical cord blood, eggs, semen, or other stem cells serves to reify the economic relation to one's own body (see Waldby, 2006).

In Foucault's terms, the neoliberal subject is "an entrepreneur and an entrepreneur of him- or herself" (Foucault, 2004, p. 232; our translation). The individual becomes a producer-consumer in the sense that she is imagined to produce the satisfactory health and well-being that she will enjoy and "consume." Under neoliberalism, the subject's own self-improvement is internalized as a moral duty to one and all; health care models are increasingly fueled by the self-care ideology. The person who is ill accrues a kind of social debt that must be redeemed by locating herself within compensatory discourses and praxes that are both rhetorical and corporeal.

Biomedical and bioeconomic discourses work together to inform wider cultural perceptions of health and the individual's public relation to his or her body and to the health care system and industry in general. Here we identify a third link to "fascism" that is sociocultural. It has less to do with biomedical "facts" or with economic "imperatives" and their measures than with shifting popular perceptions toward the acceptable terms and widely held beliefs that circulate and on the ways in which such terms shape our self-understanding in the quotidian. Consider, for example, the ways in which the word "gene" has entered popular discourse and has come to inform how we understand human life and the body. As Murray suggests, genes are considered to be:

> the most elementary particles of the body, the very authors of who we are, from eye colour to personality. The "genetic" discourse is compelling. In a world of disenchantment, where transcendent truths are increasingly unfashionable, genomics fulfills a deep cultural desire for Truth. [...] DNA has become fundamental to identity, charged with the tremendous power to explain individual differences, moral order, and human fate. [...] The gene thus operates as a cultural science fiction, offering what is at times a deeply moralistic vocabulary that masquerades as Science and Truth. (2009, p. 103)

In our arguments so far, we have connected with the term "fascism" to emphasize the ideological obedience to, and the totalizing terrain of, what might loosely be termed "scientific" authority. We see in health research and sciences that such authority is neither objective nor straightforward, but situated within the constellation of the biomedicalized, bioeconomic, and biocultural ideologies that we have sketched above. In other words, biofascism invites a totalitarian obedience to scientific authority, to the ideological political economic coordinates of neoliberalism, and to the cultural science fiction of biomedical "truths." These spheres overlap; they are mutually implicated in complex ways. Together, they form a totalizing ideology that governs the *bios*. We propose that it is this latter aspect that is of the greatest rhetorical significance in biofascism: It is "life itself," as the Master Signifier, that gets filled in by fantasy, ensuring that this value can be deployed differentially across a range of social spheres in the project of biopolitical governance. Our use of the term fascism aligns with Foucault when he suggests that:

> the major enemy, the strategic adversary is fascism [...] And not only historical fascism, the fascism of Hitler and Mussolini—which was able to mobilize and use the desire of the masses so effectively—but also the fascism in us all, in our heads and in our everyday behavior, the fascism that causes us to love power, to desire the very thing that dominates and exploits us. (Deleuze & Guattari, 1977, p. xiii)

But biofascism goes one step further and can be envisaged as both personal and public. Biofascism exploits the slippage between these classic but obsolesced categories, first locating power here, then there, but always as a ruse to ensure maximal compliance and buy-in. The three discourses we associate to bio-fascism *appear* to safeguard the civil and human rights as well as the ethical treatment of autonomous persons, offering them the tools for self-surveillance and self-regulation so that they can become entrepreneurial managers in the development and main-tenance of their own health. In reality, however, the individual is increasingly tied to health research and industries, systems of health care management, and a cadre of medical authorities increasingly inculcated into a regime that ultimately hijacks the subject in the guise of freeing it (Miller & Rose, 2008; Novas & Rose, 2000; Rose, 2006).

Discursive Effects: Governing Health Inquiry, Governing Life

Biomedicalizing, bioeconomic, and biocultural discourses have a number of extremely problematic effects, particularly as far as health inquiry is concerned. We would like to summarize two pertinent and interrelated examples here: evidence-based health sciences and medical ghostwriting.

Evidence-Based Health Sciences

Our first example has to do with the evidence-based trope that is now prominent in Western countries such as Australia, Canada, the United Kingdom, and the United States. Not unrelated to this, evidence-based medicine (EBM) has gained great momentum. Although the majority of health sciences try to distinguish themselves from medicine and the biomedical model that supports it, dominant discourses within health sciences betray a strong subjection to the biomedical paradigm and have become part of the evidence-based movement. As we argue elsewhere (Holmes et al., 2006), evidence-based health sciences (EBHS, which we mean to encompass EBM) reflect clinical practice based on scientific inquiry. The premise is that if health care professionals perform an action, there should be evidence that the action will produce the desired outcomes. These outcomes are desirable because they are believed to be beneficial to patients (Sackett, 2000).

In 1993, the Cochrane Collaboration, serving as an international research review board, was founded to provide clinicians with a resource aimed at increasing clinician–patient interaction time by facilitating clinicians' access to valid research (Holmes, Perron, & O'Byrne, 2006). The Cochrane database was established to provide this resource, and it comprises a collection of articles that have been selected according to specific criteria (Winch, Creedy, & Chaboyer, 2002). For example, the collection works with the assumption that the randomized control trial (RCT) is the gold standard and that all other research (i.e., non-RCT research, which is actually 98% of health research) is below standard (Traynor, 2002). Although EBHS acknowledges that health care professionals possess discrete bodies of knowledge, EBHS defends its rigid approach by rationalizing that the process improves health care and health care funding (Bonell, 1999; Sackett, 2000).

One of the most disturbing consequences of EBHS's methodological fundamentalism is that health sciences come to be gradually reduced to EBHS. In the starkest terms, we are currently witnessing the health sciences engaged in a strange process of devaluing and disregarding some ways of knowing, qualitative inquiry being on the losing end of this process. As Denzin, Lincoln, and Giardina suggest, qualitative researchers need to address the implications of such attempts to regulate scientific inquiry by defining what good science is: "Around the world, governments are attempting to regulate scientific inquiry by defining what counts as "good" science. These regulatory activities raise fundamental, philosophical epistemological, political and pedagogical issues for scholarship and freedom of speech in the academy" (2006, p. 769).

In terms of *epistemological issues*, we note that EBHS is built on a single (positivist) paradigm. EBHS advocates who are wedded to the concept of "evidence" maintain what is essentially a Newtonian, mechanistic worldview: They tend to believe that reality is objective, which is to say that it exists, "out there," absolutely independent of the human observer, and of the observer's intentions and observations. They fondly point to "facts," while they dismiss "values" as unscientific. EBHS becomes an ideologically driven practice that tends to ignore contexts of experience and certain types of evidence (e.g., evidence generated from qualitative inquiry or based on participants' narratives). Creativity and plurality in health research are disregarded in the name of efficiency and effectiveness. It is not so surprising, then, that EBHS has been presented as a possible answer to the crisis of legitimation confronting health care practitioners: "EBHS is predicated on an internally consistent ideology that "hard" science (via empiricism, positivism, economic rationalism and pragmatism) is the best and only way to further our understandings and the practices which flow from those understandings" (Walker, 2003, p. 152).

Of course, we would argue that there is great danger when health sciences and inquiry become governed by technicians and bureaucrats and when qualitative researchers and critical thinkers are driven to the margins or altogether expelled. The result, as Denzin, Lincoln, and Giardina have suggested, "turns subjects into numbers" and "turns social inquiry into the handmaiden of a technocratic, globalizing managerialism" (2006, p. 772).

The crisis of legitimation also speaks to *political issues* as suggested by Holmes et al. (2006). Indeed, in an age of financial turmoil that demands cost effectiveness and the efficient use of scarce resources, allied health care professions had to struggle to safeguard their position and professional contribution within the health care system. The extension of EBM to EBHS and the establishment of strict practice guidelines ("best practices guidelines" or BPGs) arrive "ready-made" and "ready-to-use": they provide the illusion of legitimacy and accountability because they tend to standardize and quantify health care work. Murray and colleagues (2007; Murray, Holmes, & Rail, 2008; Murray et al, 2008) further argue that EBHS's way-of-seeing is informed by a politically dangerous ideology as it wholeheartedly adopts neoliberal models of efficiency and accountability, right down to a corporate lexicon.

Finally, in terms of *practical and pedagogical issues*, EBHS constitutes an ossified language that maps the landscape of the professional disciplines as a whole. The Cochrane taxonomy and its derived BPGs denigrate clinical expertise and evacuate the social and ethical responsibilities that ought to distinguish health care professions. As BPGs become ingrained in the policies and normal everyday procedures that make up health care pedagogies and practices, the knowledge that health providers utilize becomes highly regulated and increasingly automatic. The price of this purported efficiency is very steep: Thoughts and actions are increasingly governed by guidelines based on specific and "acceptable" forms of knowledge, which impedes critical thinking. Given the lack of critical thinking, the individual internalizes certain practices, discourses, and types of knowledge that are supposedly "necessary" and desirable. The disciplined health care provider, then, embodies and reproduces the practices and discourses that fit within and maintain the dominant epistemic, sociopolitical, and economic power matrixes within which she navigates and operates. The blind obedience to protocols and procedures is the new ethos upon which the health care *dispositif* functions.

Medical Ghostwriting

With regard to the effects of biomedicalizing, bioeconomic and biocultural discourses, our second example concerns medical ghostwriting. In 2009, Goldacre, a self-anointed medical watchdog, broke the story in the British press about the recent ghostwriting scandal at the academic journal publisher Elsevier. In his column for *The Guardian*, Goldacre expresses moral indignation that Elsevier published no fewer than six "journals" sponsored by the pharmaceutical industry. In this case, Merck & Co. recruited scientists, medical doctors, and academics, paying them an undisclosed sum to put their name to the company's own ghostwritten research—infomercials effectively marketing Merck's products in the guise of independent research (Grant, 2009; Rout, 2009). This is not a new phenomenon; the ethical problem of ghostwriting in medical literature has been widely discussed (e.g., Angell, 2004; Blumsohn, 2006; Fugh-Berman, 2005; Gøtzsche et al., 2007; Kassirer, 2005; Larkin, 1999; Lexchin et al., 2003; Moffatt, & Elliott, 2007; Mowatt et al., 2002; Ngai et al., 2005; Sismondo, 2007; Smith, 2006).

We bring this example here and make connections to the issue of EBHS because less than 3 years earlier, the same Goldacre, in the same British newspaper, published a commentary expressing moral indignation at our recently published article in the *International Journal of Evidence-Based Healthcare* (Goldacre, 2006a). A journalist and medical doctor, Goldacre generated a good deal of press for us from his blog *badscience.net* (Goldacre, 2006b). Our article (Holmes et al., 2006) sought to expose some of the hidden political and economic dimensions of EBM and EBHS. We did not hesitate to draw some disturbing links between medicine's administrative systems, its machineries of power, and its microfascist political discourse. The political economy of microfascism, we wrote, operates ideologically, which is to say, through subtle, diffuse, and invisible forms of control that become internalized and naturalized. Our critique was lost on Goldacre, who chose instead to excoriate us for our writing style and research methods, rather than attending to the substantive claims we made. Indeed, had Goldacre understood our article, he would have seen the recent ghostwriting and marketing scandal at Elsevier as an obvious instance of the kind of political power that we discussed. A cultural critic and qualitative inquirer would have further seen that the biomedicalizing, bioeconomic, and biocultural discourses present in contemporary Western societies provide the epistemic conditions for more or less ethical ways of doing and "banking on" health inquiry.

In expressing moral indignation, Goldacre was not alone. Many researchers working within the dominant (positivist, quantitative, biomedical) paradigm denounced our critiques of EBM and EBHS (e.g., Buetow, 2007; Couto, 2007; Jefferson, 2006; Miettinen & Miettinen, 2007). For them, apparently, some forms of power, some vested interests, and some backroom dealings are worthy of moral censure, but others are not. The last line of one published response to our original paper sums this up nicely: "We do not care what paradigm is chosen, we care what works" (Jefferson, 2006, p. 393). According to this perspective, what does it matter who speaks or who writes? Those who defend the (modernist, positivist, economically rationalist) logic of EBM find themselves in contradiction when they censure Elsevier on these grounds. Interestingly, their moral condemnation is usually framed by the kinds of terms and commitments we find in qualitative (postmodernist, poststructuralist) research. If proponents of EBM were true to their quantitative methods of probabilistic induction, wouldn't they be forced to accept that many ghostwritten articles are quantitatively sound? They should not worry that research sponsored by the pharmaceutical industry is more likely to have outcomes favoring the sponsor (Lexchin et al., 2003). And they should not be concerned with critiques of RCTs that indicate a "high prevalence of ghost authorship in industry-initiated randomised trials" (Gøtzsche et al., 2007, p. 49) or in the Cochrane Collection (e.g., Mowatt et al., 2002). Shouldn't they be willing to submit ghostwritten articles to meta-analyses and to accept or reject them on the usual grounds alone? Isn't the evidence supposed to speak for itself? It is more than ironic, then, that some of the greatest defenders of the epistemological paradigm underlying EBM, EBHS, and BPGs are those who express the greatest moral outrage at Elsevier. They protest too much.

Bad Faith and the Politics of Health Inquiry

Elsevier is an easy target because the ghostwriting scandal is not an instance of subtle, diffuse, or particularly invisible forms of power and its abuse. Moral outrage is the easy response: It is politically correct posturing and it glibly and publicly performs the very the kind of moral rectitude that is expected. But is this enough? Clearly the answer is "no." The outraged individuals are often those who are unwilling or unable to turn a critical gaze back on their own endeavors, which continue quietly behind their public protests to support the very methodological and epistemological conditions that are truly outrageous. We have called this an instance of "bad faith" (Murray et al., 2007). Our original article (Holmes et al., 2006) sought to probe what remains hidden behind the seemingly benevolent face of power. Fascist regimes are not without a benevolent face; the Nazi regime, for instance, had a very public and progressive campaign for animal rights, while human rights were systematically violated (e.g., Proctor, 2000). How many researchers are not embedded within—and thus, forcibly in bed with—a tangled web of interests, the vectors of power of which are subtle, diffuse and invisible? Our work asks that researchers cease self-deception and begin to take account of the tangled web that includes Big Pharma, innumerable government lobbies, academia and its research sponsors, the convergence of research and business with public and private "takeholders, paradigms rewarding the "bioentrepreneurship" of biotech companies, service industries from the human genome sciences to multinational pharmaceutical and agribusiness complexes, corporate models from the ground up, the legal-juridical complex, and the insurance industry (Murray et al., 2007).

We cannot hope to generate a theory—let alone a practice—of human rights without an ethical commitment to expose the many guises of power in the production of scientific knowledge. We are responsible not only for what we say or write, not only for abstract scientific "matters of fact," but also for the myriad conditions under which we say what we say, the conditions under which free speech is possible, human knowledge can be generated, and human freedoms ensured. Here we leave the ethic of abstract reason and autonomy behind; we begin to acknowledge that individuals extend into the world and that they are responsible to that world and for that world. We have begun to envisage such an ethics as "an ethic of authentic practice" (Murray et al., 2008).

To be perfectly clear, we agree that Elsevier ought to be the subject of moral censure, but this alone is insufficient. We ought to take account of the attitudes and practices that aid and abet these practices—looking at the conditions of possibility for the production of scientific knowledge, in its many forms, to acknowledge that we are, each of us, responsible. Elsevier's recent ghostwriting and "ghost management" (Sismondo, 2007) scandal is only the tip of the iceberg. Even the "normal" practices of academic publishing are riven by economic and ethical conflicts. Which multinational corporations own *MedLine, BioMed,* and *PubMed,* for instance? How do certain journals justify charging a "publication fee" to authors (or their research sponsors)? What administrative systems and machineries of power are at work in the indexing, cataloging, and ranking ("index factors") of scholarly journals? Which will count for academic tenure and promotion? Research is "policed," but this is a sloppy metaphor. As Foucault remarks, power does not subjugate through blatant or obvious means, but it is *productive*, strategic, capillary, and, not least of all, seductive.

As utopian as it may sound, qualitative inquirers are perhaps best positioned to address the matters of speech and authenticity because these pose ethical and rhetorical questions that deal with the way in which power circulates in and through the production of scientific knowledge. Quantitative research can help us support these arguments, but it is less equipped to reflect on the significance of research in the life-world because such reflection calls for a deeper understanding of the historical, political, social, cultural, and economic production of scientific regimes of truth. As Shapin has argued, "speech about natural reality is a means of generating knowledge about reality, of securing assent to that knowledge, and of bounding domains of certain knowledge from areas of less certain standing" (1984, p. 482; also see Shapin & Shaffer, 1989). Securing assent is a multivalent endeavor, Shapin argues, relying on the intersection of material, social, and literary technologies—communication strategies that establish the communal conditions in and through which scientific knowledge will be produced, debated, disseminated and delivered. This is more reason, then, to be vigilant about the politics of health inquiry and the production of health knowledge.

"Fearless Speech":
On the Importance of *Parrhesia* in Academia

Given the political dimension of health inquiry and contra the superficial critique of problems such as ghostwriting, we believe that the qualitative inquirer's engagement must be more direct and courageous: It must inscribe itself in the role of the "specific intellectual" (Foucault, 1980). This fundamental role of the professor-researcher is closely linked to a freedom of speech given to our society's intellectuals (academic freedom); it involves the demanding (and often risky) duty prescribed to them of intervening and providing critique when it seems required for the public good. Critique thus constitutes not only an intellectual activity but a public duty. To "critique" means to use politically charged concepts as tools to disrupt the status quo and unpack the play of power: a theoretical/practical revolt (Eribon, 2003). This is also the duty of educators, who must foster such courage in their students—and it is particularly crucial in medicine and allied health sciences (see Papadimos & Murray, 2008). We know too well that career academics are often reluctant to critique from such a radical standpoint, and this is especially true for those who believe that there is an unassailable truth "out there." Current scientific production emerges under the yoke of complex political games in which intermingled stakeholders impose political agendas often irrelevant to scientific methods. Ghostwriting is a trenchant example in this regard: "Under contract" scientific articles find their way into so-called rigorous systematic reviews. This scaffolding of "knowledge" is elevated to the rank of truth, whereas the whole process has evidently escaped the rigor of an elementary critique. We agree with our University of Toronto colleagues that, within academia, this most fundamental human right must be exercised and defended:

> Within the unique university context, the most crucial of all human rights are freedom of speech and freedom of research and we affirm that these rights are meaningless unless they entail the right to raise deeply disturbing questions and provocative challenges to the cherished beliefs of society at large and the university itself. It is this human right to radical, critical teaching and research with which

the university has a duty above all to be concerned; for there is no one else, no other institution and no other office, in our modern neo-liberal democracy, which is the custodian of this most precious and vulnerable right of the liberated human spirit. (University of Toronto, 2010, np)

Universities are not the vassals of health institutions, pharmaceutical companies, corporations, or governmental and para-governmental agencies. As such, they must maintain a safe distance vis-à-vis these structures that might compromise, even pervert, their social function. In reality, though, this distance is threatened by the financing of universities by powerful systems (military, Big Pharma, etc.) capable of positioning an institution's guiding principles regarding education and research (Giroux, 2007). As intellectuals, professors-researchers must ensure that the university remains a fertile site of multiple pedagogical and political resistance. We must be present in the public arena and help thwart the ascent of silencing ideologies; we must expose the fetishization of global capitalism in all of health sciences' spheres and the end result in terms of the contamination of every step of health inquiry, from the allocation of research funds to the publication of results.

In this spirit of resistance and using multiple *assemblages* (or noncoordinated associations) of all kinds, intellectuals must institute *espaces de liberté* (spaces of freedom) in which the formation of alliances would permit the development of new political arrangements capable of resisting truth regimes like those highlighted in this chapter. The privileged relation between the qualitative health inquirer and certain spheres of knowledge, often foreign to the general population, makes it possible to bring back to public spaces these knowledges that must be deconstructed and critiqued. This demanding, but important back and forth, between the world of the initiate and that of the profane, makes it possible for the specific intellectual to demonstrate how some political rationalities, associated with powerful disciplinary technologies, compete to legitimize dominant knowledges at the detriment of other disparaged and marginalized knowledges. In this way, the task of the specific intellectual is directly inscribed in what Foucault calls "*parrhesia*" (2001). Foucault defines *parrhesia* as:

[A] kind of verbal activity where the speaker has a specific relation to truth through frankness, a certain relationship to his own life through danger, a certain type of relation to himself or other people through criticism (self-criticism or criticism of other people), and a specific relation to moral law through freedom and duty. More precisely, *parrhesia* is a verbal activity in which a speaker expresses his personal relationship to truth [...] because he recognizes truth-telling as a duty to improve or help other people (as well as himself). In *parrhesia*, the speaker uses his freedom and chooses frankness instead of persuasion, truth instead of falsehood or silence, the risk of death instead of life and security, criticism instead of flattery, and moral duty instead of self-interest and moral apathy. (2001, pp. 19–20)

This fearless speech, undoubtedly linked to an aesthetics of existence characterized by a constant concern over rights, ethics, and social justice, is the product of a *travail de déprise* (endeavors to get "unstuck") regarding mainstream health sciences and research. In an article entitled "Towards an Ethics of Authentic Practice," Murray et al. (2008) discuss the ways in which the self is constituted and how this determines the modes of its resistance, the avenues that are open to that self for dissent and criticism whereby that self will struggle to define new, more ethically just, modes of existence for itself and for others. Such thinking must be clearly distinguished from technological know-how, from the mindless implementation of (best practice) guidelines or the fulfillment of moral codes. Instead, as Murray and colleagues note, it entails an ethics of *authentic* risk—a risk that involves a meditation on human finitude (existential, ethical, intellectual). It is the risk of the self itself, when it dares to call itself into question, when it dares to speak its name, and when the very meaning of its existence is tied to that meaningful speech. This kind of speech does not blindly advocate the rejection of authority, but it questions the manifold of authority and power, despite the risks and dangers. We believe that scholars, as specific intellectuals, have this duty. Ethical speech is only possible when we are free to choose from a plurality of points of view, when speech and meaning are not foreclosed, as they are in methodological and epistemological fundamentalism.

Conclusion: On Deconstruction and the Creation of *Espaces de Liberté*

The poststructuralist program we propose for health inquiry is not only epistemological and methodological, but also theoretical, practical, pedagogical, and political. Is this a "positive program"? Yes. First, deconstruction and critique are necessary activities that allow for the creation of *espaces de liberté*—space for new possibilities. Viewed from this perspective, they serve a positive function. As there currently exists a "regime of truth" surrounding health research funding and inquiry, there exists a scientific and ethical obligation to deconstruct this regime. Given the privileged relation of knowledge to the intellectual mission, intellectuals are well located to "speak truth to power," to use Foucault's expression. They must open up critical debate and question those mechanisms that work to seduce health inquirers into complacency. Deconstruction is essential to bring to light the biomedicalizing, bioeconomic, and biocultural discourses at work in the health field, promoting a dangerous ideology that threatens to reproduce the justificatory rhetoric of human pharmaceutical testing in developing nations and of eugenic programs intended to "better man's lot," to offer two gruesome instances where human rights are so explicitly violated. Research *is* a political enterprise, and health inquirers must not recoil from this reality.

Of course, most would prefer not to hear resistant discourses because the latter tend to expose the very power relations that create the current situation and prop up those health inquirers with a vested interest in the status quo. However, we believe that one of the roles of the intellectual is to engage in *parrhesia* and help deterritorialize the vast field of health sciences. In neoliberal societies, such deterritorialization also entails struggles against "corporate epistemology" in health inquiry. Indeed, institutions of higher learning are currently being colonized by corporations involved in the production of knowledge and associated discourses of truth, deviance and normalization. The private ownership of knowledge is being made possible through the intellectual property regimes that are part of national laws (e.g., the Bayh-Dole

Act in the United States) and international trade agreements (e.g., GATT, APEC, CBI, AGOA). Companies such as Pfizer, Merck, Johnson & Johnson, Bristol-Myers Squibb, Wyeth, GlaxoSmithKline, AstraZeneca, Novartis, and Aventis have invested in a great number of universities and seriously impacted on knowledge creation and dissemination in the field of "health." In light of this, health inquirers must interrogate the production of hegemonic knowledge and ask a number of necessary political questions: Who decides what is health? Who controls health inquiry? Who establishes "truths" and in whose interest?

Second, our program is positive because it involves creation—the creation of breaking points to prise open the dominant bio- and health discourses and to work to imagine how things might be other than what they have become, no matter how "naturally" they present themselves, no matter how forcibly the so-called evidence speaks to us. It also involves the creation of a space of freedom within which a plurality of discourses and knowledges is encouraged. In this way, we hope to resist the Orwellian "Newspeak" that reigns in the health sciences and that works to impose a highly normative, uniform and rigidly circumscribed way of seeing, speaking, and thinking. Creation involves the provision of epistemological support for counterdiscourses, of an epistemological basis from which marginalized individuals (i.e., people, patients, health professionals, and qualitative health inquirers) can respond to the institutions of power and thus legitimize alternative evidence and expand their rights in the process. This aligns with Foucault's (2003) call for the promotion of *savoirs assujettis* or subjugated forms of knowledge. Paradoxically, an honest plurality of voices will open up a space of freedom for the radical singularity of individual and disparate knowledge. When we can witness the emergence of health discourses within which diversity takes center stage; when stories and histories of health and the everyday relations of power, domination, resistance, and struggle may circulate in *espaces de liberté*, then we can better unpack the play of power in health inquiry and guard against the project of biopolitical governance.

References

Angell, M. (2004). *The truth about the drug companies: How they deceive us and what to do about it.* New York: Random House.

Barry, A., Osborne, T., & Rose, N. S. (1996). *Foucault and political reason: Liberalism, neoliberalism, and rationalities of government.* Chicago: University of Chicago Press.

Blumsohn, A. (2006). Authorship, ghost-science, access to data and control of the pharmaceutical scientific literature: Who stands behind the word? *American Association for the Advancement of Science Professional Ethics Report, 19,* 3, 1–4.

Bonell C. (1999). Evidence-based nursing: A stereotyped view of quantitative and experimental research could work against professional autonomy and authority. *Journal of Advanced Nursing, 30,* 1, 18–23.

Buetow, S. (2007). Yes, to intellectual integrity, but without the Sartrean existentialist attitude: A commentary on Murray et al. (2007) "No exit? Intellectual integrity under the regime of 'evidence' and 'bestpractices.'" *Journal of Evaluation in Clinical Practice, 13,* 4, 526–528.

Bunton, R., & Petersen, A. R. (1997). *Foucault, health and medicine.* New York: Routledge.

Clarke, A. E., Shim, J. K., Mamo, L., Fosket, J. R., & Fishman, J. R. (2003). Biomedicalization: Technoscientific transformations of health, illness, and U.S. biomedicine. *American Sociological Review, 68,* 2, 161–194.

Cohen, A. M., Stavri, P. Z., & Hersh, W. R. (2004). A categorization and analysis of the criticisms of evidence-based medicine. *International Journal of Medical Informatics, 73,* 1, 35–43.

Couto, J. (2007) Where is Sancho? A commentary on Murray et al. (2007) "No exit? Intellectual integrity under the regime of 'evidence' and 'bestpractices.'" *Journal of Evaluation in Clinical Practice, 13,* 4, 522–523.

Crawford, R. (1980). Healthism and the medicalization of everyday life. *International Journal of Health Services, 10,* 3, 365–388.

Deleuze, G., & Guattari, F. (1977). *Anti-Oedipus: Capitalism and schizophrenia* (R. Hurley, M. Seem, and H. R. Lane, Trans.). New York: Viking Press.

Denzin, N. K., Lincoln, Y. S., & Giardina, M. D. (2006). Disciplining qualitative research. *International Journal of Qualitative Studies in Education, 19,* 6, 769–782.

Eribon, D. (2003). *Hérésies.* Paris: Fayard.

Foucault, M. (1977 [1975]). *Discipline and punish: The birth of the prison* (A. Sheridan, Trans.). New York: Pantheon Books.

Foucault, M. (1980). Truth and power. In C. Gordon (Ed.), *Power/knowledge: Selected interviews and other writings, 1972–1977* (pp. 126–127). New York: Pantheon.

Foucault, M. (1997). The birth of biopolitics. In P. Rabinow (Ed.), *Michel Foucault: Ethics, subjectivity, truth* (pp. 73–80). New York: New Press.

Foucault, M. (2001). *Fearless speech* (J. Pearson, Ed.). Los Angeles: Semiotext(e).

Foucault, M. (2003). *Society must be defended: Lectures at the Collège de France, 1975–1976.* New York: Picador.

Foucault, M. (2004). *Naissance de la biopolitique: Cours au Collège de France, 1978–1979.* Paris: Gallimard/Seuil.

French, P. (2002). What is the evidence on evidence-based nursing? An epistemological concern. *Journal of Advanced Nursing, 37,* 3, 250–257.

Freshwater, D., & Rolfe, G. (2004). *Deconstructing evidence-based practice.* London: Routledge.

Fugh-Berman, A. (2005). The corporate coauthor. *Journal of General Internal Medicine, 20,* 6, 546–548.

Giroux, H. A. (2007). *The university in chains: Confronting the military-industrial-academic complex.* Boulder, CO: Paradigm Publishers.

Goldacre, B. (2006a). Objectionable "objectives." *The Guardian,* August 19, p. 8. http://www.guardian.co.uk/science/2006/aug/19/badscience.uknews (accessed February 7, 2010).

Goldacre, B. (2006b). Archie Cochrane: "Fascist." http://www.badscience. net/2006/08/archie-cochrane-fascist/ (accessed February 7, 2010).

Goldacre, B. (2009). The danger of drugs ... and data. *The Guardian,* May 9, p. 10. http://www.guardian.co.uk/commentisfree/2009/may/09/bad-science-medical-journals-companies (accessed February 7, 2010).

Goldenberg, M. J. (2006). On evidence and evidence-based medicine: Lessons from the philosophy of science. *Social Science and Medicine, 62,* 11, 2621–2632.

Gøtzsche, P. C., Hróbjartsson, A., Johansen, H. K., Haahr, M. T., Altman, D. G., & Chan, A. (2007). Ghost authorship in industry-initiated randomised trials. *PLoS Medicine, 4,* 1, 19.

Grant, B. (2009). Merck published fake journal. *TheScientist.com.* http://www. the-scientist.com/templates/trackable/display/blog.jsp?type=blog&o_ url=blog/display/55671&id=55671 (accessed September 28, 2009).

Holmes, D., Murray, S. J., Perron, A., & Rail, G. (2006). Deconstructing the evidence-based discourse in health sciences: Truth, power, and fascism. *International Journal of Evidence-Based Healthcare, 4,* 3, 180–186.

Holmes, D., Perron, A, & O'Byrne, P. (2006). Necrospective: Evidence, virulence, and the disappearance of nursing knowledge. *Worldviews on Evidence-Based Nursing, 3*, 1, 95–102.

Jefferson, T. (2006). How to grab a headline: Lots of smoke and little meat (Response to Holmes et al.). Letter to the Editor. *International Journal of Evidence-Based Healthcare, 4*, 4, 392–393.

Kassirer, J. P. (2005). *On the take: How medicine's complicity with big business can endanger your health.* Oxford: Oxford University Press.

Koch, A. M. (2007). *Poststructuralism and the politics of method.* New York: Lexington Books.

Larkin, M. (1999). Whose article is it anyway? *The Lancet, 354*, 9189, 136.

Lexchin, J., Bero, L. A., Djulbegovic, B., & Clark, O. (2003). Pharmaceutical industry sponsorship and research outcome and quality: Systematic review. *British Medical Journal, 326*, May, 1167–1170.

Miettinen, O. S., & Miettinen, K. S. (2007). A commentary on Murray et al. (2007) "No exit? Intellectual integrity under the regime of 'evidence' and 'best-practices.'" *Journal of Evaluation in Clinical Practice, 13*, 4, 524–525.

Miller, P., & Rose, N. (2008). *Governing the present: Administering economic, social and personal life.* Cambridge: Polity Press.

Moffatt, B., & Elliott, C. (2007). Ghost marketing: Pharmaceutical companies and ghostwritten journal articles. *Perspectives in Biology and Medicine, 50*, 1, 18–31.

Mowatt, G., Shirran, L., Grimshaw, J. M., Rennie, D., Flanagin, A., Yank, V., MacLennan, G., Gøtzsche, P., & Bero, L. A. (2002). Prevalence of honorary and ghost authorship in Cochrane Reviews. *Journal of the American Medical Association, 287*, 21, 2769–2771.

Murray, S. J. (2009). The perils of scientific obedience: Bioethics under the spectre of biofascism. In S. J. Murray and D. Holmes (Eds.), *Critical interventions in the ethics of healthcare: Challenging the principle of autonomy in bioethics* (pp. 97–113). Burlington, VT: Ashgate.

Murray, S. J., Holmes, D., Perron, A., & Rail, G. (2007). No exit? Intellectual integrity under the regime of "evidence" and "best-practices." *Journal of Evaluation in Clinical Practice, 13*, 4, 512–516.

Murray, S. J., Holmes, D., Perron, A., & Rail, G. (2008). Toward an ethics of authentic practice. *Journal of Evaluation in Clinical Practice, 14*, 5, 682–689.

Murray, S. J., Holmes, D., & Rail, G. (2008). On the constitution and status of "evidence" in the health sciences. *Journal of Research in Nursing, 13*, 4, 272–280.

Ngai, S., Gold, J. L., Gill, S. S., & Rochon, P. A. (2005). Haunted manuscripts: Ghost authorship in the medical literature. *Accountability in Research, 12*, 3, 103–114.

Novas, C., & Rose, N.S. (2000). Genetic risk and the birth of the somatic individual. *Economy and Society, 29*, 4, 485–513.

Papadimos, T. J., & Murray, S. J. (2008). Foucault's "fearless speech" and the transformation and mentoring of medical students. *Philosophy, Ethics & Humanities in Medicine, 3*, 12. http://www.peh-med.com/content/3/1/12 (accessed February 7, 2010).

Proctor, R. (2000). Nazi science and Nazi medical ethics: Some myths and misconceptions. *Perspectives in Biology and Medicine, 43*, 3, 335–346.

Rail, G. (2009a). Canadian youth's discursive constructions of health in the context of obesity discourse. In J. Wright and V. Harwood (Eds.), *Biopolitics and the "obesity epidemic": Governing bodies* (pp. 141–156). London: Routledge.

Rail, G. (2009b). Psychose en matière de santé et colonisation du corps féminin. In S. Yaya (Ed.), *Pouvoir médical et santé totalitaire: Conséquences socio-anthropologiques et éthiques* (pp. 251–266). Québec: Presses de l'Université Laval.

Rail, G., & Lafrance, M. (2009). Confessions of the flesh and biopedagogies: Discursive constructions of obesity on Nip/Tuck. *Medical Humanities, 35*, 2, 76–79.

Rose, N. (1999). *Powers of freedom: Reframing political thought*. Cambridge: Cambridge University Press.

Rose, N. (2006). *The politics of life itself: Biomedicine, power, and subjectivity in the twenty-first century*. Princeton, NJ: Princeton University Press.

Rout, M. (2009). Doctors signed Merck's Vioxx studies. *The Australian*. http://www.theaustralian.news.com.au/story/0,25197,25311725-5013871,00.html (accessed September 28, 2009).

Sackett D. (2000). *Evidence-based medicine: How to practice and teach EBM*. New York: Churchill Livingstone.

Savio, M. (1964). Untitled speech. Berkeley, CA. http://www.fsm-a.org/stacks/mario/mario_speech.html (accessed February 7, 2010).

Shapin, S. (1984). Pump and circumstance: Robert Boyle's literary technology. *Social Studies of Science, 14*, 4, 481–520.

Shapin, S., & Shaffer, S. (1989). *Leviathan and the air-pump*. Princeton, NJ: Princeton University Press.

Sismondo, S. (2007). Ghost management: How much of the medical literature is shaped behind the scenes by the pharmaceutical industry? *PLoS Medicine, 4*, 9, 286.

Skrabanek, P. (1994). *The death of humane medicine and the rise of coercive healthism*. London: The Social Affairs Unit.

Smith, R. (2006). *The trouble with medical journals*. London: Royal Society of Medicine Press.

Staller, K. M. (2006). Railroads, runaways and researchers: Returning evidence rhetoric to its practice base. *Qualitative Inquiry, 12*, 3, 503–522.

Sunder Rajan, K. (2006). *Biocapital: The constitution of postgenomic life*. Durham, NC: Duke University Press.

Traynor, M. (2002). The oil crisis, risk and evidence-based practice. *Nursing Inquiry, 9*, 3, 162–169.

University of Toronto. (2010). Statement of institutional purpose. http://www.governingcouncil.utoronto.ca/policies/mission.htm#_Toc190598501 (accessed January 18, 2010).

Waldby, C. (2006). Umbilical cord blood: From social gift to venture capital. *BioSocieties, 1*, 1, 55–70.

Walker, K. (2003). Why evidence-based practice now?: A polemic. *Nursing Inquiry, 10*, 3, 145–155.

Winch, S., Creedy, D., & Chaboyer, W. (2002). Governing nursing conduct: The rise of evidence-based practice. *Nursing Inquiry, 9*, 3, 156–161.

Coda

Meaningful Research, Aging, and Positive Transformation

Carolyn Ellis

Laurel Richardson

Mary Gergen

Kenneth Gergen

Norman K. Denzin

Arthur P. Bochner

Telling Moments in an Autoethnographer's Life

Carolyn Ellis

This session seemed so easy when I first thought it up. I'd tell a story about a moment when I felt my research was meaningful. What's so hard about that? But when I sat down to actually do this, I couldn't decide on which moment to choose. Instead I began thinking about the trajectory of my career and the many meaningful moments that had transpired. To start, there was that day, July 14, 1984, at age 34, when I picked up a pen and wrote my first word of autoethnography. I wrote about the pain I felt for my dying partner who was having a particularly bad day. That acute pain was coupled with the long-term pain of losing my brother 2 years before in an airplane crash, a loss I could not cope with and certainly could not get over, a loss I felt every day. That pain was coupled with finding out the day before that I needed knee surgery, signaling for the first time that my body was mortal and that I, too, would deteriorate and die. My life felt like clashing cymbals. The notes I wrote provided the only possibility of muffling the clamor. I have continued doing autoethnography since that day—writing notes, telling my own stories, encouraging others to tell theirs reflexively, listening closely to peoples' tales of pain, loss, and renewal, and writing about how we might do this well and ethically.

At first, because of the critiques I received, I worried about whether my work would be seen as sociology. I soon came to concentrate on whether what I did was sociologically interesting. Then I questioned whether what I was doing was research. I soon came to care only that what I did was meaningful to me, my students, and my readers. Later, I wondered if what I was doing was just therapy. I soon came to believe that everything I wrote should be therapeutically useful, capable of helping and changing people, providing companionship and healing. I worried that my stories were seen as being only about me. I soon came to understand that the self and other are intertwined and that you can't know one without the other. I worried whether what I wrote was representative. I soon came to care more about whether what I wrote evoked recognition, stories, and responses from others. Did it stimulate us to keep talking? Later, I worried that my work did not address social injustice and social change. I soon came to believe that social change involves emotionality and can occur one person at a time, as one thing leads to another. Finally, I would be concerned that what I wrote would be seen as fixed, as choking out the movement of stories and interpretation. I would soon come to write revised and revisioned stories that called forth other stories and showed the self and stories in motion, refusing to be finalized.

More concrete moments now come into focus. Staring at the TV hoping to see my brother among the survivors floundering in the icy Potomac River; breathing with my partner Gene as he gasps his last breath; hearing my sister-in-law say into the phone, "Your father has died." "Are you sure?" I ask. Reading Norman Denzin's review of my article on introspection and being unable to read beyond the word schizophrenic that he uses to describe what I am proposing. Noticing Art for the first time, his brash questions intriguing me; taking in Art's critique about my defensiveness: "Let the story do its work," he says.

Then, our first kiss, ahhh my lips barely touch his cheek. We are standing in front of my house at his car. We have just had a "business" meeting. Then later his holding me as I cry because a sociologist who had read *Final Negotiations* (1995) claims I took Gene's death from his children. I realize then for the first time how risky autoethnography can be. Through it all, hearing Laurel's encouragement—and Art's—to submit "There Are Survivors" (1993) to a journal; getting the letter, Norman again, saying that "Survivors" is accepted for publication; celebrating with unbridled joy; thinking I can write anything about anything; then euthanizing three of our dogs in nine months and not being able to write about the pain, so deep and present. "You can write anything you want," says my mother, "anything," and with that I feel I have her permission to write about my relationship with her, her illness, but not her death, not then anyway. And all along the way, writing, writing, whenever I can, whenever it seems right, sharing stories, hearing others, comparing, feeling companionship, giving companionship, writing to care, love, be with, change the community of qualitative methods, academia, the larger world even. Then turning to ethics as relational; how to think that way, yet not deny injustice; to write of racism even when it might hurt those I write about; because it is the right thing to do and that is what matters more. To reenvisioning the stories I have told, after listening to readers, critics, some of them anyway. And now to write the stories of others' lives—Holocaust survivors—I hope with the same empathy and compassion with which I have written my own stories, knowing that my stories are entangled in theirs—*and need to be*—in order to have hope that future generations will not forget those who suffered and died, and so that we/I will not stand back while another Holocaust takes place.

As I grow older, I long to spend more time looking out over the mountains, returning to where I came from, and I do, feeling spiritually connected with those I love and the work that inspires me to go on, writing, caring, hoping to revision and transform myself first and positively impact others and the world I live in. "Is what I do research?" I ask myself. "Sociology? Representative? Apolitical? Egotistical? Just therapy?"

"What absolutely meaningless, useless, irrelevant questions," the impatient yet happy woman shouts out from the covered porch wrapping around their mountain cabin and then listens to the echoes reverberating from the wooded hillsides. She cups her ear and thinks she hears the clouds, sun, sky, and mountains holding a discussion.

"The meaning is in the experience, the experience, the experience," the mountain groans.

"There's nothing quite like walking through the woods."

"No, the meaning is the story," says the cloud, its billowing wisps of white sounding out the words. "Without a story to tell, what is the meaning of hearing a thunder clap, for example?"

"No, no, the meaning comes in writing the story about the experience," says the sun, dancing across the horizon. "It's the process, the revision that is important. I should know. I reinvent myself anew every morning."

"You're all right," says the big blue sky. "Don't you know, we're all in this together?"

The aging woman smiles at the chatter, takes a sip of her favorite New Zealand Sauvignon Blanc, and lets it roll sensually around her mouth. What a wonderful luxury to have the time to think these thoughts and the opportunity to do this work. She grabs her pen and writes this sentence as she speaks it out loud, "Writing the story is part of the experience of living the story time and time again."

"What did you say?" asks her partner Art, who is in the kitchen cooking.

"Carry onnnnnnnn," the sky, cloud, sun, and mountain respond in harmony.

And she does.[1]

Stories of Aging, Age, and Positive Transformation

Mary Gergen

1965: Finding the Magic

My career in social psychology began as a research assistant in the Department of Social Relations at Harvard University. Without realizing what I was getting into, I landed in the heart of experimental social psychology. In my first months I learned to use a Monroe calculator to do analyses of variance. Each day I strove to come up with an F ratio that would reach the magical level of .05. Finding basic laws of human behavior was the goal of the game. In the summer of 1966, I was sent up to a top floor of William James Hall to learn to use Data Text, one of the first word-based computer programs for data analysis. This was indeed an amazing program; data that were once scrawling script and scores on forms were instantly transformed without effort or error. Later, across the river at the Business School, I analyzed data from a marketing survey for Professor Raymond Bauer. I was branching out, and my skills as part of an analytic team were admired. This was the wave of the future, and I was onboard.

1974: Conformity and Curiosity— Graduate School Style

Having moved to Philadelphia, I joined the Ph.D. program in psychology at Temple University, where I took the four required statistics courses, from simple chi-squares to multivariate analysis. I also worked as a TA in statistics and methods courses, did research with several professors, and worked at the survey research center. It was more of the same in terms of the empirical traditions, but I do admit to experiencing a thrill at making a code book that organized how all the variables could be found in a large study. I recognized an unfamiliar streak of compulsivity I didn't know I had. It was a sweet feeling, akin to balancing a checkbook.

Along the way, I took a seminar in the History & Systems of Psychology with Willis Overton and audited one in the Philosophy of the Behavioral Sciences, led by Joseph Margolis. In both of these courses, aspects of empirical psychology were strongly contested. I must credit my friend and fellow traveler, Walter Paynter, a grad student in the rat lab, of all places, for leading me astray and highlighting the disconnect between my life in Weiss Hall as a social psychology student and as a kibitzer in the philosophy of science. The threads of experimental social psychology were slowly being unraveled, and I was left holding the yarn.

My dissertation, based on the "hit" of the day, attribution theory, had a focus on older people's explanations for why they stopped engaging in a variety of activities. The choice of this subject population was suggested by my desire to find a sample in decline. From my perspective, old people were inevitably going downhill, and so much the better for my research. The question I was exploring was on the relationship of types of attributions to wellbeing. My dissertation was built on a theme of negativity. My plan was to interview a group of about forty people between the ages of 63 and 93, living in private homes and retirement communities, about why they had given up various activities—church, romance, hobbies, jobs, and physical activities, including sports.

The data were rich and nuanced, filled with many sad stories of depression, disease, and disability. My questions led them on. They were designed to reveal shortcomings and losses. I coded these complex stories of living into a 2 x 2 matrix (internal vs. external and voluntary vs. involuntary attribution cells). "I am too old" was an answer coded as internal-involuntary, the worst response one might give. That is, the reason one gave up some activity was internal to oneself and could not be helped. Other information, squeezed into the scales I gave, had to do with well-being, life satisfaction, and health. Not surprisingly, involuntary-internal attributions led to feelings of less happiness, less satisfaction with life, and fewer healthy self-reports. To make my professors really take note, I managed to find the right program and fed the computer with enough variables to produce elegant-looking path analyses, which seemed to suggest a route for downward life experiences for some and upward ones for others. I never exactly understood the data crunching that took place within the vast computer that would generate such sophisticated-looking outcomes, but I did get pleasure out of discovering that my hunches about attributions worked out.

That said, my greatest source of pleasure was spending time with some of the participants I met along the way. Listening to their stories, having conversations with them, and visiting them at home were exhilarating experiences, although I knew that the interviews were not ends in themselves, but just the beginning of data production. A horrible metaphor keeps coming to mind: It was something like enjoying the lambs on their way to market, but knowing it was the lamb chops I was really after. Despite these sensitivities, I earned my Ph.D. Looking back later, I could reframe this research as social constructionist discourse analysis, but that's jumping ahead of my story. I was beginning to see how I might transform myself beyond the limits of the "slaughter house," but that outcome was still in the future.

1980: Living with the Rebels

Social constructionist ideas were fomenting in my house. I remember dinner parties where people, including John Shotter and Rom Harré, from England, and Erving Goffman, from Penn, had spoken of plotting revolution. (I must admit I secretly laughed at their "rebel" proclamations, although they were deadly serious in many respects. I also was a bit nervous whenever the rhetoric was too strident, mostly because I was reluctant to give up my personal ties to some of the luminaries in the opposite camp and I was always hoping for a bloodless transformation.) Ken [Gergen] had drummed himself out of favor of the Society for Experimental Psychology with his revolutionary articles, which helped to bring on the "crisis in social psychology." (Naturally, it was later declared "over" by those within the ranks.)

For me, feminist theory also was brewing. (Although I had been a practicing feminist since high school when I worked as a carhop at Bud's Big Boy Drive-in and chafed under the domination of the sexist boss, my new feminism was a more sophisticated version of the same impulse, derived from reading women's studies texts.) Here, at the crossroads of these two related areas, I was forming a new identity. This newly minted self felt both exciting and challenging. I was going to discover what this new combination of highly contentious and often uncongenial wavelengths might bode for me. The postmodern turn, as understood by American feminists, was primarily populated by French feminists, who often declared they were not feminists, not psychologists, and not allied with one another. (In fact, one Parisian faction burned down the offices of another, they were so alienated from one another.) I was on fire, but pyrotechnics was not then my style.

1984: My Almost Brilliant Career

Fortunately, I did not have a professional commitment that prevented me from exploring new ways of doing psychology. In 1984, I began working at Penn State University, Brandywine, a campus near my home in suburban Philadelphia. My chief commitments were to teach and also to do research (not to mention service). The obligations were high, but the freedom from departmental standards was helpful. Far from my colleagues at University Park, I could explore and write as I chose. It was invigorating to see that I might define myself uniquely and make a difference within the psychology of gender as a social constructionist. I had certain advantages in pursuing this risky path. I did not have to get grants, support graduate students in empirical research, or publish or perish. Thus, my way was open to some rather outlandish explorations.

In 1986, I organized a conference at my campus called "Feminist Thought and the Structure of Knowledge." I invited well-known feminist scholars from a variety of disciplines—religion, anthropology, social sciences, and biology—to speak and write on the influence of feminist thinking on their disciplines. When it was concluded, I edited a book of the same name, and included a chapter of my own that spelled out a new research orientation, one that was critical of standard notions of scientific rigor and that laid out a feminist-inspired set of alternatives (Gergen, 1988). The emphases included valuing the relationship between the researcher and the researched, recognizing the value investments inherent in the research process, and acknowledging the embeddedness of the participants in their relational networks. I rejected objectivity, value-neutrality, and the autonomous individual. I was definitely on the path toward losing my respectability within the Society for Experimental Social Psychology, but, more significantly, on my way to developing a viable feminist postmodernism in psychology.

I decided that if I was really committed to my quest for an alternative feminist psychology, I had to engage in the role I envisioned for such research. How was I going to instantiate the equality, mutuality, and value-laden feminist/constructionist research I desired? To satisfy these purposes, I designed a simple study. To ensure equality, I invited friends from my tennis club to my house for lunch, after which I engaged them in a conversation on the topic of menopause. Again, harkening back to the issue of aging, my research goal was to challenge the medical model of menopause that insisted that we were all entering a "disease" phase of life and to suggest that menopause was a normal, and even positive, phase of life. Also, I must confess that in a moment of self-doubt, I included some preformulated questionnaires and prepost evaluations of the event.

The manner in which I wrote up the piece, as a book chapter (Gergen, 1989), took me back out on the ledge again. As I began my analysis, I experienced a great deal of freedom. The story I created was a wonderfully complex yet coherent report of the dramatic form the action had taken. I even could admit that the event took twists and turns I never could have predicted. The discourse analysis was thematic and revealing of the various speakers, but it remained, after all, my interpretation. I was the singular voice of authority, and there was no challenge to my version of the event. To contend with this, I invented a coauthor, a character whose voice was that of the critic. Its role was to reduce my authorial power by questioning my interpretations, cajoling me to reveal my efforts at persuasion, and making other comments about the text. I fell eagerly into conversation with my adversarial self and had an intriguing time writing up our conversations. Sometimes our interactions had the feeling of a séance as I entered a dream-space with my alter. What lavish fun this was, and how much this dual authoring junket felt PC: Philosophically Correct.

1988

Ken and I were selected as Fellows at the Netherlands Institute for Advanced Study in Wassenaar. Designed after the Center for Advanced Study at Stanford University, but closer to the beach (with lunchtime volleyball), I finally had a room of my own, furnished with original oils, carpets, and contemporary furniture. My room was all Virginia Woolf asked for (including a stipend) and more (a free lunch and stimulating colleagues). When I had a project to do, nothing interfered with my doing it. One diversion that jump-started my career as a performance social scientist involved writing a playlet in a feminist postmodern style. It came into being in response to a paper by a postmodern sociologist, Steven Tyler, which I thought was utterly and annoyingly macho, despite its brilliance. Later, Ken and I were invited to a postmodern conference in Denmark, hosted by Steinar Kvale, and I decided to do a performance of my paper there. Ken was quite worried about what I was daring to do. I was less so, partly because I didn't understand the gravity of the occasion and the antipathy that many speakers had to postmodern ideas, and also because I thought what I had done was really quite good! I would act "the critic" of Tyler's postmodernism in my performance, but appear feminine at the same time. To this end, I wore a red boa 10 feet long, with black, slim trousers and a turtleneck, along with high heels, earrings, and makeup. The performance seemed to go well, and afterward many women in the audience came up to compliment me. (I was the only woman on the program, and I felt they were supporting my presence, if nothing else.)

Later, my piece almost didn't get published, but in the end it did (mostly thanks to Ken's intervention; see Gergen, 1990). After that, it was even appreciated by those who were at first quite skeptical. It was the only postmodern piece in the entire conference on postmodernism. I felt vindicated in my approach and that

I had created something that truly did stand in the crossroads of feminism and social constructionism. My dreams of this identity seemed realized.

1995 and Beyond:
Carrying On—Striptease and "If You Please"

Once I started performance work, I didn't want to stop. Being able to combine youthful interests in acting, creative writing, and psychology over the past 20 years has been totally alluring. There is even justification for doing performance work in terms of social constructionism. We ask: Who has the right to make the rules for how one does research, writing, or presenting? Aren't they established by people in disciplinary enclaves, and thus not foundational or forever. There are many forms of rhetoric that can fashion our realities. We are not so constrained as we may have believed. In these many endeavors, Ken has been a partner in crime with me, and we have now expanded our range of performances from philosophy and psychological theorizing to therapy and communication (Gergen & Gergen, 2001).

For many years now, I have been doing performance work with an emphasis on aging. I return to this topic, but now with a special, personal investment. I am no longer the young researcher looking for old people to study. I am an oldie myself. I have a special investment in wanting to change the way the world and its aging population (and everyone counts on that score) think about this stage of life. I want us all to appreciate the joys of growing older. For me, it is a bittersweet time, in a sense, because life becomes so precious and intriguing, so full of promise, but also, I come to realize with more intensity, so finite. In my repertoire of performance pieces, my favorite is a strip tease (modified greatly since I discovered that it is not easy to remove pantyhose without losing one's dignity) in which I challenge the stereotype associated with older women, that they are meant to disappear (Gergen, 2001). Far from disappearing, I have discovered that the aging process has been one of continuous appearing—that is, of growing and developing in unexpected ways. Sometimes I even feel embarrassed at how old I am to still be learning so much and feel I must redouble my efforts to master the world I've been in so long.

I also have become involved in promoting other forms of qualitative methods within psychology. So many wonderful possibilities, and yet these approaches have been shunned by many psychologists, including those from my home base, the Society for the Psychology of Women. The promises and predictions of an empirical psychology have not paid off as expected according to the dreams of the natural sciences, and the seduction of qualitative approaches beckons one and all. They offer the possibility of freedom of expression, of creating new paradigms, of promoting social values, of encouraging collaboration, and of maintaining the integrity of people who are studied.

Then, too, it seems that everyone is getting older and wiser and less willing to jump through hoops set up by the disciplinary gatekeepers, who are themselves tiring of keeping so many gay spirits outside. I am growing in confidence that a "new look" in psychology is forthcoming, and I hope to be there to celebrate as one of the rebels, after all.

The Polyphonic Passions of a Scholarly Profession

Kenneth Gergen

How much I have cherished this lifetime immersion in the world of scholarship. It has been nothing less than an adventure in co-creating life with others. To be sure, there have been frustrations and failures. In the absence of such events there would be no adventure. In the present offering, I wish to recount some significant chapters in this unfolding narrative, but with a particular focus on the varied sources of professional passion. My life as a scholar has offered many rewards, but the joys of one phase of life are not always suited or desirable in another.

Awakening Fires: Some from Hell

In my days of youthful enthusiasm, the prospect of probing the mind was an intoxicating elixir. It was not only the thrill of discovery that drew me to the field of psychology, but the opportunity to make a significant contribution to human well-being. After all, were the causes of aggression, oppression, altruism, moral responsibility, and other crucial ingredients of well-being not to be found in the mental make-up of individual actors? And, did the tools of empirical science not offer the best available means for securing knowledge of the largely uncharted territory of the inner world? Undergraduate life at Yale pointed me to the path, and after 2 years of required service as a naval officer, I was "raring to go." And, with a wife and an infant daughter in my life, it was imperative to move quickly and effectively forward to a career.

The Department of Psychology at Duke University offered me the perfect venue for moving forward: a highly visible and productive mentor, an enthusiastic faculty, financial support, and laboratory facilities at my disposal. And so, with my professors and fellow students, the research machine cranked into overdrive. We "ran subjects" by the hundreds and generated tomes of data, statistical tables, and multiple manuscripts. There was enormous joy in finding myself now a fully engaged and highly productive young scientist. And were we not simultaneously laying foundational stones in the edifice of human knowledge?

But there were also subtler and less admirable enjoyments beginning to emerge. I was becoming increasingly aware that there was a certain game-like quality to generating publishable manuscripts. More points were acquired by creating statistical interactions than main effects, validating ironic as opposed to more obvious hypotheses, establishing make-believe conditions that tricked subjects into believing they were real, massaging statistics until the .05 level of significance was achieved, and so on. The game was also welded to the professional hierarchy, and winning meant situating one's ideas and findings in such a way that they approached the top of the pyramid. Slowly, I began to find that winning the game became more important than the content and social contribution of the research. I sensed a slow decay in my enthusiasm. Yet, the sum total of my energetic pursuits was the reward of my first teaching position at Harvard University. I was a player!

Consciousness Expanding: The Pleasure and the Pain

I had the great fortune at Harvard of teaching in the Department of Social Relations. The department had been formed as a grand attempt to cross-fertilize and synthesize thinking in psychology, sociology, and social anthropology. I thus found myself in collegial relations with mythic figures such as Talcott Parsons, David Riessman, and Erik Erikson, along with a host of younger and very talented professionals. I did take a certain pride in my background as an experimental social psychologist. I could defend very well the virtues of rigor, precision, experimentation, and sophisticated statistical analysis. But the doors were now open to an enormously rich landscape of thought, and the delight of traveling the terrain was consuming.

Yet as the dialogs developed across the spheres, and friendships blossomed, I was also finding my experimental training increasingly confining. It was as if the thinking of the field I represented seldom ventured beyond the doors of the laboratory enclosure. What the laboratory walls were shutting out as "extraneous variables" essentially constituted the social world at large. There was virtually nothing to be said in my discipline about politics, social policy, cultural dynamics, social movements, moral deliberation, poverty, religion, ethnic traditions, or societal transformations in value—for starters. Thus, with the new intellectual riches as supports, I began to tread a path of critical self-reflection. I began to see that social psychological research was largely reflecting culturally contingent patterns of behavior, and not the timeless verities that were promised. Further, because theory and methods were saturated with value, research could actually bring about changes in social patterns. The sciences were not standing outside culture—as if studying a distant object—but were active participants in shaping cultural life. Subsequently, I published my critical reflections in the flagship journal of the discipline (Gergen, 1973). I could not have imagined the intensity of my peer's irritation. Therein began my progressive banishment from the field.

Revolution and Righteousness

Swarthmore College provided a wonderful new home. It had also been so to other disciplinary "outsiders," at one time serving as the center of psychology's Gestalt resistance to the then dominant behaviorism. More importantly, it was a rich intellectual environment, offering the scholar opportunities for moving across all departmental boundaries, with no over-arching demands that one should remain true to any discipline. It was also a season for revolution. There was not only the massive resistance to the Vietnam War, but the compelling movements of African Americans, feminists, and the gay community—among others—for social justice. This generalized resistance to traditional authority was also reflected in widespread intellectual critique of Western modernism and the empiricist view of science that it had spawned. It was now "life at the barricades," that heady feeling of putting our identities on the line for a higher cause. There was no doubting the value of the changes we were seeking, and just possibly we might succeed.

It was this sense of valued mission that fired my explorations into an alternative to empiricist science. Sewing together strands of critical theory, literary and rhetorical theory, and developments in the history and sociology of science, the contours of a social constructionist alternative began to take shape. Could we not see scientific truths as byproducts of culturally and historically situated communities, communities in which moral and political values colored theory, methods, and results? And could we not assay the outcomes of these communal efforts in terms of their pragmatic and political value across the spectrum of society, and indeed across the global spectrum of cultures? What might knowledge making become if we understood it as a process of social construction?[2] Such questions established an exciting agenda for exploration.

Liberation and the Lightness of Being

One of the most wondrous outcomes of a social constructionist view of life is that there are no "musts," no necessary authorities, no bodies of truth or reason, no traditions of value, and so on, to which we must necessarily adhere. In effect, one discovers an enormous sense of liberation. This is not, however, a liberation without responsibility. For one also realizes that there is no move into the future that does not draw from resources provided by preceding communities of meaning. And, too, there is no move into the future that does not depend on collaboration among persons. At the outset, the fuel of freedom largely fed the flames of deconstruction. I, along with colleagues from across the disciplines, critically probed the constructed character of one taken for granted reality after another. Perhaps this movement was essential to secure the newfound freedom. But much like the French Revolution, spilling the blood of the tyrannical could not nourish the flowering of an alternative way of being. As Mary Gergen admonished, it is high time for me to replace the struggle with the past with the exploration of promising potentials for the future.

The subsequent years were a sumptuous feast of innovation. There were first explorations with Mary into the narrative basis of self-construction and into replacing the individualism implied in the writing of autobiography with a relation-centered "duography." There was also the adventure of writing my first book for a more general audience. This work, *The Saturated Self* (Gergen, 1991), allowed me to think freely about the transformation in social life invited by the emerging technologies of communication. This work, in turn, opened up a new range of relations with scholars and practitioners in therapy, organizational change, education, communication, and more. There was an open invitation, as well, to explore the potentials of the full range of nontraditional research practices. Discourse study, collaborative inquiry, action research, and performance-based inquiry were especially enticing. In an attempt to reconstruct the vision of aging, Mary and I developed the *Positive Aging Newsletter*, an electronically distributed newsletter that now goes to thousands of recipients in five languages. And, with colleagues from both the academic and practical world, we formed The Taos Institute. Here we launched exploration into the outcomes of bringing together social constructionist theory with collaborative practices in the culture at large. It was firecracker time!

Reveling in Relational Being

There are joys—more and less admirable—in dedicated research, professional competition, expanding consciousness, righteous revolution, and scatter-shot creativity. However, there is a more serene pleasure that has entered my life in recent years. It is not one to which I ever aspired. Indeed, in my early professional years I could neither imagine nor indulge in it. Resonant with the title of a book I recently published, I shall call it the joy of *relational being* (Gergen, 2009a). In my early career, I embraced the individualist tradition, with its compelling vision of individual heroism and the attendant thrill of competition. However, with the development of social constructionist theory, both the conceptual and ideological flaws in this tradition became increasingly clear. Slowly, I began to see how all my professional efforts were not "my doing," but the outcome of relational processes in which I was embedded—with colleagues, friends, family, textual companions, and indeed the technical and natural environment in which I existed. My writings, research, and performances increasingly explored the potentials—both conceptual and practical—of relational process as the source of all meaning and value. And as this work took shape, so was there a sea change in the quality of my relations. Increasingly, the source of my joy was to be found in the quality of the relational activities in which I was engaged. Rather than finding myself in an ocean in which I was desperately trying to swim in a single direction, I could float with limbs outstretched and move more harmoniously with the shifting currents of relationship. For a one-time existentialist, this was unexpected bliss.

Outsider

Laurel Richardson

Everything Has Changed and Everything Has Stayed the Same

I read a novel this year called *Still Alice* (Genova, 2007). The narrator is a professor of neural-linguistics who is herself developing Alzheimer's. No matter what she loses—her sense of direction, her nouns, her citations, her children's names—she experiences herself as STILL Alice. There is still something inside her that she recognizes as her signature—maybe her soul, her self, her center.

As I age, I realize that—although thankfully I do not have dementia—I have become more interested in knowing about that which makes me "me"—what makes me Laurel and not Laurie or Lauren—or anyone else.

No matter the changes, I am essentially who I am and have been and will be.

ooooo

I grew up on the margins of communities—half Jewish, half gentile—fully accepted into neither category; half a child of my father's English-Irish forbearers, settled in Virginia circa 1770, making him a Son of the American Revolution; half a child of my mother's family, herself a Russian immigrant to America, making me a first-generation American. I'm half from a family of privilege and half from one of hardships.

Because of my marginality, I have always felt like an outsider. My academic work has reflected this. Like my father, I wanted to do something good for those less fortunate than I; like my mother, I wanted to escape the lot that had been given me. From both my parents, I learned that I wanted whatever I did to be meaningful. This meant that I would have to step over my marginality—the margins of academia, too—and be out front as a *conscious* outsider. I hoped that I would not do it alone; I hoped to find a way of belonging that had eluded me during my childhood.

Reviewing my academic career for this panel, I have been struck by how in my earlier career I cared about three things: (1) being on the forefront of knowledge—at the margins; (2) being with like-minded folk; and (3) getting approval for my work.

Let me relate three significant early examples and then talk about how it is for me now.

My first meaningful "outsiderness" occurred while I was in graduate school. There, I happened into two new specialties: ethnomethodology and the sociology of science. Neither of these at the time were accepted into the sociological genre, but I loved how each of these questioned the hoity-toityness of science—its arrogance and hubris and above-it-all claim to authoritative knowledge. Important scholars in those specialties—Harold Garfinkel in one, Robert K. Merton, in the other—took note of me and my work and praised me. I liked that, and I liked that I was on the ground-floors of new edifices that would soar. I was not a lone outsider. Our work felt meaningful, forcing social science into a critique of itself.

A second meaningful "outsiderness" experience occurred when I was still an untenured professor at The Ohio State University. I had been in a major car accident and had suffered a coma. After I came out of the coma, I could not do mathematics or speak. But I could write. I turned to the rewriting of sociology from a feminist perspective, in part to propagate feminist analysis and in part to re-teach myself sociology. The resultant textbook, *The Dynamics of Sex and Gender* (1977), went into seven editions and helped define the field. It spoke to students of both genders and it spoke to their mothers. The book was on the margins, new, and impacted thousands of students. I was an outsider, but not alone: I was member of a community of feminist activists.

A third meaningful "outsiderness" happened when I was a full professor. I was suffering (as were so many of us) the "crisis of representation." I couldn't write. I couldn't accept the limits that positivistic sociology had imposed on qualitative research findings and on me. An abiding pull toward poetry had been thwarted by my years of writing "scientific" sociology. To get past my impasse and to honor my "otherness" voice, I decided to explore how truth-value was propagated through the prose trope. "Why prose for the re-telling of interviews?" I asked. "Nobody speaks in prose, after all. Everyone—the world over—speaks poetically, in phrases with pauses, like line-breaks." As an experiment, I decided to write an in-depth interview with an unwed mother as a narrative poem and present it to a sociology conference (Richardson, 1992). My questioning of format had a major unanticipated impact on the audience. Some of the audience maligned me, swore at me, and accused me of fabricating the interview. But others were positively excited about the possibilities of telling the sociological story in alternative ways. Since that time, countless numbers of research articles using poetic representation, ethnodrama, autoethnography, and so on have been published (see Bochner & Ellis, 2002; Ellis & Bochner, 1996; Richardson & St. Pierre, 2005). That is, I am a member of a vast conspiracy of like-minded people. Some of you are in that conspiracy, too.

And then, I took early retirement from sociology and became an adjunct professor of Cultural Studies in Education. Although I had been an outsider in my highly quantitative sociology department, I was a full professor. And although Cultural Studies provided me with an intellectual home, I was an institutional outsider—an adjunct. Getting approval and being on the forefront with like-minded people no longer propelled me. Instead, I wanted to work collaboratively with my husband, the novelist Ernest Lockridge, on what became a genre-breaking book—*Travels with Ernest: Crossing the Literary/Sociological Divide* (2004). Telling of our travels together in separate narratives, complemented with transcribed conversations, we explore the boundaries of fiction/nonfiction, and how gender, personal biography, and disciplinary perspectives shape our writing choices. The reader sees the negotiation of a two-career partnership, academic collaboration, and a blended family. The special joy of this book, I think, is that it offers a writing model for breaching power differentials, honoring individual voices, and writing for both discovery and empowerment. I like that it was written late in my career, when I was an adjunct.

My best friend died two years ago. To deal with her dying and death, I wrote *Last Writes: A Daybook for a Dying Friend* (2007). That is, I turned to writing to deal with my pain. I used the diary format and told "true" stories flourished by literary devices to keep the reader reading. What I had learned in my earlier collaboration, I applied to this solo work.

But alongside all the writing I was doing and have done, a road I had not taken beckoned—namely, the visual expression world. My visual work is once again on the margins, outsider-art, like altered books, mixed-media, art quilts, and recycling left-overs—like the buttons in my mother's button box. I'm experimenting bringing the written and the visual together. I know that this art-world work is having an impact on me, how I think, how I see, what I want from life. But I'm going to have to wait and see what it says to the world.

Last August my older sister died—a month after she was diagnosed with three primary cancers. The horror around her dying, my deep sense of loss, and my inability after her death to put even three words together sent me to a hospice grief counselor. Sue encouraged me in visual arts. I've created a small art quilt and a dos-e-dos *Grief* book, composed of my painting, poetry, and dreams. One side opens to my sister's life; the other to mine.

With the death of my sister, our plans for a shared home—a second home for me—also died. I would not be moving to Arizona. Or Chicago. I would be living where I have lived for the past 30 years in Worthington, an historical village north of Columbus, Ohio. How could I handle my grief, loss, and imagined future? I resolved to pay attention to where I did live, and to live there with intention. For me, "intention" translated into writing about it.

I decided to explore what I did with my life—"seven minutes from home." One's life is known through what one does and through the relationships one establishes. I planned to use my ethnographic skills of participant observation, looking to find the lightheartedness in my life. But soon my writing took me to deeper parts of myself as the quotidian stimulated my memories and unresolved issues. The accounts got longer, deeper, more fleshed out. Before long, I was adding poems, drawings, and photos. I've been putting everything (not in my file cabinet, as I usually do with my work), but in plastic sleeves in a three-ring notebook. For some reason, I want to be able to hold the entire project in my hand, move pieces around and add to it. Themes of permanence and change have emerged. To my surprise, I have discovered that I am creating a complex mixed-media book I'm calling *Seven Minutes from Home*.

When I told an urban planner about my project, he said, "How did you know that '7 minutes from home' is the time we use for urban renewal projects? That's all the time that displaced and fragile people can accept to get to their groceries, doctors, schools."

Seven minutes from my home is all the farthest I want to go by foot or car. In less than 7 minutes, I can walk to a block party and discover people who can recite Shakespeare; I can walk to La Chat to have lunch with a friend with congestive heart failure; I can walk to our Dairy Queen and witness the heroin sales by teenagers to undercover cops. In 7 minutes, I can drive to the Stitching Post and witness the liquidators eliminate personnel; I can drive to a Surface Design workshop and tell my birth story in cloth; I can drive to my integrative medicine doctor and plan on 20 more years of robust health; I can drive to my health club and eavesdrop on really old men; I can drive to all of my friends' houses, my children's houses, Anthem Lake, Worthington Mall, my art groups, and writing group. And I can drive to Kobacker House Hospice to meet with Sue, my grief counselor.

At one of those meetings, I told Sue that I had spent an hour and half looking at cards at a card shop in the mall and that I felt I was wasting my time. She replied, "What do you know? Someone might have been passing by that shop and said, 'Well, look at that light beaming out of there,' and their day or even their life may have been changed."

So, today, I am (thankfully) much less concerned with external approval—delighted and surprised and humbled when it is there. I am applying my skills to my own life and times. I am in my life. And I am not trying to be an outsider or on the margins or doing something new: I just am. It's just who I am.

Everything has changed and everything has stayed the same.

Writing as Transformation

Norman K. Denzin

C. Wright Mills urged scholars to write out of their own biographies, to write in ways that connect the personal with the political, the historical, personal troubles, and institutional apparatuses. Paulo Freire urged us to perform pedagogies that overcome systems of oppression. In "It's Alright, Ma (I'm only Bleeding)," Bob Dylan said, "Even the President of the United States must stand naked sometime," and Janis Joplin made a lot of money for Kris Kristofferson when she sang these lines from "Me and Bobby McGee": "Freedom is just another word for nothin' left to lose."

These are ethical injunctions. If there is nothing left to lose, then there is everything to be gained by being free. Being free means being free of these oppressive structures, free of these cops in my head (as Augusto Boal would say) that tell me I cannot be free.

In the academy, the cops are everywhere—hiring and promotion committees, journal editors, students in the classroom, colleagues next door, administrators. These are people who tell us not to write out of the personal, not to be political, not to be experimental, or perfomative, or to write autoethnography. They tell us to keep the personal at home, to keep it quiet, in the closet, act as if it never happened.

Somehow, this Midwest farm boy looked for a way to work from Mills to Freire, from Dylan to Kristofferson, to not be afraid to stand naked, with nothin' left to lose, to write in ways that said the personal must always be political and transformative. And the personal must come from the heart, the soul, the places of pain, injury, failure, deep hurt. There is nothing to hide, the personal has been stripped clean, even the "president of the United States must stand naked sometime!"

The personal should not be indulged, no romanticism, no celebration of tragic or fallen heroes. No self-help, up from the gutter narratives: The personal can only be used to advance a social justice agenda.

My engagement with transformative writing began in the mid-1980s with an essay on epiphanies, or turning-point encounters in people's lives. I argued that an interpretive social science should address those moments that transform lives; meaningful social science is about meaningful events in peoples' lives. Underneath these lines was the fact that I was writing my way out of a set of experiences that had transformed my life, and this is what I wanted to be writing about. I disguised myself in my texts, and in *On Understanding Emotion* (1984), *The Alcoholic Self* (1987a), and *The Recovering Alcoholic* (1987b) I gave my stories to other people. I was afraid to take up the challenge of either Dylan or Kristofferson. I was all too ready to hide behind Mills and Freire.

So there was a disconnect between the personal in the abstract and the personal at the level of the personal.

Fast forward to the present, to *Flags in the Window: Notes from the American War Zone* (2007) and *Searching for Yellowstone: Race, Gender, Family, and Memory in the Postmodern West* (2008). *Flags in the Window* was written out of a 9/11/01 rage, a belief that I had a responsibility to speak out against the Bush wars, terrorism, new surveillance regimes, Islamophobia, Axis of Evil, lies, deception. So I wrote a series of performance pieces, dated them, and called them dispatches from the field. My model was Ernie Pyle (1900–1945), the American journalist of World War II who sent daily dispatches from the European battlefields. My essays were intended to be transformative, to rethink what democracy might mean under the Bush nightmare.

Searching for Yellowstone (2008) worked outward from childhood memories and from the present. I was struggling with a new method, a way of writing myself into history. I wrote from the sting of memory—childhood experiences—and collisions between the personal and the public. I wrote about the Lewis and Clark expedition, Sacagawea, Yellowstone, Indians as college mascots, art and the transcontinental railroad. After Ulmer (1989), I experimented with a writing form called the mystory, suturing my epiphanies into the bicentennial celebrations of Lewis and Clark, tracing out the rhizomatic threads that knitted my personal history—my personal Yellowstone—with these national celebratory events that seemed to be occurring outside our cabin door.

Fast forward to another present. 2005: the first International Congress Qualitative Inquiry, and 2008–09: a new journal, *International Review of Qualitative Research*. The journal and the congress draw a circle around a project started in 1959 when I first read C. Wright Mills (1959). The critical interpretive community now has a global apparatus that can help make the utopian dream of a transformative social science happen. A hard-fought freedom is within our grasp.

Meaning and Method in a University Life

Arthur P. Bochner

The organizer of the session, his partner and frequently coauthor, says to him, "Just tell a story about moments in your academic life when you felt your work was *meaningful*, then tell how what you think of as meaningful has changed as you've aged. "Oh, one more thing," she adds, "Be brief!"

This is the pot calling the kettle black. Wasn't she the one who brought him a 700-page manuscript to read a few weeks after they met in 1990? How often has he gently prodded her to cut her papers and presentations? He grins when he recalls the many times he has cautioned her, "You better cut a page or two. You're going to end up way over time." Oh well, turnaround is fair play.

He thinks about her charge to the panelists, about his age, and about the meaning of *meaningful*. He feels blocked by the word. What can it mean? He thumbs through his thesaurus arriving at *meaningful*. Looking down, he reads, "ADJS. Significant; Suggestive; Eloquent; Pregnant; Meaty... He dwells for a few seconds on each:

Significant: Ah, that would be my most important research. Or would it be my most trenchant, striking, consequential, and urgent?

Suggestive: Ah, my most generative publications. Like seed to flower, these are the publications that gave rise to other works. I could emphasize the most original, most embryonic, most gestating monographs.

Eloquent: Ah, how I would love to talk about my life as a writer—how I've worked to make my prose more colorful, elegant, flourishing, fluent, lively, and graceful.

Pregnant: Ah, here I could focus on the fullest and densest work, the chapters that I've packed and loaded with meanings.

Meaty: Ah, the thickness of the work. Go deep, Art, that's what you so often strive for, isn't it? Tell them about your most challenging, vexing, demanding, and exhaustive inquiry into the human condition.

So many possibilities; so little time.

He thinks about this thing called "meaning." Why is he so puzzled by it? He reminds himself that meaning is not an object—not an it. Meaning is an idea. He recalls Mendel's essay on meaning written so many years ago (Menzel, 1978). "Meaning, who needs it?" Mendel asked. *I do,* he whispers to himself.

He likes this assignment (except the part about being brief), though he realizes how nostalgic he gets when he looks back on his life. He has spent the last three summers writing his academic memoirs, each chapter an exercise in expressing what was meaningful *then* seen through the lens of what appears meaningful *now*. His is a project she would call "revisioning" (Ellis, 2009), a fallible effort to try to correct one's own incapacity to see and understand what was going on *when it was going on*. The difficulty of the task should not be underestimated. Each day, he trudges up the stairs to his office and enters the dominion of narrative memory, a finite province of meaning (Berger & Luckmann, 1967) in which he is perpetually uncertain where the next turn on the highway of reminiscence will take him. He struggles to achieve an honest account of the past without betraying the friends and colleagues and lovers he has known and without giving in uncritically to the need to reassure himself that his life has been meaningful, coherent, and honorable. He is painfully aware of the temptation of exaggeration, the fallibility of language, the frailty of memory, and the fiction inherent in any true story. As his project unfurls, he begins to understand that he cannot just tell his life, he must examine it, mull it over, toss it, turn it, squeeze it, embrace it, doubt it, adore it, trust it, and caress it to discover, explain, explore, and interpret what he may have been thinking, what had inspired him, and what he cared about.

How he has labored over every page, every sentence, every word—wanting to get it right, tell it well, shine a light—writing not about what he knows but to find out what he knows and what it means, keeping his butt in the chair, chaining himself to his computer voluntarily—the self-imposed penalty he must pay for pleading guilty to the crime with which he was charged of wanting to make sense, figure out, understand. Here, in the quiet of the sacred space of his home office, he has found a safe place to revisit and feel deeply again the disappointments and the triumphs, the sorrowful and the sweet, the losses and the gains, the defeats and the victories; a place where he can dwell in the details of how he was conditioned by his Jewish upbringing, by a strict and critical immigrant father, by the affirmation of certain teachers, mentors, colleagues, friends, journal editors, and elders in the field; how he became other-directed, ambitious, demanding, angry, and self-indulged; how he liked to work hard and play hard, experimenting with drugs, with women, with unorthodox teaching, with gambling and adventure-seeking; how he could be abrasive, defiant, and stern and, at the same time, appear aloof, remote, and unapproachable; how he had been awakened from his absorption in himself when his first wife, a woman he adored and admired, lost her mind, had a psychotic break, no longer recognized him, couldn't care for herself, regressed, split, suffered, diminished, and lost herself, a self; how in that moment he saw how precarious, tentative, uncertain, precious, sorrowful, painful, absurd, fateful, and mysterious life could be; how this experience forced him to question what one could know, what was worth knowing, being, doing, wanting, and loving; how his own philosophy of science kept evolving as he moved through a demanding reading program from Comte (Harrison, 1886) to Popper (1950) to Feyerabend (1975) to Kuhn (1962) to Lyotard (1984), to Heidegger (1971) to Rorty (1979, 1982) to Levinas (Hand, 1989) to Gadamer (1989)—from the Vienna Circle to the hermeneutic circle; how his methodological orientation had shifted from experimental, quasi-experimental, and survey designs to ethnomethodology to interviews, to co-constructed narratives, to personal narratives to autoethnographies; how he had once thought it best to interview a thousand people once to how he now thought it better to interview one person a thousand times (Greenspan, 1998); how in the 1960s and early 1970s he had been inspired by the writings of Erving Goffman (1959), R. D. Laing (1961), and Tom Szasz (1961), and energized by Slater's *The Pursuit of Loneliness* (1971), Reich's *The Greening of America* (1970), and Roszak's *The Making of a Counterculture* (1970); how in the mid-1970s he'd been stunned by the courage of Ken Gergen (1973), the eloquence of Clifford Geertz (1973, 1980), the originality and electrifying intelligence of Ernest Becker (1973), the imagination and incisive empiricism of Jules Henry (1973), and the pragmatic theorizing of Gregory Bateson (1972); how in the 1980s he's learned from Richard Rorty that the question, "How do we know?" is not as important as the question, "What kind of world can we make?"

Rorty (1979, esp. p. 383) reaffirmed his belief that there is no escape from time and chance; that only dialog can save us (unless we see a philosophy of despair as preferable to a philosophy of solidarity); and that we needed to take seriously the question, "What will we do with ourselves (once we) know the laws of our own behavior?" And then he came across Alasdair MacIntyre's *After Virtue* (1981), where he confronted again the dilemma of moral choices such as the one he faced when had to face the troubling choice of whether to leave or stay with his first wife, a choice in which different virtues appeared to make rival and incompatible claims on him, and the fact he had to choose did not, could never, release him from the authority of the claim that he chose to go against. And, it was about at this time in his life, a time he was exploring the possibilities for a social science of narrative identity grounded in MacIntyre's question (1981, pp. 216–217), "Of what story or stories do I find myself a part" and in what fashion am I "accountable for the actions and experiences which compose my self as a narratable life?" that he entered a new story, a more hopeful, engaged, passionate, emotional story, when he met, by chance, by luck, or by fate, one Carolyn Ellis, the rose of his heart, who appeared suddenly, like the first daffodil of spring peeking through the still frozen tundra—a surprise, a gift, a generative, generous, gentle, kindred spirit with whom he could, he should, he did, begin again, awakened, aroused, stirred up, connected together in dialog, collaborating, composing, inventing, hiking up and down smoky mountains, planting lush green places, together seeking, wondering, and singing now worn clichés: "Yes, we can!"

Yes, we can build a bridge between the imagination of the humanities and the rigor of the social sciences. Yes, we can open new opportunities for others to tell stories shrouded in secrecy; we can embrace and privilege the particular, the marginal, and the oppressed; we can write against the conventions and center our work on the question of how we should live instead of what we can know; we can collaborate with Norman Denzin, Laurel Richardson, Ken and Mary Gergen, Mitch Allen, and numerous students and scholars here and across the oceans who seek to build a counterculture of inquiry that appeals to kindness, affirmation, and appreciation, one that places the personal, the emotional, the aesthetic, and the poetic at the center of inquiry and eschews a social science untouched by love, tenderness, and social science; and one that gives no special authority to tabulating, pigeonholing, calculating, or distancing one's self from one's inquiry. Yes, indeed, these are the experiences and dreams that have made his life—a life of writing, teaching, and being human—feel meaningful.

He looks over his paper and sees he has painted with a broad brush abstractly and briefly. But he notices that he has left out something she wanted. She asked him to mention a particular point, one turn in the road that truly made a difference, a meaningful, inspiring moment that sticks in his mind. He remembers one very well, one brief moment when he felt he had turned the corner and his academic life had a new promise and mission. The year was 1978. The occasion was a conference held in Asilomar, California in honor of the legacy of Gregory Bateson. At the conference, he gave a passionate presentation of a paper he titled "Forming Warm Ideas" (Bochner, 1981) and in which he emphatically insisted that "heart and head must go hand in hand" (p. 70) and after which he himself was warmed by Gregory's affectionate affirmation. "You get it," Gregory whispered in his ear, "not many do."

Notes

1. Another version of this text also appears as part of "Fighting Back or Moving On: An Autoethnographic Response to Critics," 2009, *The International Review of Qualitative Research, 2,* 3, 371–378.
2. These explorations were more fully elaborated in Gergen (1994, 2009b).

References

Bateson, G. (1972). *Steps to an ecology of mind.* New York: Ballantine.

Becker, E. (1973). *The denial of death.* New York: Free Press.

Berger, P. L., & Luckmann, T. (1967). *The social construction of reality: A treatise in the sociology of knowledge.* Garden City, NY: Anchor.

Bochner, A. P. (1981). Forming warm ideas. In C. Wickler-Mott and J. H. Weakland (Eds.), *Rigor and imagination: Essays from the legacy of Gregory Bateson* (pp. 65–82). New York: Praeger.

Bochner, A. P., & Ellis, C. (Eds.). (2002). *Ethnographically speaking: Autoethnography, literature, and aesthetics.* Thousand Oaks, CA: AltaMira.

Denzin, N. K. (1984). *On understanding emotion.* San Francisco: Jossey-Bass (re-issue, with new introduction, 2007. New Brunswick, NJ: Transaction Books.)

Denzin, N. K. (1987a). *The alcoholic self.* Newbury Park, CA: Sage.

Denzin, N. K. (1987b). *The recovering alcoholic.* Newbury Park, Ca: Sage.

Denzin, N. K. (2007). *Flags in the window: Dispatches from the American war zone.* New York: Peter Lang.

Denzin, N. K. (2008). *Searching for Yellowstone: Race, gender, family, and memory in the postmodern West.* Walnut Creek, CA: Left Coast Press.

Ellis, C. (1993). "There are survivors": Telling a story of a sudden death. *The Sociological Quarterly, 34,* 4, 711–730.

Ellis, C. (1995). *Final negotiations: A story of love, loss, and chronic illness.* Philadelphia: Temple University Press.

Ellis, C. (2009). *Revision: Autoethnographic reflections on life and work.* Walnut Creek, CA: Left Coast Press.

Ellis, C., & Bochner, A. (Eds.). (1996). *Composing ethnography: Alternative forms of qualitative writing.* Thousand Oaks, CA: Sage.

Feyerabend, P. (1975). *Against method.* New York: Schocken Books.

Geertz, C. (1973). *The interpretation of cultures: Selected essays.* New York: Basic Books.

Geertz, C. (1980). Blurred genres: The refiguration of social thought. *American Scholar, 49,* 2, 165–179.

Gadamer, H. G. (1989). *Truth and method*. (2nd rev. ed., J. Weinsheimer and D. G. Marshall, Trans.). New York: Crossroads.

Genova, L. (2007). *Still Alice*. New York: Simon and Shuster.

Gergen, K. J. (1973). Social psychology as history. *Journal of Personality and Social Psychology, 26*, 1, 309–320.

Gergen, K. J. (1994). *Realities and relationships: Soundings in social construction*. Cambridge, MA: Harvard University Press.

Gergen, K. J. (1991). *The saturated self*. New York: Basic Books.

Gergen, K. J. (2009a). *An invitation to social construction* (2nd ed.). London: Sage.

Gergen, K. J. (2009b). *Relational being: Beyond self and community*. New York: Oxford University Press.

Gergen, M. (1988). Towards a feminist methodology. In M. Gergen (Ed.), *Feminist thought and the structure of knowledge* (pp. 87–104). New York: New York University Press.

Gergen, M. (1989). Talking about menopause: A dialogic analysis. In L. E. Thomas (Ed.), *Research on adulthood and aging: The human sciences approach* (pp. 65–87). Albany: State University of New York Press.

Gergen, M. (1990). From mod masculinity to post-mod macho: A feminist re-play. *The Humanist Psychologist, 18*, 1, 95–104.

Gergen, M. (2001). *Feminist reconstructions in psychology: Narrative, gender, and performance*. Thousand Oaks, CA: Sage.

Gergen, M., & Gergen, K. J. (2001). Ethnographic representations as relationship. In C. Ellis and A. Bochner (Eds.), *Ethnographically speaking* (pp. 11–33). Walnut Creek, CA: AltaMira.

Goffman, E. (1959). *The presentation of self in everyday life*. New York: Doubleday.

Greenspan, H. (1998). *On listening to Holocaust survivors: Recounting and life history*. Westport, CT.: Praeger.

Hand, S. (1989). *The Levinas reader: Emmanuel Levinas*. Oxford, UK: Blackwell Publishing.

Harrison, F. (1886). *The positivist library of Auguste Comte*. London: Reeves and Turner.

Heidegger, M. (1971). *On the way to language* (P. D. Hertz and J. Stambaugh, Trans.). New York: Harper & Row.

Henry, J. (1973). *Pathways to madness*. New York: Vintage Books.

Kuhn, T. (1962). *The structure of scientific revolutions*. Chicago: University of Chicago Press.

Laing, R. D. (1961). *The self and others*. New York: Pantheon.

Lyotard, J. (1984). *The postmodern condition: A report on knowledge.* Minneapolis: University of Minnesota Press.

MacIntyre, A. (1981). *After virtue: A study in moral theory.* Notre Dame, IN: University of Notre Dame Press.

Menzel, H. (1978). Meaning—Who needs it? In M. Brenner, P. Marsh, and M. Brenner (Eds.), *The social contexts of method* (pp. 140–171). New York: St. Martin's Press.

Mills, C. Wright. (1959). *The sociological imagination.* New York: Oxford.

Popper, K. (1950). *The open society and its enemies.* Princeton, NJ: Princeton University Press.

Reich, C. (1970). *The greening of America.* New York: Random House.

Richardson, L. (1977). *The dynamics of sex and gender: A sociological perspective.* Chicago: Rand McNally.

Richardson, L. (1992). The poetic representation of lives: Writing a postmodern sociology. *Studies in Symbolic Interaction, 13,* 1, 19–29.

Richardson, L. (2007). *Last writes: A daybook for a dying friend.* Walnut Creek, CA: Left Coast Press.

Richardson, L., & Lockridge, E. (2004). *Travels with Ernest: Crossing the literary/sociological divide.* Walnut Creek, CA: AltaMira Press.

Richardson, L., & St. Pierre, E. (2005). Writing: A method of inquiry. In N. K. Denzin and Y. S. Lincoln (Eds.), *Handbook of qualitative research* (3rd ed., pp. 959–978). Thousand Oaks, CA: Sage.

Rorty, R. (1979). *Philosophy and the mirror of nature.* Princeton, NJ: Princeton University Press.

Rorty, R. (1982). *Consequences of pragmatism (essays 1972–1980).* Minneapolis: University of Minnesota Press.

Roszak, T. (1970). *The making of a counterculture: Reflections on the technocratic society and its youthful opposition.* New York: Doubleday.

Slater, P. (1971). *The pursuit of loneliness: American culture at the breaking point.* Boston: Beacon Press.

Szasz, T. (1961). *The myth of mental illness: Foundations for a theory of personal conduct.* New York: Hoeber-Harper.

Ulmer, G. L. (1989). Mystory: The law of idiom in applied grammatology. In R. Cohen (Ed.), *The future of literary theory* (pp. 304–323). London: Routledge.

Index

9/11/01, 15, 266

activist/s, 16–17, 35, 66, 78–79, 84, 127, 148-149, 261
apartheid, 26, 128, 130, 182

Bush, George W., 15, 29
   administration, 37n3, 37n4, 176, 256

citizenship, 23, 55, 61, 87, 106
civil,
   disobedience, 74
   liberties, 14, 37n3
   rights, 14, 68–70, 91–93, 221, 224
   society, 206
colonize/ation, 21, 23–26,182, 235
cultural,
   authenticity, 58
   autonomy, 22
   bio-, Chapter 12
   capital, 210
   continuity, 53, 56–61
   critique, 28
   diversity, 47, 60, 92
   identity, 51, 60, 77, 140
   knowledge, 212
   performance, 24
   politics, 15, 17
   practices, 34, 76–77, 119, 211
   relativist, 77
   supremacy, 127
   traditions, 60
   values, 166

Declaration of the Rights of Man and Citizen (1789), 67, 71
decolonize/ation, 17, 20–21, 27, 34
discrimination, 13, 16–17, 35, 54–55, 79, 83, 209
diversity, 177, 182, 236
    cultural, 47, 60, 92
    methodological, 36

essentialism, 88,
ethics,
    and logic, 46
    and media, Chapter 1
    and rationalism, 45, 51
    and review boards, 222
    communication, 45–46, 49
    consequentialist theory of, 89
    discourse, 86–87
    Enlightenment models of, 47
    Kantian, 46, 86
    modernist, 53
    of aesthetics, 167, 234
    of justice, 54
    of research, 192
    philosophical, 45
    relational, 245
    tri-level, Chapter 1
    utilitarian, 47
ethnography, 31, 109, 116–121, 263
    auto-, 31–32, 117, 208, 243–246, 270; Chapter 7
        and performance, Chapter 8
    critical, 31, 33, 117; Chapter 11
    performance, 120, 113, 118–120, 207, 265
    realist, 31, 121
exploitation, 14, 90, 224

feminist/ism, 21, 47, 115, 257, 261
    American, 250
    endarkened, 31, 175–177
    French, 250
    politics, 176
    postmodern, 208, 250–252
    psychology, 251
    theory, 249

genocide, 26, 82
global, 17, 87
    community, 15, 257, 267
    citizens, 15, 17
    economy, 54, 233
    media ethics, see Chapter 1
    sensibility, 176
    uncertainty, 16–17

homelessness, 13, 32–33, 35; Chapter 10

indigenous,
    culture, 24–25, 34
    epistemologies, 117
    knowledge, 24
    language, 127
    methodologies, 20
    models of governance, 23
    models of democracy, 23
    pedagogies, 21
    poetics, 21
    scholars, 16, 176
inequality, 15–16, 53, 186–188, 206–210, 213–214
injustice, 14–17, 21, 33, 36, 59, 61, 88, 95, 102–104, 113, 182, 207–
        208, 211, 214, 244–245
International Congress of Qualitative Inquiry (ICQI), 16–19, 34
Islamophobia, 266

justice,
    Department, 37n3, 37n4
    distributive, 54, 213
    dynamic, 59–62
    ethics of, 54, 62
    human, 17
    modernist, 53
    need-based principle of, 55
    restorative, 25–27
    social, 15–36, 45, 50–51, 53, 60, 83, 85–87, 113–114, 182, 206, 209,
        214–215,   234, 257, 265; see also Chapter 4
    theory of, 53

Kennedy, John F., 177
knowledge,
    and ethics, 134
    authoritative, 261
    collective, 212
    compulsory, 136
    construction, 161, 219
    creation, 236
    decolonizing, 20
    discursive, 211
    embodied, 160, 167
    health, 231
    hegemonic, 236
    human, 230, 255
    indigenous, 24
    marginalized, 233
    politics of, 159–163
    production, 209, 219, 235
    scientific, 230–231
    systems, 24, 31, 126
    theory of, 46–51
    translation, 103–106

Mandela, Nelson, 121, 133
Maori, 22–23, 101

neoliberal/ism, 17, 214, 227
    economics, 209, 223
    individualism, 30, 83, 222
    institutions, 206
    political economy, 222
    societies, 219, 235

Obama, Barack, 15, 32, 120; Chapter 9
oppression, 13, 17, 20–21, 27, 29, 100, 102, 117, 182, 255, 265
Orwell, George, 113, 121
    Orwellian, 222, 236

pain, 13, 24–25, 28–29, 35, 160–161, 167–168, 199, 243–245, 256, 262, 265, 269
pedagogy/ies,
    and resistance, 223
    and rights, 160, 169

critical, 20–22, 27
indigenous, 21
of freedom, 27
of hope, 28–29, 167
of oppression, 29
performance/ative, 15, 32, 159, 161, 169, 265
social justice, 22
spectacle, 15
persecution, 13, 35, 74
politics, 19–20, 35, 50, 53, 59, 137, 140, 147, 150, 178, 256
American, 181
biopolitics, 220–221
cultural, 15, 17
feminist, 176
indigenous, 21
international, 55
intimate, 163
of difference, Chapter 9
of funding, 108
of health, Chapter 12
of hope, 27–29
of knowledge, 217
of representation, 159
of resistance, 28
principled, 58–60
radical, 35
racial, 32
sexual, 17
poverty, 13, 15, 21, 24, 32–33, 35, 58, 176, 186, 256; see also Chapter 11

relativism, 85, 87–88
reliability, 85
Revolution,
American, 67, 73–76, 93, 260
French, 67, 73–76, 93, 258

suffering, 13–14, 24, 26, 29, 35, 61–62, 71, 88, 92, 95, 97, 132, 182,
197–198, 245, 261, 269
slavery, 82, 89–90
social,
change, 20, 28, 36, 58, 244
construction/ism/ist, 84–87, 90, 167, 249, 252–253, 257–259
economies, 20

exclusion, 33, 186, 189, Chapter 11
identity, 212
inquiry, 20, 84–85, 114, 207, 214, 226
institutions, 59, 89
isolation, 187
justice, 15–36, 45, 50–51, 53, 60, 83, 85–87, 113–114, 182, 206,
    209, 214–215, 234, 257, 265; see also Chapter 4
life, 20, 84, 88, 93–97, 258
norms, 212
policy, 15, 18, 70, 256
practices, 30, 67, 73, 75–76, 90–91, 94, 102, 148, 161
psychology, 247–251, 256
responsibility, 55, 227
science/s, 20, 36, 82–88, 93–95, 109, 115, 118, 208, 250–252, 261,
    266–267, 270–271
sustainability, 106
vulnerabilities, 213
work/ers, 16, 20, 117, 162, 194, 198–202
sovereignty, 23
subaltern, 127–130, 134, 163
surveillance, 144, 220–224, 266

terror/ism, 15, 67, 74, 266
torture, 13–14, 35, 37n4, 69, 82
transnational/ism,
    and social justice, 60
    corporations, 45, 57
    ethical frameworks, 47, 51, 62
Truth and Reconciliation Commission (South Africa), 26, 31, 127–128
Tutu, Desmond, 121, 133

Universal Declaration of Human Rights (1948), 13, 51, 69–70, 88,
    126, 186

validity, 85, 117, 120

war, 13, 15–16, 35–36, 54, 82
    Afghanistan, 178, 266
    Bosnia, 82
    Cold War, 70
    Iraq, 14, 36, 77, 79, 178, 266
    Vietnam, 14, 257
    WWII, 14, 76, 266

Editor Bios

Norman K. Denzin is Distinguished Professor of Communications, College of Communications Scholar, and Research Professor of Communications, Sociology, and Humanities at the University of Illinois, Urbana-Champaign. One of the world's foremost authorities on qualitative research and cultural criticism, Denzin is the author or editor of more than two dozen books, including *Performance Ethnography, Reading Race, Interpretive Ethnography, The Cinematic Society, Images of Postmodern Society, The Recovering Alcoholic, The Alcoholic Self,* and *Searching for Yellowstone.* He is past editor of *The Sociological Quarterly,* coeditor of the landmark *Handbook of Qualitative Research* (1st, 2nd, and 3rd editions, Sage Publications, with Yvonna S. Lincoln), and coeditor of the *Handbook of Critical & Indigenous Methodologies* (2008, Sage, with Yvonna S. Lincoln and Linda Tuhiwai Smith). With Michael D. Giardina, Denzin is coeditor of *Contesting Empire/Globalizing Dissent: Cultural Studies after 9/11* (Paradigm, 2006) and a series of books on qualitative inquiry published by Left Coast Press: *Qualitative Inquiry and the Conservative Challenge: Confronting Methodological Fundamentalism* (2006), *Ethical Futures in Qualitative Research: Decolonizing the Politics of Knowledge* (2007), *Qualitative Inquiry and the Politics of Evidence* (2008), and *Qualitative Inquiry and Social Justice: Toward a Politics of Hope* (2009). He is also the editor of the journal *Qualitative Inquiry* (with Yvonna S. Lincoln), founding editor of *Cultural Studies/Critical Methodologies,* series editor of *Studies in Symbolic Interaction,* and *Cultural Critique* series editor for Peter Lang Publishing. He is the founding president of the International Association for Qualitative Inquiry and the director of the International Congress of Qualitative Inquiry.

Michael D. Giardina is visiting assistant professor of advertising and affiliate faculty of Cultural Studies & Interpretive Research at the University of Illinois, Urbana-Champaign. He is the author of *Sporting Pedagogies: Performing Culture & Identity in the Global Arena* (Peter Lang, 2005), which received the 2006 Most Outstanding Book award from the North American Society for the Sociology of Sport. In addition to a series of books edited with Norman K. Denzin on qualitative inquiry and interpretive research, he is the editor of *Youth Culture & Sport: Identity, Power, and Politics* (Routledge, 2007, with Michele K. Donnelly) and *Globalizing Cultural Studies: Methodological Interventions in Theory, Method and Policy* (Peter Lang, 2007, with Cameron McCarthy, Aisha Durham, Laura Engel, Alice Filmer, and Miguel Malagreca). He is currently the associate editor of the *Sociology of Sport Journal*, and sits on the editorial board of *Cultural Studies/ Critical Methodologies*. With Joshua I. Newman, he is completing a book titled *Consuming NASCAR Nation: Sport, Spectacle, and the Cultural Politics of Neoliberalism.*

Contributors

Tony E. Adams is an assistant professor in the Department of Communication, Media & Theatre at Northeastern Illinois University (Chicago). He teaches courses on relationships, gender, persuasion, identity, and communication theory. His work has appeared in journals such as *Qualitative Inquiry, Soundings, Cultural Studies/Critical Methodologies*, and *The Review of Communication.*

Arthur P. Bochner is professor of communication and codirector of the Institute for Human Interpretive Studies at the University of South Florida. He has written extensively on ethnography, autoethnography, and narrative inquiry, and has published such books as *Ethnographically Speaking: Autoethnography, Literature, and Aesthetics* (AltaMira, 2002, with Caroyln Ellis), *Composing Ethnography: Alternative Forms of Qualitative Writing* (AltaMira, 1996, with Carolyn Ellis), and *Understanding Family Communication* (Gorsuch, 1990/1995, with Janet Yerby and Nancy Buerkele-Rothfuss). His work has also appeared in journals such as *Qualitative Inquiry, Journal of Contemporary Ethnography, Communication Theory,* and *Studies in Symbolic Interaction*. He served as president of the National Communication Association.

Svend Brinkmann is a professor of psychology at Aalborg University, Denmark, where he is the codirector of the Center for Qualitative Research. He is author of many books, including *John Dewey—En introduktion* (*John Dewey: An Introduction*) (Copenhagen, Hans Reitzels Forlag, 2006) and *Psyken: Mellem synapser og samfund* (Aarhus University Press, 2009) and editor of such books as *Selvrealisering—Kritiske diskussioner af en grænseløs udviklingskultur* (*Self-realization—Critical Discussions of a Boundless Culture of Development*, 2005, with Cecilie Eriksen), *Psykologi: Forskning og profession* (*Psychology: Research and Profession*) (Copenhagen, Hans Reitzels Forlag, 2007, with Lene Tanggaard), and *InterViews: Learning the Craft of Qualitative Research Interviewing* (Sage, 2008, with Steiner Kvale).

Julianne Cheek is a professor at Atlantis Medical College in Oslo, Norway. She also holds honorary professorships in South Africa and the United Kingdom and was previously the director of the Early Career Researcher Development Program at the University of South Australia. She is the author of *Postmodern and Poststructuralist Approaches to Nursing Research* (Sage, 2000) and coauthor of *Finding out: Information Literacy for the 21st Century* (Macmillan, 1995) and *Society and Health: Social Theory for Health Workers* (Longman Chesire, 1996), which won the prize for the best Tertiary Single Book (wholly Australian) in the prestigious Australian Awards for Excellence in Educational Publishing for 1996. She is also coeditor of the journal *Health: An Interdisciplinary Journal for the Social Study of Health, Illness, and Medicine*, associate editor of *Qualitative Health Research*, and is on the editorial boards of many other journals.

Clifford G. Christians is Research Professor of Communications and former director of the Institute of Communications Research at the University of Illinois, Urbana-Champaign. He has also been a visiting scholar in philosophical ethics at Princeton University and in social ethics at the University of Chicago and a PEW Fellow in Ethics at Oxford University. He is the author or editor of numerous books, including *Good News: Social Ethics and the Press* (Oxford University Press, 1993, with John Ferre and Mark Fackler), *Communication Ethics and Universal Values* (Sage, 1997, with Michael Trabor), and *Normative Theories of the Media* (University of Illinois Press, forthcoming). He also serves on the editorial boards of a dozen academic journals, is the former editor of *Critical Studies in Media Communication*, and currently edits *The Ellul Forum*.

Cynthia B. Dillard is a professor of multicultural education in the School of Teaching and Learning at The Ohio State University. Her major research interests include critical multicultural education, spirituality in teaching and learning, epistemological concerns in research and African/African American feminist studies. Most recently, her research has focused in Ghana, West Africa, where she established a preschool and was enstooled as Nana Mansa II, Queen Mother of Development, in the village of Mpeasem, Ghana, West Africa. She is the author of *On Spiritual Strivings: Transforming an African American Woman's Life* (State University of New York Press, 2007).

Carolyn Ellis is professor of communication and codirector of the Institute for Human Interpretive Studies at the University of South Florida. She is the author or editor of many books, including *Revision: Autoethnographic Reflections on Life and Work* (Left Coast Press, 2009); *The Ethnographic I: A Methodological Novel about Autoethnography* (AltaMira, 2004); *Composing Ethnography: Alternative Forms of Qualitative Writing* (AltaMira, 1996, with Arthur P. Bochner); and *Final Negotiations: A Story of Love, Loss and Chronic Illness* (Temple University Press, 1995). Her current research projects investigate autoethnograpy, narrative writing, issues of illness and loss, and the Holocaust.

Frederick Erickson is professor of social research methodology and director of CONNECT: A Center for Research and Innovation in Elementary Education, at the University of California, Los Angeles and Seeds University Elementary School. He is the author of many books, including most recently *Arts, Humanities, and Sciences in Educational Research—and Social*

Engineering in Federal Education Policy (Teachers College Record, in press) and *Talk and Social Theory: Ecologies of Speaking and Listening in Everyday Life* (Polity Press, 2004).

A. Belden Fields is Professor Emeritus of political science at the University of Illinois, Urbana-Champaign. He is the author of many books, including *Trotskyism and Maoism: Theory and Practice in France and the United States* (Praeger, 1988), *Education and Democratic Theory* (SUNY Press, 2001, with Walter Feinberg), and *Rethinking Human Rights for the New Millennium* (PalgraveMacmillan, 2003).

Uwe Flick is professor of qualitative research at the Alice Salomon University of Applied Sciences in Berlin, Germany. He is the author most recently of *An Introduction to Qualitative Research* (4th ed., Sage, 2009), *Qualitative Research in Psychology* (Sage, 2009), *Managing Quality in Qualitative Research* (Sage, 2008), and *Designing Qualitative Research* (Sage, 2008). Dr. Flick has also been a visiting scholar at various universities, including the London School of Economics, Cambridge University, École des Hautes Études en Sciences Sociales, Paris, and Massey University, Palmerston North, New Zealand.

Kenneth J. Gergen is Senior Research Professor of Psychology at Swarthmore College. He is the author or editor of a number of key texts in the field of social constructionism, including most recently *Relational Being* (Oxford University Press, 2009), *Realities and Relationships, Soundings in Social Construction* (Harvard University Press, 1994), and *Social Construction in Context* (Sage, 2001). He is also an affiliate professor at Tilburg University, honorary professor at the University of Buenos Aires, and president of The Taos Institute.

Mary Gergen is Emerita Professor of Psychology and Women's Studies at Pennsylvania State University, Brandywine. She is the author or editor of many landmark books on feminist theory, social constructionism, and performative psychology, including *Feminist Reconstructions in Psychology: Narrative, Gender & Performance* (Sage, 2001), *Social Constructionism: A Reader* (Sage,

2003, edited with Kenneth Gergen), *Toward a New Psychology of Gender* (Routledge, 1997, with Sara N. Davis), and *Feminist Thought and the Structure of Knowledge* (New York University Press, 1988). She is also one of the founders of The Taos Institute, a nonprofit educational organization concerned with the social processes essential for the construction of reason, knowledge, and human value.

Stacy Holman Jones is associate professor and director of graduate studies in the Department of Communication at the University of South Florida. She is the author of *Torch Singing: Performing Resistance and Desire from Billie Holiday to Edith Piaf* (AltaMira, 2007) and *Kaleidoscope Notes: Writing Women's Music and Organizational Culture* (AltaMira, 1998).

Dave Holmes is full professor and vice-dean (Academic) at the University of Ottawa's Faculty of Health Sciences. He is also University Research Chair in Forensic Nursing (2009–2014) and nurse-researcher at the University of Ottawa's Institute of Mental Health Research (Forensic Psychiatry Program). After completing his Ph.D. in nursing (Montreal/McGill, 2002), Professor Holmes completed a Canadian Institute of Health Research (CIHR) postdoctoral fellowship at the University of Toronto (2003). To date, he has received funding from CIHR and from the Social Sciences and Humanities Research Council of Canada to conduct his research program on risk management in the fields of Public Health and Forensic Nursing. His work has been published in top-tier journals in nursing, criminology, sociology, and medicine, and he is coeditor of *Critical Interventions in the Ethics of Health Care* (Ashgate, 2009) and *Abjectly Boundless: Boundaries, Bodies and Health Care* (Ashgate, 2010).

Antjie Krog is a poet, writer, journalist, and Professor Extraordinary in the Faculty of Arts at the University of the Western Cape, South Africa. She has published twelve volumes of poetry in Afrikaans, two volumes in English, and two non-fiction books: *Country of My Skull*, on the South African Truth and Reconciliation Commission, and *A Change of Tongue*, about the transformation in South Africa after 10 years. Her work has been translated into English, Dutch, Italian, French, Spanish, Swedish, Serbian, and Arabic. *Country of My Skull* is widely used at universities as part of the curriculum dealing with writing about the past. She was also asked to translate the autobiography of Nelson Mandela, *Long Walk to Freedom*, into Afrikaans. She has been awarded most of the prestigious awards for nonfiction, translation and poetry available in Afrikaans and English as well as the Award from the Hiroshima Foundation for Peace and Culture for the year 2000 and the Open Society Prize from the Central European University. Her most recent book, *There Was This Goat*, written with Nosisi Mpolweni and Kopano Ratele and published by KZN Press in March 2009, investigates the Truth Commission testimony of Notrose Nobomvu Konile.

Stuart J. Murray is assistant professor of rhetoric and writing in the Department of English at Ryerson University in Toronto, Canada. He also holds concurrent appointments in the Faculty of Health Sciences at the University of Ottawa and in the Dalla Lana School of Public Health at the University of Toronto. He publishes widely in nursing, health sciences, and the medical humanities and, with Dave Holmes, he is the editor of *Critical Interventions in the Ethics of Healthcare* (Ashgate, 2009). He is currently completing a book-length project on the rhetorical dimensions of biopolitics and thanatopolitics, tentatively titled, *The Living from the Dead.*

Elisabeth Niederer is the scientific leader of the Carinthian Network Against Poverty and Social Discrimination. Her book *Die Kultur der Armut (The Culture of Poverty)* will be published in 2010 (Transcript).

Geneviève Rail is professor and principal of the Simone de Beauvoir Institute at Concordia University, Canada, where she does research on young women's discursive constructions of the body and health in the context of obesity discourses and biopedagogies. Her work as appeared in scholarly journals such as *Journal of Evaluation in Clinical Practice, Journal of Research in Nursing, Sociology of Sport Journal, International Journal of Evidence Based Healthcare,* and *Journal of Women and Aging.*

Laurel Richardson is Professor Emeritus of Sociology at The Ohio State University. She is an international leader in qualitative research, gender, and the sociology of knowledge. She has written numerous groundbreaking books, including the landmark *Fields of Play: Constructing an Academic Life* (Rutgers University Press, 1997), which received the 1998 Charles Cooley award from the Society for the Study Symbolic Interaction. Other publications include *Travels with Ernest: Crossing the Literary/Sociology Divide* (AltaMira, 2004, with Ernest Lockridge), *Writing Strategies: Reaching Diverse Audiences* (Sage, 1990), *Feminist Frontiers* (1st–7th editions) (McGraw-Hill, 2003, with Verta Taylor and Nancy Whittier), *The New Other Woman: Contemporary Single Women in Affairs with Married Men* (Macmillan, 1985), and *Last Writes: A Daybook for a Dying Friend* (Left Coast Press, 2007).

Tami L. Spry is professor of communication studies at St. Cloud State University, where she teaches courses in performance studies and communication theory. Dr. Spry performs her autobiographical and autoethnographic work around the country, focusing on issues of gender violence, mental illness, race relationships, shamanic healing, and loss. She is currently working on a book, *Paper and Skin: Writing and Performing the Autoethnographic Life.* Her publications appear in journals such as *Text and Performance Quarterly, Qualitative Inquiry*, and *Women and Language,* as well as chapters in various anthologies.

Rainer Winter is professor of cultural and media theory at Klagenfurt University, Austria, where he writes and teaches on cultural studies, qualitative research, and media anlaysis. He is the editor of *Global America? The Cultural Consequences of Globalization* (Liverpool University Press, 2004, with Ulrich Beck and Nathan Sznaider) and the Cultural Studies book series for Transcipt Press, Germany. His latest book is titled *Widerstand im Netz. Das Internet und die Herausbildung einer transnationalen Öffentlichkeit* (*Resistance in the Network: The Internet and the Emergence of a Transnational Public*) (Transcript, 2010).